Selections from the

Personal, Political, Philosophical, and

Epistolary Writings of

Thomas Jefferson

THE
WRITINGS OF
Thomas Jefferson

Selected and Edited by
Saul K. Padover

Illustrated with Lithographs
by Lynd Ward

THE HERITAGE PRESS
New York

JEFFERSON: THE PERSONAL SIDE

THOMAS JEFFERSON the statesman and many-sided genius is well and justly remembered by posterity. He spent some forty years in public life, serving his state and country in numerous capacities, and always with distinction. Let us recall that he was a Member of Congress, Governor, Ambassador, Secretary of State, Vice-President of the United States, President of the United States, and University Rector. His contributions to America were manifold. An inventor, pioneer, scholar, and sage, he enriched whatever he touched.

Many of Jefferson's writings—reports, statutes, inaugural addresses, letters—have become an integral part of the American tradition and of the philosophy of democracy. In the realm of action, his services were no less notable. One need only mention the founding of the Democratic (then called the Republican) Party, the purchase of the Louisiana Territory, the creation of the University of Virginia, to realize the extent of his gifts to America.

But Jefferson's importance does not stop there. He was probably the first statesman in history to develop democratic ideas and their implications with amplitude and consistency. He not only made the ideal of democracy—freedom and self-government—the goal of his political life, but he also explored its meaning and formulated its basic tenets. His conception of democracy was rooted in a truly noble belief in the goodness and decency of the human being. It was Jefferson's unshakable trust in man's dignity and capacity for the full development of his personality that has made him the central figure in American democratic thought. It may be truly said that Jefferson symbolizes what is finest in the American ideal. Abraham Lincoln said truly that Jefferson's principles were "the definitions and axioms of a free society." Nowadays, indeed, when Americans proudly speak of the system under which they live and have flourished, they are likely to refer to it as "Jeffersonian democracy."

For all of these achievements, Jefferson is rightly appreciated—in a sense, perhaps too well. His public image has come down to us as a staid Founding Father, a powdered-hair political figure, solemn of visage, earnest and humorless. But that is not the true Jefferson.

He was, to be sure, hard-working and disciplined, unswervingly dedicated to his democratic ideals, which he systematically strove to shape into reality. But there was also another, less known side to Jefferson—the gay and entertaining side. Sweet-tempered and unfailingly considerate of others, he was a fun-loving, life-loving, merry man. Friends and intimates knew him as a jolly gentleman and vivacious companion. He appreciated good food and fine wines (which he drank in moderation), loved dancing, fiddling, and singing. Outdoors, he nearly always hummed some tune. Isaac, his Negro servant, recalled years after his master's death: "Mr. Jefferson always singin' when ridin' or walkin'; hardly see him anywhar outdoors but what he was a-singin'; had a fine clear voice, sung minnits [minuets] and such." The ever-cheerful Mr. Jefferson was also an amusing storyteller, a whimsical commentator, and a scintillating conversationalist. Let us look at this facet of his character.

First, his physical appearance.

Jefferson was big—about six feet two and a half inches in height— lean and wide-shouldered. In the words of his Negro servant, he was a "tall, straight-bodied man . . . , a straight-up man." He had, according to a contemporary, "uncommonly long" legs and "very large" hands and feet. Angular and strong, Jefferson walked with an elastic, swinging stride, indicating power under perfect control. When he sat and talked, it was in a "lounging manner," easy and relaxed.

Jefferson was not handsome by ordinary standards. His chin was long; his nose small, regular, with slightly raised nostrils—"long face, high nose," as his servant described him. The skin was thin, delicate, tending to peel and crack. The hair was reddish in youth, sandy in later years. The hazel eyes were kindly and quizzical. There was an air of benignity about him. Senator William Maclay, who knew Jefferson as Secretary of State, said of him in his *Journal* that "his face has a sunny aspect."

Jefferson attracted people also by his strength and vitality. He rode horseback daily, and retained his vigor to the very end. Daniel Webster, visiting Monticello when Jefferson was eighty-one, was struck by his "extraordinary" health. Grandson Thomas Jefferson Randolph tells that when his grandfather died in his eighty-fourth year, "he had not lost a tooth, or had one defective." The old gentleman's hearing and eyesight were in fine shape too.

He was an optimist who enjoyed life and cherished it in all its aspects. Even family tragedies, such as the loss of his wife after ten happy years of marriage (he never remarried), did not permanently dampen his spirits. An admirer and follower of the Stoic philosophers and of Epicurus—to whom he referred, in a letter to a like-minded friend, as "our master"—Jefferson accepted the gift of life, the good as well as the bad, with reasoned cheerfulness. "My temperament," he said, "is sanguine." Unless stirred to momentary anger by acts of injustice or oppression, his basic attitudes were positive and good-humored. He considered the latter, in fact, a major social and personal virtue, as he repeatedly told members of his family. When he was seventy-three, his sprightly friend John Adams, then eighty-one, asked him what he called a "frivolous" question, namely, whether he would be willing to go back to the cradle and live his life over again. Jefferson replied: ". . . I say, yea. I think with you, that it is a good world on the whole; that it has been framed on a principle of benevolence, and more pleasure than pain dealt out to us. . . . I steer my bark with hope in the head, leaving fear astern."

Jefferson, although not a wit like his friend, Benjamin Franklin, did have humor and whimsy. At first meeting he seemed to be somewhat reserved, especially with strangers, but he warmed to those he came to know, sometimes even on short acquaintance. He loved conversation, but shunned argumentativeness. When opinions threatened to become heated, Jefferson, a good and courteous listener, tactfully changed the subject. Controversy, he felt was an idle exercise of the emotions; it was no road to truth or wisdom. He used to point out the inutility of argumentation by the anecdote of "two men who sat down candidly to discuss a subject, and each converted the other."

Jefferson preferred to follow the rule of Benjamin Franklin: "Never to contradict anybody." If requested to express an opinion, Franklin, whom Jefferson called "the most amiable of men in society," parried it by himself asking a question or requesting information, or by subtly suggesting doubts. Avoidance of controversial conversation was, of course, in line with Jefferson's serene temperament. But there was also principle involved in this. He believed strongly that every person was entitled to his opinion, no matter how erroneous. In a letter to his grandson in 1808, President Jefferson wrote: "When I hear another express an opinion which is not mine, I say to myself, he has a right to his opinion, as I to mine; why should I question it? His error does me no injury. . . . If a fact be misstated, it is probable he is gratified by a belief of it. . . . If he wants information . . . , I will give it in measured terms; but if he . . . shows a desire to dispute the fact with me, I hear him and say nothing."

Jefferson would not indulge in argumentation, not only because he found it personally distasteful but also because he did not think it necessary. He was convinced that truth was invincible in the long run. Misinformation or aberrant notions entertained by individuals were temporary and, in any case, not of great moment. Truth, he used to say, was in itself so powerful and eternal that nothing could resist its ultimate triumph. There was, therefore, as he put it, no need for him to "become a Don Quixote" in private conversation to set everybody right.

His talk was varied, occasionally playful and paradoxical, often fecundated by formidable learning. It was likely to touch upon almost anything—natural history, fine arts, travel, philosophy, education, technology, or whatever happened to interest him or his interlocutor at the moment. A French aristocrat, the Duc de La Rochefoucauld-Liancourt, visiting Monticello in 1796, wrote of his host: "His conversation is of the most agreeable kind, and he possesses a stock of information not inferior to that of any other man. In Europe he would hold a distinguished rank among men of letters."

Jefferson had the gift of repartee. Perhaps his most memorable *mot* was the one he made in Paris when he arrived to succeed the celebrated Benjamin Franklin as American Minister. Asked, "C'est vous, Monsieur, qui remplace le Docteur Franklin?" Jefferson replied: "No one can replace him, Sir: I am only his successor." This phrase, widely reported, quickly established Jefferson's reputation among the witty French as a man of *esprit*.

Jefferson appreciated good jokes even at his own expense; sometimes he would laugh at them until he had tears in his eyes. On occasion he could not resist the temptation of taking sly digs at those whom he considered stuffy. A case in point is that of Senator William Plumer of New Hampshire, who visited the President sometime in 1803 and recorded their conversation. The humorless New Englander relates how Jefferson, after touching upon crops and weather, proceeded with a straight face to make "an elaborate defence of Horse-racing—he said it was an effectual means to improve the breed of horses—that all people will have their amusements—that horse racing is less injurious to the people than playing cards or dice as the Bostonians do. . . ." Jefferson, incidentally, never played cards and permitted none at Monticello.

He could tell tall tales with a straight face just to see what effect they would have on the solemn and the unmirthful. The grimly earnest John Quincy Adams, for example, notes in his *Diary* that he heard Jefferson tell that before he went to Europe he left in Virginia some ripe pears sewed in bags—and when he returned six years later he found them perfectly preserved and self-candied! In Paris, Jefferson also reported witnessing a hailstorm that pelted big stones. At another time, he said, the thermometer in Paris stood at twenty degrees below zero—for six weeks! Uncertain whether Jefferson was serious or not, the bemused Adams concluded: "You never can be an hour in this man's company without something of the marvelous, like these stories."

These facets of Jefferson's character—the humane, life-loving, and entertaining—deserve remembrance because they, too, are part of the great American tradition. His appeal over the years, growing with every generation, lies not merely in his brilliantly formulated philosophy of democracy but also in the fact that he was a radiant personality. Indeed, the more one knows Jefferson the more one cherishes him. He was truly a man for all seasons and all times.

THERE IS always a certain difficulty involved in selecting the works of any author of ample output. In the case of Jefferson, there is the additional challenge of his being not merely a writer but also a major historic figure and a man of protean intellectual interests. To do justice to the multiform Jefferson, and to present him with a measure of roundness, the editor has sought to strike a balance between the statesman and the thinker.

The selections covering Jefferson the statesman include also his personal writings, among which are the *Autobiography* and the political diary which he called *The Anas*. These are of such obvious importance that their inclusion needs no explanation. The same may be said of Jefferson's self-evaluation and his *Testament*.

In regard to the other selections, including the Letters, the editor was guided by three main criteria—relevance, representativeness, and variety. In other words, the test for the selections was their meaningfulness, their exemplification of Jefferson, and illustration of the range of his interests. The editor believes that the writings presented in this volume show Jefferson in his multiformity as well as his timelessness.

Saul K. Padover

CONTENTS

PART THREE
LETTERS

PART ONE

Autobiographic

PREFACE

THESE personal papers are basic materials for any understanding of Jefferson. While not as complete as one might have wished, there are nevertheless enough of them to provide us with a true portrait of Jefferson, as seen by himself. In what these papers say or omit to say, they constitute significant forms of self-evaluation.

Jefferson was not an introspective man. He wasted little time on his own ego. His preoccupation was not primarily with his soul or his self. Superbly rational and balanced, he was not tormented by self-doubt and had no need for self-assertiveness. There was, in short, little of Jean Jacques Rousseau in Jefferson. Personal drama was not an integral part of his makeup.

The essential Jefferson was an activist, a doer, and a problem-solver. One of the most widely read men of his, or any other, age, he loved ideas and had a strong taste for philosophical and scientific speculation, but within limits and always with an eye for the practical. An idealistic pragmatist, Jefferson was at the same time, in Aristotle's words, an inveterate "political animal," as these autobiographic papers show. "Politics," he once said, "is my duty." It was also, of course, a virtually lifelong profession.

Jefferson's *Autobiography* cannot be ranked with that of his admired friend Benjamin Franklin. It is not only relatively short but also incomplete. Written at the age of 77 in retirement at Monticello, the *Autobiography* was designed not for posterity but for the information of his own family. It covers only the first half of his life, terminating quite abruptly with the year 1790 (March), when Jefferson went to New York to take up his duties as Secretary of State in George Washington's Cabinet. Despite its brevity, the *Autobiography* tells a good deal about him, including one unexpectedly sardonic remark about his mother's family, the Randolphs. Referring to the boasted maternal pedigree, the son of the modestly born Peter Jefferson, a self-made and self-taught man, commented with dry irony that such a genealogy was something "to which let everyone ascribe the faith and merit he chooses." On another occasion, Jefferson quoted the English novelist Laurence Sterne's humorous observation that "a coat of arms may be purchased as cheap as any other coat."

The Anas, a collection of what Jefferson called "loose scraps," is in a sense a continuation of the *Autobiography*. It is a kind of diary covering not quite three of his four years as Secretary of State (1791–1793), plus a few additional entries of a subsequent period. An explanation of the background of *The Anas*, which Jefferson added a quarter century later (1818), is found in its introductory pages, especially the first two paragraphs.

The Anas is of interest on several counts. It is probably the first "diary" of an American Cabinet member. It records the strains and stresses of America's first National Administration. It conveys the sharp flavor of political conflict among the strong-minded men who surrounded President Washington and who pioneered in the establishment of the American Republic. There are notes of partisanship and gossip in the "scraps" of *The Anas*, but it should be kept in mind that the politics of the period was permeated with passion and verbal violence, which spared nobody. Jefferson was, if anything, likely to be more restrained than his personal or political enemies.

Altogether, these autobiographical materials, including his tentative assessment of his services to America and also his *Testament*, go far to help us understand Jefferson, the political leader par excellence.

S. K. P.

The Autobiography

⋙ JANUARY 6, 1821 ⋘ At the age of 77, I begin to make some memoranda, and state some recollections of dates and facts concerning myself, for my own more ready reference, and for the information of my family.

The tradition in my father's family was, that their ancestor came to this country from Wales, and from near the mountain of Snowdon, the highest in Great Britain. I noted once a case from Wales, in the law reports, where a person of our name was either plaintiff or defendant; and one of the same name was secretary to the Virginia Company. These are the only instances in which I have met with the name in that country. I have found it in our early records; but the first particular information I have of any ancestor was of my grandfather, who lived at the place in Chesterfield called Ozborne's, and owned the lands afterwards the glebe of the parish. He had three sons; Thomas who died young, Field who settled on the waters of Roanoke and left numerous descendants, and Peter, my father, who settled on the lands I still own, called Shadwell, adjoining my present residence. He was born February 29, 1707–8, and intermarried 1739, with Jane Randolph, of the age of 19, daughter of Isham Randolph, one of the seven sons of that name and family, settled at Dungeness in Goochland. They trace their pedigree far back in England and Scotland, to which let everyone ascribe the faith and merit he chooses.

My father's education had been quite neglected; but being of a strong mind, sound judgment, and eager after information, he read much and improved himself, insomuch that he was chosen, with Joshua Fry, Professor of Mathematics in William and Mary college, to continue the boundary line between Virginia and North Carolina, which had been begun by Colonel Byrd; and was afterwards employed with the same Mr. Fry, to make the first map of Virginia which had ever been made, that of Captain Smith being merely a conjectural sketch. They possessed excellent materials for so much of the country as is below the blue ridge; little being then known beyond that ridge. He was the third or fourth settler, about the year 1737, of the part of the country in which I live. He died, August 17th, 1757, leaving my mother a widow, who lived till 1776, with six daughters and two sons, myself the elder. To my younger brother he left his estate on James River, called Snowdon, after the supposed birth-place of the family: to myself, the lands on which I was born and live.

He placed me at the English school at five years of age; and at the Latin at nine, where I continued until his death. My teacher, Mr. Douglas, a clergyman from Scotland, with the rudiments of the Latin and Greek languages, taught me the French; and on the death of my father, I went to the Reverend Mr. Maury, a correct classical scholar, with whom I continued two years; and then, to wit, in the spring of 1760, went to William and Mary college, where I continued two years. It was my great good fortune, and what probably fixed the destinies of my life, that Dr. William Small of Scotland, was then professor of Mathematics, a man profound in most of the useful branches of science, with a happy talent of communication, correct and gentlemanly manners, and an enlarged and liberal mind. He, most happily for me, became soon attached to me, and made me his daily companion when not engaged in the school; and from his conversation I got my first views of the expansion of science, and of the system of things in which we are placed. Fortunately, the philosophical chair became vacant soon after my arrival at college, and he was appointed to fill it *per interim*: and he was the first who ever gave, in that college, regular lectures in Ethics, Rhetoric and Belles lettres. He returned to Europe in 1762, having previously filled up the measure of his goodness to me, by procuring for me, from his most intimate friend, George Wythe, a reception as a student of law, under his direction, and introduced me to the acquaintance and familiar table of Governor Fauquier, the ablest man who had ever filled that office. With him, and at his table, Dr. Small and Mr. Wythe, his *amici omnium horarum,** and myself, formed a *partie quarrée*, and to the habitual conversations on these occasions I owed much instruction. Mr. Wythe continued to be my faithful and beloved mentor in youth, and my most affectionate friend through life. In 1767,

he led me into the practice of the law at the bar of the General court, at which I continued until the Revolution shut up the courts of justice.

In 1769, I became a member of the legislature by the choice of the county in which I live, and so continued until it was closed by the Revolution. I made one effort in that body for the permission of the emancipation of slaves, which was rejected: and indeed, during the regal government, nothing liberal could expect success. Our minds were circumscribed within narrow limits, by an habitual belief that it was our

* Friends of all hours.

duty to be subordinate to the mother country in all matters of government, to direct all our labors in subservience to her interests, and even to observe a bigoted intolerance for all religions but hers. The difficulties with our representatives were of habit and despair, not of reflection and conviction. Experience soon proved that they could bring their minds to rights, on the first summons of their attention. But the King's Council, which acted as another house of legislature, held their places at will, and were in most humble obedience to that will: the Governor too, who had a negative on our laws, held by the same tenure, and with still greater devotedness to it: and, last of all, the Royal negative closed the last door to every hope of amelioration.

On the 1st of January, 1772, I was married to Martha Skelton, widow of Bathurst Skelton, and daughter of John Wayles, then twenty-three years old. Mr. Wayles was a lawyer of much practice, to which he was introduced more by his great industry, punctuality, and practical readiness, than by eminence in the science of his profession. He was a most agreeable companion, full of pleasantry and good humor, and welcomed in every society. He acquired a handsome fortune, and died in May, 1773, leaving three daughters: the portion which came on that event to Mrs. Jefferson, after the debts should be paid, which were very considerable, was about equal to my own patrimony, and consequently doubled the ease of our circumstances.

When the famous Resolutions of 1765, against the Stamp-act, were proposed, I was yet a student of law in Williamsburg. I attended the debate, however, at the door of the lobby of the House of Burgesses, and heard the splendid display of Mr. Henry's talents as a popular orator. They were great indeed; such as I have never heard from any other man. He appeared to me to speak as Homer wrote. Mr. Johnson, a lawyer, and member from the Northern Neck, seconded the resolutions, and by him the learning and the logic of the case were chiefly maintained. My recollections of these transactions may be seen on page 60 of the life of Patrick Henry, by Wirt, to whom I furnished them.

In May, 1769, a meeting of the General Assembly was called by the Governor, Lord Botetourt. I had then become a member; and to that meeting became known the joint resolutions and address of the Lords and

Commons, of 1768–9, on the proceedings in Massachusetts. Counter-resolutions, and an address to the King by the House of Burgesses, were agreed to with little opposition, and a spirit manifestly displayed itself of considering the cause of Massachusetts as a common one. The Governor dissolved us: but we met the next day in the Apollo of the Raleigh tavern, formed ourselves into a voluntary convention, drew up articles of association against the use of any merchandise imported from Great Britain, signed and recommended them to the people, repaired to our several counties, and were re-elected without any other exception than of the very few who had declined assent to our proceedings.

Nothing of particular excitement occurring for a considerable time, our countrymen seemed to fall into a state of insensibility to our situation; the duty on tea, not yet repealed, and the declaratory act of a right in the British Parliament to bind us by their laws in all cases whatsoever, still suspended over us. But a court of inquiry held in Rhode Island in 1762, with a power to send persons to England to be tried for offences committed here, was considered, at our session of the spring of 1773, as demanding attention. Not thinking our old and leading members up to the point of forwardness and zeal which the times required, Mr. Henry, Richard Henry Lee, Francis L. Lee, Mr. Carr and myself agreed to meet in the evening, in a private room of the Raleigh, to consult on the state of things. There may have been a member or two more whom I do not recollect. We were all sensible that the most urgent of all measures was that of coming to an understanding with all the other colonies, to consider the British claims as a common cause to all, and to produce a unity of action: and, for this purpose, that a committee of correspondence in each colony would be the best instrument for intercommunication: and that their first measure would probably be, to propose a meeting of deputies from every colony, at some central place, who should be charged with the direction of the measures which should be taken by all. We, therefore, drew up the resolutions which may be seen in Wirt, page 87. The consulting members proposed to me to move them, but I urged that it should be done by Mr. Carr, my friend and brother-in-law, then a new member, to whom I wished an opportunity should be given of making known to the house his great worth and talents. It was so agreed; he moved them, they were agreed to *nem. con.*, and a committee of correspondence appointed, of whom Peyton Randolph, the speaker, was chairman. The Governor (then Lord Dunmore) dissolved us, but the committee met the next day, prepared a circular letter to the speakers of the other colonies, inclosing to each a copy of the resolutions, and left it in charge with their chairman to forward them by expresses.

The origination of these committees of correspondence between the colonies has been since claimed for Massachusetts, and Marshall* has given into this error, although the very note of his appendix to which he refers, shows that their establishment was confined to their own towns. This matter will be seen clearly stated in a letter of Samuel Adams Wells to me of April 2nd, 1819, and my answer of May 12th. I was corrected by the letter of Mr. Wells in the information I had given Mr. Wirt, as stated in his note, page 87, that the messengers of Massachusetts and Virginia crossed each other on the way, bearing similar propositions; for Mr. Wells shows that Massachusetts did not adopt the measure, but on the receipt of our proposition, delivered at their next session. Their message, therefore, which passed ours, must have related to something else, for I well remember Peyton Randolph's informing me of the crossing of our messengers.

The next event which excited our sympathies for Massachusetts, was the Boston port bill, by which that port was to be shut up on the 1st of June, 1774. This arrived while we were in session in the spring of that year. The lead in the House, on these subjects, being no longer left to the old members, Mr. Henry, R. H. Lee, Fr. L. Lee, three or four other members, whom I do not recollect, and myself, agreeing that we must boldly take an unequivocal stand in the line with Massachusetts, determined to meet and consult on the proper measures, in the council-chamber, for the benefit of the library in that room. We were under conviction of the necessity of arousing our people from the lethargy into which they had fallen, as to passing events; and thought that the appointment of a day of general fasting and prayer would be most likely to call up and alarm their attention. No example of such a solemnity

---

* In his *Life of Washington.*

had existed since the days of our distresses in the war of '55, since which a new generation had grown up. With the help, therefore, of Rushworth, whom we rummaged over for the revolutionary precedents and forms of the Puritans of that day, preserved by him, we cooked up a resolution, somewhat modernizing their phrases, for appointing the 1st day of June, on which the port bill was to commence, for a day of fasting, humiliation, and prayer, to implore Heaven to avert from us the evils of civil war, to inspire us with firmness in support of our rights, and to turn the hearts of the King and Parliament to moderation and justice. To give greater emphasis to our proposition, we agreed to wait the next morning on Mr. Nicholas, whose grave and religious character was more in unison with the tone of our resolution, and to solicit him to move it. We accordingly went to him in the morning. He moved it the same day; the 1st of June was proposed; and it passed without opposition. The Governor dissolved us, as usual. We retired to the Apollo, as before, agreed to an association, and instructed the committee of correspondence to propose to the corresponding committees of the other colonies, to appoint deputies to meet in Congress at such place, *annually*, as should be convenient, to direct, from time to time, the measures required by the general interest: and we declared that an attack on any one colony, should be considered as an attack on the whole. This was in May. We further recommended to the several counties to elect deputies to meet at Williamsburg, the 1st of August ensuing, to consider the state of the colony, and particularly to appoint delegates to a general Congress, should that measure be acceded to by the committees of correspondence generally. It was acceded to; Philadelphia was appointed for the place, and the 5th of September for the time of meeting. We returned home, and in our several counties invited the clergy to meet assemblies of the people on the 1st of June, to perform the ceremonies of the day, and to address to them discourses suited to the occasion. The people met generally, with anxiety and alarm in their countenances, and the effect of the day, through the whole colony, was like a shock of electricity, arousing every man, and placing him erect and solidly on his centre. They chose, universally, delegates for the convention. Being elected one for my own county, I prepared a draught of instructions to be given to the delegates whom we should send to the Congress, which I meant to propose at our meeting. In this I took the ground that, from the beginning, I had thought the only one orthodox or tenable, which was, that the relation between Great Britain and these colonies was exactly the same as that of England and Scotland, after the accession of James, and until the union, and the same as her present relations with Hanover, having the same executive chief, but no other necessary political connection; and that our emigration from England to this country gave her no more rights over us, than the emigrations of the Danes and Saxons gave to the present authorities of the mother country, over England. In this doctrine, however, I had never been able to get anyone to agree with me but Mr. Wythe. He concurred in it from the first dawn of the question, What was the political relation between us and England? Our other patriots, Randolph, the Lees, Nicholas, Pendleton, stopped at the half-way house of John Dickinson, who admitted that England had a right to regulate our commerce, and to lay duties on it for the purposes of regulation, but not of raising revenue. But for this ground there was no foundation in compact, in any acknowledged principles of colonization, nor in reason: expatriation being a natural right, and acted on as such, by all nations, in all ages. I set out for Williamsburg some days before that appointed for our meeting, but was taken ill of a dysentery on the road, and was unable to proceed. I sent on, therefore, to Williamsburg, two copies of my draught, the one under cover to Peyton Randolph, who I knew would be in the chair of the convention, the other to Patrick Henry. Whether Mr. Henry disapproved the ground taken, or was too lazy to read it (for he was the laziest man in reading I ever knew) I never learned: but he communicated it to nobody. Peyton Randolph informed the convention he had received such a paper from a member, prevented by sickness from offering it in his place, and he laid it on the table for perusal. It was read generally by the members, approved by many, though thought too bold for the present state of things; but they printed it in pamphlet form, under the title of "A Summary View of the Rights of British America."* It found its way to

* See Part ii, page 243.

England, was taken up by the opposition, interpolated a little by Mr. Burke so as to make it answer opposition purposes, and in that form ran rapidly through several editions. This information I had from Parson Hurt, who happened at the time to be in London, whither he had gone to receive clerical orders; and I was informed afterwards by Peyton Randolph, that it had procured me the honor of having my name inserted in a long list of proscriptions, enrolled in a bill of attainder commenced in one of the Houses of Parliament, but suppressed in embryo by the hasty step of events, which warned them to be a little cautious. Montague, agent of the House of Burgesses in England, made extracts from the bill, copied the names, and sent them to Peyton Randolph. The names, I think, were about twenty, which he repeated to me, but I recollect those only of Hancock, the two Adamses, Peyton Randolph himself, Patrick Henry, and myself. The convention met on the 1st of August, renewed their association, appointed delegates to the Congress, gave them instructions very temperately and properly expressed, both as to style and matter; and they repaired to Philadelphia at the time appointed. The splendid proceedings of that Congress, at their first session, belong to general history, are known to everyone, and need not therefore be noted here. They terminated their session on the 26th of October, to meet again on the 10th of May ensuing. The convention, at their ensuing session of March, '75, approved of the proceedings of Congress, thanked their delegates, and reappointed the same persons to represent the colony at the meeting to be held in May: and foreseeing the probability that Peyton Randolph, their president, and speaker also of the House of Burgesses, might be called off, they added me, in that event, to the delegation.

Mr. Randolph was, according to expectation, obliged to leave the chair of Congress, to attend the General Assembly summoned by Lord Dunmore, to meet on the 1st day of June, 1775. Lord North's conciliatory propositions, as they were called, had been received by the Governor, and furnished the subject for which this assembly was convened. Mr. Randolph accordingly attended, and the tenor of these propositions being generally known, as having been addressed to all the governors, he was anxious that the answer of our Assembly, likely to be the first, should harmonize with what he knew to be the sentiments and wishes of the body he had recently left. He feared that Mr. Nicholas, whose mind was not yet up to the mark of the times, would undertake the answer, and therefore pressed me to prepare it. I did so, and, with his aid, carried it through the House, with long and doubtful scruples from Mr. Nicholas and James Mercer, and a dash of cold water on it here and there, enfeebling it somewhat, but finally with unanimity, or a vote approaching it. This being passed, I repaired immediately to Philadelphia, and conveyed to Congress the first notice they had of it. It was entirely approved there. I took my seat with them on the 21st of June. On the 24th, a committee which had been appointed to prepare a declaration of the causes of taking up arms, brought in their report (drawn I believe by J. Rutledge) which, not being liked, the House recommitted it, on the 26th, and added Mr. Dickinson and myself to the committee. On the rising of the House, the committee having not yet met, I happened to find myself near Governor W. Livingston, and proposed to him to draw the paper. He excused himself and proposed that I should draw it. On my pressing him with urgency, "we are as yet but new acquaintances, sir," said he, "why are you so earnest for my doing it?" "Because," said I, "I have been informed that you drew the Address to the people of Great Britain, a production, certainly, of the finest pen in America." "On that," says he, "perhaps, sir, you may not have been correctly informed." I had received the information in Virginia from Colonel Harrison on his return from that Congress. Lee, Livingston, and Jay had been the committee for that draught. The first, prepared by Lee, had been disapproved and recommitted. The second was drawn by Jay, but being presented by Governor Livingston, had led Colonel Harrison into the error. The next morning, walking in the hall of Congress, many members being assembled, but the House not yet formed, I observed Mr. Jay speaking to R. H. Lee, and leading him by the button of his coat to me. "I understand, sir," said he to me, "that this gentleman informed you, that Governor Livingston drew the Address to the people of Great Britain." I assured him, at once, that I had not received that information from Mr. Lee, and that not a word had ever passed on the subject between Mr. Lee and myself; and after some explanations the subject was dropped. These gentlemen had had some sparrings in debate before, and continued ever very hostile to each other.

I prepared a draught of the declaration committed to us. It was too strong for Mr. Dickinson. He still retained the hope of reconciliation with the mother country, and was unwilling it should be lessened by offensive statements. He was so honest a man, and so able a one, that he was greatly indulged even by those who could not feel his scruples. We therefore requested him to take the paper, and put it into a form he could approve. He did so, preparing an entire new statement, and preserving of the former only the last four paragraphs and half of the preceding one. We approved and reported it to Congress, who accepted it. Congress gave a signal proof of their indulgence to Mr. Dickinson, and of their great desire not to go too fast for any respectable part of our body, in permitting him to draw their second petition to the King according to his own ideas, and passing it with scarcely any amendment. The disgust against this humility was general; and Mr. Dickinson's delight at its passage was the only circumstance which reconciled them to it. The vote being passed, although further observation on it was out of order, he could not refrain from rising and expressing his satisfaction, and concluded by saying, "there is but one word, Mr. President, in the paper which I disapprove, and that is the word *Congress*"; on which Ben Harrison rose and said, "There is but one word in the paper, Mr. President, of which I approve, and that is the word *Congress*."

On the 22d of July, Dr. Franklin, Mr. Adams, R. H. Lee, and myself, were appointed a committee to consider and report on Lord North's conciliatory resolution. The answer of the Virginia Assembly on that subject having been approved, I was requested by the committee to prepare this report, which will account for the similarity of feature in the two instruments.

On the 15th of May, 1776, the convention of Virginia instructed their delegates in Congress, to propose to that body to declare the colonies independent of Great Britain, and appointed a committee to prepare a declaration of rights and plan of government.

In Congress, Friday, June 7, 1776. The delegates from Virginia moved, in obedience to instructions from their constituents, that the Congress should declare that these United colonies are, and of right ought to be, free and independent states, that they are absolved from all allegiance to the British crown, and that all political connection between them and the state of Great Britain is, and ought to be, totally dissolved; that measures should be immediately taken for procuring

the assistance of foreign powers, and a Confederation be formed to bind the colonies more closely together.

The House being obliged to attend at that time to some other business, the proposition was referred to the next day, when the members were ordered to attend punctually at ten o'clock.

Saturday, June 8. They proceeded to take it into consideration, and referred it to a committee of the whole, into which they immediately resolved themselves, and passed that day and Monday, the 10th, in debating on the subject.

It was argued by Wilson, Robert R. Livingston, E. Rutledge, Dickinson, and others—

That, though they were friends to the measures themselves, and saw the impossibility that we should ever again be united with Great Britain, yet they were against adopting them at this time:

That the conduct we had formerly observed was wise and proper now, of deferring to take any capital step till the voice of the people drove us into it:

That they were our power, and without them our declarations could not be carried into effect:

That the people of the middle colonies (Maryland, Delaware, Pennsylvania, the Jerseys and New York) were not yet ripe for bidding adieu to British connection, but that they were fast ripening, and, in a short time, would join in the general voice of America:

That the resolution, entered into by this House on the 15th of May, for suppressing the exercise of all powers derived from the crown, had shown, by the ferment into which it had thrown these middle colonies, that they had not yet accommodated their minds to a separation from the mother country:

That some of them had expressly forbidden their delegates to consent to such a declaration, and others had given no instructions, and consequently no powers to give such consent:

That if the delegates of any particular colony had no power to declare such colony independent, certain they were, the others could not declare it for them; the colonies being as yet perfectly independent of each other:

That the assembly of Pennsylvania was now sitting above stairs, their convention would sit within a few days, the convention of New York was now sitting, and those of the Jerseys and Delaware counties would meet on the Monday following, and it was probable these bodies would take up the question of Independence, and would declare to their delegates the voice of their state:

That if such a declaration should now be agreed to, these delegates must retire, and possibly their colonies might secede from the Union:

That such a secession would weaken us more than could be compensated by any foreign alliance:

That in the event of such a division, foreign powers would either refuse to join themselves to our fortunes, or, having us so much in their power as that desperate declaration would place us, they would insist on terms proportionably more hard and prejudicial:

That we had little reason to expect an alliance with those to whom alone, as yet, we had cast our eyes:

That France and Spain had reason to be jealous of that rising power, which would one day certainly strip them of all their American possessions:

That it was more likely they should form a connection with the British court, who, if they should find themselves unable otherwise to extricate themselves from their difficulties, would agree to a partition of our territories, restoring Canada to France, and the Floridas to Spain, to accomplish for themselves a recovery of these colonies:

That it would not be long before we should receive certain information of the disposition of the French court, from the agent whom we had sent to Paris for that purpose:

That if this disposition should be favorable, by waiting the event of the present campaign, which we all hoped would be successful, we should have reason to expect an alliance on better terms:

That this would in fact work no delay of any effectual aid from such ally, as, from the advance of the season and distance of our situation, it was impossible we could receive any assistance during this campaign:

That it was prudent to fix among ourselves the terms on which we should form alliance, before we declared we would form one at all events:

And that if these were agreed on, and our Declaration of Independence ready by the time our Ambassador should be prepared to sail, it would be as well as to go into that Declaration at this day.

On the other side, it was urged by J. Adams, Lee, Wythe, and others, that no gentleman had argued against the policy or the right of separation from Britain, nor had supposed it possible we should ever renew our connection; that they had only opposed its being now declared:

That the question was not whether, by a Declaration of Independence, we should make ourselves what we are not; but whether we should declare a fact which already exists:

That, as to the people or parliament of England, we had always been independent of them, their restraints on our trade deriving efficacy from our acquiescence only, and not from any rights they possessed of imposing them, and that so far, our connection had been federal only, and was now dissolved by the commencement of hostilities:

That, as to the King, we had been bound to him by allegiance, but that this bond was now dissolved by his assent to the last act of Parliament, by which he declares us out of his protection, and by his levying war on us, a fact which had long ago proved us out of his protection; it being a certain position in law, that allegiance and protection are reciprocal, the one ceasing when the other is withdrawn:

That James the II never declared the people of England out of his protection, yet his actions proved it, and the Parliament declared it:

No delegates then can be denied, or ever want, a power of declaring an existing truth:

That the delegates from the Delaware counties having declared their constituents ready to join, there are only two colonies, Pennsylvania and Maryland, whose delegates are absolutely tied up, and that these had, by their instructions, only reserved a right of confirming or rejecting the measure:

That the instructions from Pennsylvania might be accounted for from the times in which they were drawn, near a twelvemonth ago, since which the face of affairs has totally changed:

That within that time, it had become apparent that Britain was determined to accept nothing less than a *carte-blanche*, and that the King's answer to the Lord Mayor, Aldermen and Common Council of London, which had come to hand four days ago, must have satisfied everyone of this point:

That the people wait for us to lead the way:

That *they* are in favor of the measure, though the instructions given by some of their *representatives* are not:

That the voice of the representatives is not always consonant with the voice of the people, and that this is remarkably the case in these middle colonies:

That the effect of the resolution of the 15th of May has proved this, which, raising the murmurs of some in the colonies of Pennsylvania and Maryland, called forth the opposing voice of the freer part of the people, and proved them to be the majority even in these colonies:

That the backwardness of these two colonies might be ascribed, partly to the influence of proprietary power and connections, and partly, to their having not yet been attacked by the enemy:

That these causes were not likely to be soon removed, as there seemed no probability that the enemy would make either of these the seat of this summer's war:

That it would be vain to wait either weeks or months for perfect unanimity, since it was impossible that all men should ever become of one sentiment on any question:

That the conduct of some colonies, from the beginning of this contest, had given reason to suspect it was their settled policy to keep in the rear of the confederacy, that their particular prospect might be better, even in the worst event:

That, therefore, it was necessary for those colonies who had thrown themselves forward and hazarded all from the beginning, to come forward now also, and put all again to their own hazard:

That the history of the Dutch Revolution, of whom three states only confederated at first, proved that a secession of some colonies would not be so dangerous as some apprehended:

That a declaration of Independence alone could render it consistent with European delicacy, for European powers to treat with us, or even to receive an Ambassador from us:

That till this, they would not receive our vessels into their ports, nor acknowledge the adjudications of our courts of admiralty to be legitimate, in cases of capture of British vessels:

That though France and Spain may be jealous of our rising power, they must think it will be much more formidable with the addition of Great Britain; and will therefore see it their interest to prevent a coalition; but should they refuse, we shall be but where we are; whereas without trying, we shall never know whether they will aid us or not:

That the present campaign may be unsuccessful, and therefore we had better propose an alliance while our affairs wear a hopeful aspect:

That to wait the event of this campaign will certainly work delay, because, during the summer, France may assist us effectually, by cutting off those supplies of provisions from England and Ireland, on which the enemy's armies here are to depend; or by setting in motion the great power they have collected in the West Indies, and calling our enemy to the defence of the possessions they have there:

That it would be idle to lose time in settling the terms of alliance, till we had first determined we would enter into alliance:

That it is necessary to lose no time in opening a trade for our people, who will want clothes, and will want money too, for the payment of taxes:

And that the only misfortune is, that we did not enter into alliance with France six months sooner, as, besides opening her ports for the vent of our last year's produce, she might have marched an army into Germany, and prevented the petty princes there, from selling their unhappy subjects to subdue us.

It appearing in the course of these debates, that the colonies of New York, New Jersey, Pennsylvania, Delaware, Maryland, and South Carolina were not yet matured for falling from the parent stem, but that they were fast advancing to that state, it was thought most prudent to wait a while for them, and to postpone the final decision to July 1st; but, that this might occasion as little delay as possible, a committee was appointed to prepare a Declaration of Independence. The committee were John Adams, Dr. Franklin, Roger Sherman, Robert R. Livingston, and myself. Committees were also appointed, at the same time, to prepare a plan of confederation for the colonies, and to state the terms proper to be proposed for foreign alliance. The committee for drawing the Declaration of Independence, desired me to do it. It was accordingly done, and being approved by them, I reported it to the House on Friday, the 28th of June, when it was read, and ordered to lie on the table. On Monday, the 1st of July, the House resolved itself into a committee of the whole, and resumed the consideration of the original motion made by the delegates of Virginia, which, being again debated through the day, was carried in the affirmative by the votes of New Hampshire, Connecticut, Massachusetts, Rhode Island,

New Jersey, Maryland, Virginia, North Carolina and Georgia. South
Carolina and Pennsylvania voted against it. Delaware had but two
members present, and they were divided. The delegates from New
York declared they were for it themselves, and were assured their
constituents were for it; but that their instructions having been drawn
near a twelvemonth before, when reconciliation was still the general
object, they were enjoined by them to do nothing which should impede
that object. They, therefore, thought themselves not justifiable in voting on either side, and asked leave to withdraw from the question;
which was given them. The committee rose and reported their resolution to the House. Mr. Edward Rutledge, of South Carolina, then requested the determination might be put off to the next day, as he
believed his colleagues, though they disapproved of the resolution,
would then join in it for the sake of unanimity. The ultimate question,
whether the House would agree to the resolution of the committee,
was accordingly postponed to the next day, when it was again moved,
and South Carolina concurred in voting for it. In the meantime, a third
member had come post from the Delaware counties, and turned the
vote of that colony in favor of the resolution. Members of a different
sentiment attending that morning from Pennsylvania also, her vote
was changed, so that the whole twelve colonies who were authorized
to vote at all, gave their voices for it; and, within a few days, the
convention of New York approved of it, and thus supplied the void
occasioned by the withdrawing of her delegates from the vote.

Congress proceeded the same day to consider the Declaration of
Independence, which had been reported and lain on the table the Friday
preceding, and on Monday referred to a committee of the whole. The
pusillanimous idea that we had friends in England worth keeping terms
with, still haunted the minds of many. For this reason, those passages
which conveyed censures on the people of England were struck out,
lest they should give them offence. The clause too, reprobating the
enslaving the inhabitants of Africa, was struck out in complaisance to
South Carolina and Georgia, who had never attempted to restrain the
importation of slaves, and who, on the contrary, still wished to continue
it. Our northern brethren also, I believe, felt a little tender under those

censures; for though their people had very few slaves themselves, yet they had been pretty considerable carriers of them to others. The debates, having taken up the greater parts of the 2d, 3d, and 4th days of July, were, on the evening of the last, closed; the Declaration was reported by the committee, agreed to by the House, and signed by every member present, except Mr. Dickinson. As the sentiments of

men are known not only by what they receive, but what they reject also, I will state the form of the Declaration as originally reported. The parts struck out by Congress shall be distinguished by a black line drawn under them;* and those inserted by them shall be placed in the margin, or in a concurrent column.

≫ The Declaration thus signed on the 4th, on paper, was engrossed on parchment, and signed again on the 2d of August.

* The Declaration is omitted here; it is printed in Part II, page 263.

[Some erroneous statements of the proceedings on the Declaration of Independence having got before the public in latter times, Mr. Samuel A. Wells asked explanations of me, which are given in my letter to him of May 12, '19, before and now again referred to. I took notes in my place while these things were going on, and at their close wrote them out in form and with correctness, and from 1 to 7 of the two preceding sheets, are the originals then written; as the two following are of the earlier debates on the Confederation, which I took in like manner.]

On Friday, July 12, the committee appointed to draw the articles of Confederation reported them, and, on the 22d, the House resolved themselves into a committee to take them into consideration. On the 30th and 31st of that month, and 1st of the ensuing, those articles were debated which determined the proportion, or quota, of money which each state should furnish to the common treasury, and the manner of voting in Congress. The first of these articles was expressed in the original draught in these words: "Art. XI. All charges of war and all other expenses that shall be incurred for the common defence, or general welfare, and allowed by the United States assembled, shall be defrayed out of a common treasury, which shall be supplied by the several colonies in proportion to the number of inhabitants of every age, sex, and quality, except Indians not paying taxes, in each colony, a true account of which, distinguishing the white inhabitants, shall be triennially taken and transmitted to the Assembly of the United States."

Mr. Chase moved that the quotas should be fixed, not by the number of inhabitants of every condition, but by that of the "white inhabitants." He admitted that taxation should be always in proportion to property, that this was, in theory, the true rule; but that, from a variety of difficulties, it was a rule which could never be adopted in practice. The value of the property in every State, could never be estimated justly and equally. Some other measure for the wealth of the State must therefore be devised, some standard referred to, which would be more simple. He considered the number of inhabitants as a tolerably good criterion of property, and that this might always be obtained. He therefore thought it the best mode which we could adopt, with one exception only: he observed that Negroes are property, and as such, cannot be distinguished from the lands or personalities held in those States where there are few slaves; that the surplus of profit which a Northern farmer is able to lay by, he invests in cattle, horses, &c., whereas a Southern farmer lays out the same surplus in slaves. There is no more reason, therefore, for taxing the Southern States on the farmer's head, and on his slave's head, than the Northern ones on their farmers' heads and the heads of their cattle; that the method proposed would, therefore, tax the Southern States according to their numbers and their wealth conjunctly, while the Northern would be taxed on numbers only: that Negroes, in fact, should not be considered as members of the State, more than cattle, and that they have no more interest in it.

Mr. John Adams observed, that the numbers of people were taken by this article, as an index of the wealth of the State, and not as subjects of taxation; that, as to this matter, it was of no consequence by what name you called your people, whether by that of freemen or of slaves; that in some countries the laboring poor were called freemen, in others they were called slaves; but that the difference as to the state was imaginary only. What matters it whether a landlord, employing ten laborers on his farm, gives them annually as much money as will buy them the necessaries of life, or gives them those necessaries at short hand? The ten laborers add as much wealth annually to the State, increase its exports as much in the one case as the other. Certainly five hundred freemen produce no more profits, no greater surplus for the payment of taxes, than five hundred slaves. Therefore, the State in which are the laborers called freemen, should be taxed no more than that in which are those called slaves. Suppose, by an extraordinary operation of nature or of law, one half the laborers of a State could in the course of one night be transformed into slaves; would the State be made the poorer or the less able to pay taxes? That the condition of the laboring poor in most countries, that of the fishermen particularly of the Northern States, is as abject as that of slaves. It is the number of laborers which produces the surplus for taxation, and numbers, therefore, indiscriminately, are the fair index of wealth; that it is the use of the word "property" here, and its application to some of the people of the State, which produces the fallacy. How does the Southern farmer procure slaves? Either by importation or by purchase from his neighbor. If he imports a slave, he adds one to the number of laborers in his country, and proportionably to its profits and abilities to pay taxes; if he buys from his neighbor, it is only a transfer of a laborer from one farm to another, which does not change the annual produce of the State, and therefore, should not change its tax: that if a Northern farmer works ten laborers on his farm, he can, it is true, invest the surplus of ten men's labor in cattle; but so may the Southern farmer, working ten slaves; that a State of one hundred thousand freemen can maintain no more cattle, than one of one hundred thousand slaves. Therefore, they have no more of that kind of property; that a slave may indeed, from the custom of speech, be more properly called the wealth of his master, than the free laborer might be called the wealth of his employer; but as to the State, both were equally its wealth, and should, therefore, equally add to the quota of its tax.

Mr. Harrison proposed, as a compromise, that two slaves should be counted as one freeman. He affirmed that slaves did not do as much work as freemen, and doubted if two effected more than one; that this was proved by the price of labor; the hire of a laborer in the Southern colonies being from 8 to £12, while in the Northern it was generally £24.

Mr. Wilson said, that if this amendment should take place, the Southern colonies would have all the benefit of slaves, whilst the Northern ones would bear the burthen: that slaves increase the profits of a State, which the Southern States mean to take to themselves; that they also increase the burthen of defence, which would of course fall so much the heavier on the Northern: that slaves occupy the places of freemen, and eat their food. Dismiss your slaves, and freemen will take their places. It is our duty to lay every discouragement on the importation of slaves; but this amendment would give the *jus trium liberorum** to him who would import slaves: that other kinds of property were pretty equally distributed through all the colonies: there were as many cattle, horses and sheep, in the North as the South, and South as the North; but not so as to slaves: that experience has shown that those colonies have been

---

* Right of three freemen.

always able to pay most, which have the most inhabitants, whether they be black or white; and the practice of the Southern colonies has always been to make every farmer pay poll taxes upon all his laborers, whether they be black or white. He acknowledges, indeed, that freemen work the most; but they consume the most also. They do not produce a greater surplus for taxation. The slave is neither fed nor clothed so expensively as a freeman. Again, white women are exempted from labor generally, but Negro women are not. In this, then, the Southern States have an advantage as the article now stands. It has sometimes been said, that slavery is necessary, because the commodities they raise would be too dear for market if cultivated by freemen; but now it is said that the labor of the slave is the dearest.

Mr. Payne urged the original resolution of Congress, to proportion the quotas of the States to the number of souls.

Dr. Witherspoon was of opinion, that the value of lands and houses was the best estimate of the wealth of a nation, and that it was practicable to obtain such a valuation. This is the true barometer of wealth. The one now proposed is imperfect in itself, and unequal between the States. It has been objected that Negroes eat the food of freemen, and, therefore, should be taxed; horses also eat the food of freemen; therefore they also should be taxed. It has been said too, that in carrying slaves into the estimate of the taxes the State is to pay, we do no more than those States themselves do, who always take slaves into the estimate of the taxes the individual is to pay. But the cases are not parallel. In the Southern colonies slaves pervade the whole colony; but they do not pervade the whole continent. That as to the original resolution of Congress, to proportion the quotas according to the souls, it was temporary only, and related to the moneys heretofore emitted: whereas we are now entering into a new compact, and therefore stand on original ground.

August 1. The question being put, the amendment proposed was rejected by the votes of New Hampshire, Massachusetts, Rhode Island, Connecticut, New York, New Jersey, and Pennsylvania, against those of Delaware, Maryland, Virginia, North and South Carolina. Georgia was divided.

The other article was in these words: "Art. XVII. In determining questions, each colony shall have one vote."

July 30, 31, August 1. Present forty-one members. Mr. Chase observed this article was the most likely to divide us, of any one proposed in the draught then under consideration: that the larger colonies had threatened they would not confederate at all, if their weight in Congress should not be equal to the numbers of people they added to the confederacy; while the smaller ones declared against a union, if they did not retain an equal vote for the protection of their rights. That it was of the utmost consequence to bring the parties together, as, should we sever from each other, either no foreign power will ally with us at all, or the different States will form different alliances, and thus increase the horrors of those scenes of civil war and bloodshed, which in such a state of separation and independence, would render us a miserable people. That our importance, our interests, our peace required that we should confederate, and that mutual sacrifices should be made to effect a compromise of this difficult question. He was of opinion, the smaller colonies would lose their rights, if they were not in some instances allowed an equal vote; and, therefore, that a discrimination should take place among the questions which would come before Congress. That the smaller States should be secured in all questions concerning life or liberty, and the greater ones, in all respecting property. He, therefore, proposed, that in votes relating to money, the voice of each colony should be proportioned to the number of its inhabitants.

Dr. Franklin thought, that the votes should be so proportioned in all cases. He took notice that the Delaware counties had bound up their delegates to disagree to this article. He thought it a very extraordinary language to be held by any State, that they would not confederate with us, unless we would let them dispose of our money. Certainly, if we vote equally, we ought to pay equally; but the smaller States will hardly purchase the privilege at this price. That had he lived in a State where the representation, originally equal, had become unequal by time and accident, he might have submitted rather than disturb government; but that we should be very wrong to set out in this practice, when it is in our power to establish what is right. That at the time of the Union between England and Scotland, the latter had made the objection which the smaller States now do; but experience had proved that no unfairness had ever been shown them: that their advocates had prognosticated that it would again happen, as in times of old, that the whale would swallow Jonas, but he thought the prediction reversed in event, and that Jonas had swallowed the whale; for the Scotch had in fact got possession of the government, and gave laws to the English. He reprobated the original agreement of Congress to vote by colonies, and, therefore, was for their voting, in all cases, according to the number of taxables.

Dr. Witherspoon opposed every alteration of the article. All men admit that a confederacy is necessary. Should the idea get abroad that there is likely to be no union among us, it will damp the minds of the people, diminish the glory of our struggle, and lessen its importance; because it will open to our view future prospects of war and dissension among ourselves. If an equal vote be refused, the smaller States will become vassals to the larger; and all experience has shown that the vassals and subjects of free States are the most enslaved. He instanced the Helots of Sparta, and the provinces of Rome. He observed that foreign powers, discovering this blemish, would make it a handle for disengaging the smaller States from so unequal a confederacy. That the colonies should in fact be considered as individuals; and that, as such, in all disputes, they should have an equal vote; that they are now collected as individuals making a bargain with each other, and, of course, had a right to vote as individuals. That in the East India Company they voted by persons, and not by their proportion of stock. That the Belgic confederacy voted by provinces. That in questions of war the smaller States were as much interested as the larger, and therefore, should vote equally; and indeed, that the larger States were more likely to bring war on the confederacy, in proportion as their frontier was more extensive. He admitted that equality of representation was an excellent principle, but then it must be of things which are co-ordinate; that is, of things similar, and of the same nature: that nothing relating to individuals could ever come before Congress; nothing but what would respect colonies. He distinguished between an incorporating and a federal union. The union of England was an incorporating one; yet Scotland had suffered by that union; for that its inhabitants were drawn from it by the hopes of places and employments: nor was it an instance of equality of representation; because, while Scotland was allowed nearly a thirteenth of representation, they were to pay only one fortieth of the land tax. He expressed his hopes, that in the present enlightened state of men's minds, we might expect a lasting confederacy, if it was founded on fair principles.

John Adams advocated the voting in proportion to numbers. He said that we stand here as the representatives of the people: that in some States the people are many, in others they are few; that therefore, their vote here should be proportioned to the numbers from whom it comes. Reason, justice and equity never had weight enough on the face of the earth, to govern the councils of men. It is interest alone which does it, and it is interest alone which can be trusted: that therefore the interests within doors, should be the mathematical representatives of the interests without doors: that the individuality of the colonies is a mere sound. Does the individuality of a colony increase its wealth or numbers? If it does, pay equally. If it does not add weight in the scale of the confederacy, it cannot add to their rights, nor weigh in argument. A. has £50, B. £500, C. £1000 in partnership. Is it just they should equally dispose of the moneys of the partnership? It has been said, we are independent individuals making a bargain together. The question is not what we are now, but what we ought to be when our bargain shall be made. The confederacy is to make us one individual only; it is to form us like separate parcels of metal, into one common mass. We shall no longer retain our separate individuality, but become a single individual as to all questions submitted to the confederacy. Therefore, all those reasons, which prove the justice and expediency of equal representation in other assemblies, hold good here. It has been objected that a proportional vote will endanger the smaller States. We answer that an equal vote will endanger the larger. Virginia, Pennsylvania, and Massachusetts, are the three greater colonies. Consider their distance, their difference of produce, of interests, and of manners, and it is apparent they can never have an interest or inclination to combine for the oppression of the smaller: that the smaller will naturally divide on all questions with the larger. Rhode Island, from its relation, similarity and intercourse, will generally pursue the same objects with Massachusetts; Jersey, Delaware, and Maryland, with Pennsylvania.

Dr. Rush took notice, that the decay of the liberties of the Dutch republic proceeded from three causes. 1. The perfect unanimity requisite on all occasions. 2. Their obligation to consult their constituents. 3. Their voting by provinces. This last destroyed the equality of representation, and the liberties of Great Britain also are sinking from the same defect. That a part of our rights is deposited in the hands of our legislatures. There, it was admitted, there should be an equality of representation. Another part of our rights is deposited in the hands of Congress: why is it not equally necessary there should be an equal representation there? Were it possible to collect the whole body of the people together, they would determine the questions submitted to them by their majority. Why should not the same majority decide when voting here, by their representatives? The larger colonies are so providentially divided in situation, as to render every fear of their combining visionary. Their interests are different, and their circumstances dissimilar. It is more probable they will become rivals, and leave it in the power of the smaller States to give preponderance to any scale they please. The voting by the number of free inhabitants, will have one excellent effect, that of inducing the colonies to discourage slavery, and to encourage the increase of their free inhabitants.

Mr. Hopkins observed, there were four larger, four smaller, and four middle-sized colonies. That the four largest would contain more than half the inhabitants of the confederated States, and therefore, would govern the others as they should please. That history affords no instance of such a thing as equal representation. The Germanic body votes by States. The Helvetic body does the same; and so does the Belgic confederacy. That too little is known of the ancient confederations, to say what was their practice.

Mr. Wilson thought, that taxation should be in proportion to wealth, but that representation should accord with the number of freemen. That government is a collection or result of the wills of all: that if any government could speak the will of all, it would be perfect; and that, so far as it departs from this, it becomes imperfect. It has been said that Congress is a representation of States, not of individuals. I say, that the objects of its care are all the individuals of the States. It is strange that annexing the name of "State" to ten thousand men, should give them an equal right with forty thousand. This must be the effect of magic, not of reason. As to those matters which are referred to Congress, we are not so many States; we are one large State. We lay aside our individuality, whenever we come here. The Germanic body is a burlesque on government; and their practice, on any point, is a sufficient authority and proof that it is wrong. The greatest imperfection in the constitution of the Belgic confederacy is their voting by provinces. The interest of the whole is constantly sacrificed to that of the small States. The history of the war in the reign of Queen Anne sufficiently proves this. It is asked, shall nine colonies put it into the power of four to govern them as they please? I invert the question, and ask, shall two millions of people put it in the power of one million to govern them as they please? It is pretended, too, that the smaller colonies will be in danger from the greater. Speak in honest language and say, the minority will be in danger from the majority. And is there an assembly on earth, where this danger may not be equally pretended? The truth is, that our proceedings will then be consentaneous with the interests of the majority, and so they ought to be. The probability is much greater, that the larger States will disagree, than that they will combine. I defy the wit of man to invent a possible case, or to suggest any one thing on earth, which shall be for the interests of Virginia, Pennsylvania and Massachusetts, and which will not also be for the interest of the other States.

These articles, reported July 12, '76, were debated from day to day, and time to time, for two years, were ratified July 9, '78, by ten States, by New Jersey on the 26th of November of the same year, and by Delaware on the 23d of February following. Maryland alone held off two years more, acceding to them March 1, '81, and thus closing the obligation.

Our delegation had been renewed for the ensuing year, commencing August 11; but the new government was now organized, a meeting of the legislature was to be held in October, and I had been elected a member by my county. I knew that our legislation, under the regal government, had many very vicious points which urgently required reformation, and I thought I could be of more use in forwarding that work. I therefore retired from my seat in Congress on the 2d of September, resigned it, and took my place in the legislature of my State, on the 7th of October.

On the 11th, I moved for leave to bring in a bill for the establishment of courts of justice, the organization of which was of importance. I drew the bill; it was approved by the committee, reported and passed, after going through its due course.

On the 12th, I obtained leave to bring in a bill declaring tenants in tail to hold their lands in fee simple. In the earlier times of the colony, when lands were to be obtained for little or nothing, some provident individuals procured large grants; and, desirous of founding great families for themselves, settled them on their descendants in fee tail. The transmission of this property from generation to generation, in the same name, raised up a distinct set of families, who, being privileged by law in the perpetuation of their wealth, were thus formed into a Patrician order, distinguished by the splendor and luxury of their establishments. From this order, too, the king habitually selected his counsellors of State; the hope of which distinction devoted the whole corps to the interests and will of the crown. To annul this privilege, and instead of an aristocracy of wealth, of more harm and danger, than benefit, to society, to make an opening for the aristocracy of virtue and talent, which nature has wisely provided for the direction of the interests of society, and scattered with equal hand through all its conditions, was deemed essential to a well-ordered republic. To effect it, no violence was necessary, no deprivation of natural right, but rather an enlargement of it by a repeal of the law. For this would authorize the present holder to divide the property among his children equally, as his affections were divided; and would place them, by natural generation, on the level of their fellow citizens. But this repeal was strongly opposed by Mr. Pendleton, who was zealously attached to ancient establishments; and who, taken all in all, was the ablest man in debate

I have ever met with. He had not indeed the poetical fancy of Mr. Henry, his sublime imagination, his lofty and overwhelming diction; but he was cool, smooth and persuasive; his language flowing, chaste and embellished; his conceptions quick, acute and full of resource; never vanquished: for if he lost the main battle, he returned upon you, and regained so much of it as to make it a drawn one, by dexterous manœuvres, skirmishes in detail, and the recovery of small advantages which, little singly, were important all together. You never knew when you were clear of him, but were harassed by his perseverance, until the patience was worn down of all who had less of it than himself. Add to

this, that he was one of the most virtuous and benevolent of men, the kindest friend, the most amiable and pleasant of companions, which ensured a favorable reception to whatever came from him. Finding that the general principle on entails could not be maintained, he took his stand on an amendment which he proposed, instead of an absolute abolition, to permit the tenant in tail to convey in fee simple, if he chose it; and he was within a few votes of saving so much of the old law. But the bill passed finally for entire abolition.

In that one of the bills for organizing our judiciary system, which proposed a court of Chancery, I had provided for a trial by jury of all matters of fact, in that as well as in the courts of law. He defeated it by the introduction of four words only, *"if either party choose."* The consequence has been, that as no suitor will say to his judge, "Sir, I distrust you, give me a jury," juries are rarely, I might say, perhaps, never, seen in that court, but when called for by the Chancellor of his own accord.

The first establishment in Virginia which became permanent, was made in 1607. I have found no mention of Negroes in the colony until about 1650. The first brought here as slaves were by a Dutch ship; after which the English commenced the trade, and continued it until the revolutionary war. That suspended, *ipso facto*, their further importation for the present, and the business of the war pressing constantly on the legislature, this subject was not acted on finally until the year '78, when I brought in a bill to prevent further importation. This passed without opposition, and stopped the increase of the evil by importation, leaving to future efforts its final eradication.

The first settlers of this colony were Englishmen, loyal subjects to their king and church, and the grant to Sir Walter Raleigh contained an express proviso that their laws "should not be against the true Christian faith, now professed in the church of England." As soon as the state of the colony admitted, it was divided into parishes, in each of which was established a minister of the Anglican church, endowed with a fixed salary, in tobacco, a glebe house and land with the other necessary appendages. To meet these expenses, all the inhabitants of the parishes were assessed, whether they were or not members of the established church. Towards Quakers who came here, they were most cruelly intolerant, driving them from the colony by the severest penalties. In process of time, however, other sectarisms were introduced, chiefly of the Presbyterian family; and the established clergy, secure for life in their glebes and salaries, adding to these, generally, the emoluments of a classical school, found employment enough, in their farms and school-rooms, for the rest of the week, and devoted Sunday only to the edification of their flock, by service, and a sermon at their parish church. Their other pastoral functions were little attended to. Against this inactivity, the zeal and industry of sectarian preachers had an open and undisputed field; and by the time of the revolution, a majority of the inhabitants had become dissenters from the established church, but were still obliged to pay contributions to support the pastors of the minority. This unrighteous compulsion, to maintain teachers of what they deemed religious errors, was grievously felt during the regal government, and without a hope of relief. But the first republican legislature, which met in '76, was crowded with petitions to abolish this spiritual tyranny. These brought on the severest contests in which I have ever been engaged. Our great opponents were Mr. Pendleton and Robert Carter Nicholas; honest men, but zealous churchmen. The petitions were referred to the committee of the whole house on the state of the country and, after desperate contests in that committee, almost daily from the 11th of October to the 5th of December, we prevailed so far only, as to repeal the laws which rendered criminal the maintenance of any religious opinions, the forbearance of repairing to church, or the exercise of any mode of worship; and further, to exempt dissenters from contributions to the support of the established church; and to suspend, only until the next session, levies on the members of that church for the salaries of their own incumbents. For although the majority of our citizens were dissenters, as has been observed, a majority of the legislature were churchmen. Among these, however, were some reasonable and liberal men, who enabled us, on some points, to obtain feeble majorities. But our opponents carried, in the general resolutions of the committee of November 19, a declaration that religious assemblies ought to be regulated, and that provision ought to be made for continuing the succession of the clergy, and superintending their conduct. And, in the bill now passed, was inserted an express reservation of the question, Whether a general assessment should not be established by law, on everyone, to the support of the pastor of his choice; or whether all should be left to voluntary contributions; and on this question, debated at every session, from '76 to '79 (some of our dissenting allies, having now secured their particular object, going over to the advocates of a general assessment), we could only obtain a suspension from session to session until '79, when the question against a general assessment was finally carried, and the establishment of the Anglican church entirely put down. In justice to the two honest but zealous opponents who have been named, I must add, that although, from their natural temperaments, they were more disposed generally to acquiesce in things as they are, than to risk innovations, yet whenever the public will had once decided, none were more faithful or exact in their obedience to it.

The seat of our government had originally been fixed in the peninsula of Jamestown, the first settlement of the colonists; and had been afterwards removed a few miles inland to Williamsburg. But this was at a time when our settlements had not extended beyond the tide waters. Now they had crossed the Alleghany; and the centre of population was far removed from what it had been. Yet Williamsburg was still the depository of our archives, the habitual residence of the Governor and many other of the public functionaries, the established place for the sessions of the legislature, and the magazine of our military stores; and its situation was so exposed that it might be taken at any time in war, and, at this time particularly, an enemy might in the night run up either of the rivers, between which it lies, land a force above, and take possession of the place, without the possibility of saving either persons or things. I had proposed its removal so early as October, '76; but it did not prevail until the session of May, '79.

Early in the session of May, '79, I prepared, and obtained leave to bring in a bill, declaring who should be deemed citizens, asserting the natural right of expatriation, and prescribing the mode of exercising it. This, when I withdrew from the house, on the 1st of June following, I left in the hands of George Mason, and it was passed on the 26th of that month.

In giving this account of the laws of which I was myself the mover and draughtsman, I, by no means, mean to claim to myself the merit of obtaining their passage. I had many occasional and strenuous coadjutors in debate, and one, most steadfast, able and zealous; who was himself a host. This was George Mason, a man of the first order of wisdom among those who acted on the theatre of the revolution, of expansive mind, profound judgment, cogent in argument, learned in the lore of our former constitution, and earnest for the republican change on democratic principles. His elocution was neither flowing nor smooth; but his language was strong, his manner most impressive, and strengthened by a dash of biting cynicism, when provocation made it seasonable.

Mr. Wythe, while speaker in the two sessions of 1777, between his return from Congress and his appointment to the Chancery, was an able and constant associate in whatever was before a committee of the whole. His pure integrity, judgment and reasoning powers, gave him great weight. Of him, see more in some notes inclosed in my letter of August 31, 1820, to Mr. John Saunderson.*

Mr. Madison came into the House in 1776, a new member and young; which circumstances, concurring with his extreme modesty, prevented his venturing himself in debate before his removal to the Council of State, in November, '77. From thence he went to Congress, then consisting of few members. Trained in these successive schools, he acquired a habit of self-possession, which placed at ready command the rich resources of his luminous and discriminating mind, and of his extensive information, and rendered him the first of every assembly afterwards, of which he became a member. Never wandering from his subject into vain declamation, but pursuing it closely, in language pure,

---

* Letter to John Saunderson, Esq., Monticello, August 31, 1820.

Sir: Your letter of the 19th was received in due time, and I wish it were in my power to furnish you more fully, than in the enclosed paper, with materials for the biography of George Wythe; but I possess none in writing, am very distant from the place of his birth and early life, and know not a single person in that quarter from whom inquiry could be made, with the expectation of collecting anything material. Add to this, that feeble health disables me, almost, from writing; and entirely from the labor of going into difficult research. I became acquainted with Mr. Wythe when he was about thirty-five years of age. He directed my studies in the law, led me into business, and continued, until death, my most affectionate friend. A close intimacy with him, during that period of forty odd years, the most important of his life, enables me to state its leading facts, which, being of my own knowledge, I vouch their truth. Of what precedes that period, I speak from hearsay only, in which there may be error, but of little account, as the character of the facts will themselves manifest. In the epoch of his birth, I may err a little, stating that from the recollection of a particular incident, the date of which, within a year or two, I do not distinctly remember. These scanty outlines you will be able, I hope, to fill up from other information, and they may serve you, sometimes, as landmarks to distinguish truth from error, in what you hear from others. The exalted virtue of the man will also be a polar star to guide you in all matters which may touch that element of his character. But on that you will receive imputation from no man; for, as far as I know, he never had an enemy. Little as I am able to contribute to the just reputation of this excellent man, it is the act of my life most gratifying to my heart; and leaves me only to regret that a waning memory can do no more.

Of Mr. Hancock I can say nothing, having known him only in the chair of Congress. Having myself been the youngest man but one in that body, the disparity of age prevented any particular intimacy. But of him there can be no difficulty in obtaining full information in the North.

I salute you, Sir, with sentiments of great respect,

Th. Jefferson

classical and copious, soothing always the feelings of his adversaries by civilities and softness of expression, he rose to the eminent station which he held in the great National Convention of 1787; and in that of Virginia which followed, he sustained the new constitution in all its parts, bearing off the palm against the logic of George Mason, and the fervid declamation of Mr. Henry. With these consummate powers, were united a pure and spotless virtue which no calumny has ever attempted to sully. Of the powers and polish of his pen, and of the wisdom of his administration in the highest office of the nation, I need say nothing. They have spoken, and will forever speak for themselves.

So far we were proceeding in the details of reformation only; selecting points of legislation, prominent in character and principle, urgent, and indicative of the strength of the general pulse of reformation. When I left Congress, in '76, it was in the persuasion that our whole code must be reviewed, adapted to our republican form of government; and, now that we had no negatives of Councils, Governors, and Kings to restrain us from doing right, that it should be corrected, in all its parts, with a single eye to reason, and the good of those for whose government it was framed. Early, therefore, in the session of '76, to which I returned, I moved and presented a bill for the revision of the laws, which was passed on the 24th of October; and on the 5th of November, Mr. Pendleton, Mr. Wythe, George Mason, Thomas L. Lee, and myself, were appointed a committee to execute the work. We agreed to meet at Fredericksburg to settle the plan of operation, and to distribute the work. We met there accordingly, on the 13th of January, 1777. The first question was, whether we should propose to abolish the whole existing system of laws, and prepare a new and complete Institute, or preserve the general system, and only modify it to the present state of things. Mr. Pendleton, contrary to his usual disposition in favor of ancient things, was for the former proposition, in which he was joined by Mr. Lee. To this it was objected, that to abrogate our whole system would be a bold measure, and probably far beyond the views of the legislature; that they had been in the practice of revising, from time to time, the laws of the colony, omitting the expired, the repealed, and the obsolete, amending only those retained, and probably meant we should now do the same, only including the British statutes as well as our own: that to compose a new Institute, like those of Justinian and Bracton, or that of Blackstone, which was the model proposed by Mr. Pendleton, would be an arduous undertaking, of vast research, of great consideration and judgment; and when reduced to a text, every word of that text, from the imperfection of human language, and its incompetence to express distinctly every shade of idea, would become a subject of question and chicanery, until settled by repeated adjudications; and this would involve us for ages in litigation and render property uncertain, until, like the statutes of old, every word had been tried and settled by numerous decisions, and by new volumes of reports and commentaries; and that no one of us, probably, would undertake such a work, which to be systematical, must be the work of one hand. This last was the opinion of Mr. Wythe, Mr. Mason, and myself. When we proceeded to the distribution of the work, Mr. Mason excused himself, as, being no lawyer, he felt himself unqualified for the work, and he resigned soon after. Mr. Lee excused himself on the same ground, and died, indeed, in a short time. The other two gentlemen, therefore, and myself divided the work among us. The common law and statutes to the 4 James I. (when our separate legislature was established) were assigned to me; the British statutes, from that period to the present day, to Mr. Wythe; and the Virginia laws to Mr. Pendleton. As the law of Descents, and the criminal law fell of course within my portion, I wished the committee to settle the leading principles of these, as a guide for me in framing them; and, with respect to the first, I proposed to abolish the law of primogeniture, and to make real estate descendible in parcenary to the next of kin, as personal property is, by the statute of distribution. Mr. Pendleton wished to preserve the right of primogeniture, but seeing at once that that could not prevail, he proposed we should adopt the Hebrew principle, and give a double portion to the elder son. I observed, that if the eldest son could eat twice as much, or do double work, it might be a natural evidence of his right to a double portion; but being on a par in his powers and wants, with his brothers and sisters, he should be on a par also in the partition of the patrimony; and such was the decision of the other members.

On the subject of the Criminal law, all were agreed, that the punishment of death should be abolished, except for treason and murder; and that, for other felonies, should be substituted hard labor in the public works, and in some cases, the *Lex talionis*. How this last revolting principle came to obtain our approbation I do not remember. There remained, indeed, in our laws, a vestige of it in a single case of a slave; it was the English law, in the time of the Anglo-Saxons, copied probably from the Hebrew law of "an eye for an eye, a tooth for a tooth," and it was the law of several ancient people; but the modern mind had left it far in the rear of its advances. These points, however, being settled, we repaired to our respective homes for the preparation of the work.

In the execution of my part, I thought it material not to vary the diction of the ancient statutes by modernizing it, nor to give rise to new questions by new expressions. The text of these statutes had been so fully explained and defined, by numerous adjudications, as scarcely ever now to produce a question in our courts. I thought it would be useful, also, in all new draughts, to reform the style of the British statutes, and of our own acts of Assembly; which, from their verbosity, their endless tautologies, their involutions of case within case, and parenthesis within parenthesis, and their multiplied efforts at certainty, by *saids* and *aforesaids*, by *ors* and by *ands*, to make them more plain, are really rendered more perplexed and incomprehensible, not only to common readers, but to the lawyers themselves. We were employed in this work from that time to February, 1779, when we met at Williamsburg, that is to say, Mr. Pendleton, Mr. Wythe and myself; and meeting day by day, we examined critically our several parts, sentence by sentence, scrutinizing and amending, until we had agreed on the whole. We then returned home, had fair copies made of our several parts, which were reported to the General Assembly, June 18, 1779, by Mr. Wythe and myself, Mr. Pendleton's residence being distant, and he having authorized us by letter to declare his approbation. We had, in this work, brought so much of the Common law as it was thought necessary to alter, all the British statutes from *Magna Charta* to the present day, and all the laws of Virginia, from the establishment of our legislature, in the 4th Jac. 1. to the present time, which we thought should be retained, within the compass of one hundred and twenty-six bills, making a printed folio of ninety pages only. Some bills were taken out, occasionally, from time to time, and passed; but the main body of the work was not entered on by the legislature until after the general peace, in 1785, when, by the unwearied exertions of Mr. Madison, in opposition to the endless quibbles, chicaneries, perversions, vexations and delays of lawyers and demi-lawyers, most of the bills were passed by the legislature, with little alteration.

The bill for establishing religious freedom, the principles of which had, to a certain degree, been enacted before, I had drawn in all the latitude of reason and right. It still met with opposition; but, with some mutilations in the preamble, it was finally passed; and a singular proposition proved that its protection of opinion was meant to be universal. Where the preamble declares, that coercion is a departure from the plan of the holy author of our religion, an amendment was proposed, by inserting the word "Jesus Christ," so that it should read, "a departure from the plan of Jesus Christ, the holy author of our religion"; the insertion was rejected by a great majority, in proof that they meant to comprehend, within the mantle of its protection, the Jew and the Gentile, the Christian and Mahometan, the Hindoo, and Infidel of every denomination.

Beccaria, and other writers on crimes and punishments, had satisfied the reasonable world of the unrightfulness and inefficacy of the punishment of crimes by death; and hard labor on roads, canals and other public works, had been suggested as a proper substitute. The Revisors had adopted these opinions; but the general idea of our country had not yet advanced to that point. The bill, therefore, for proportioning crimes and punishments, was lost in the House of Delegates by a majority of a single vote. I learned afterwards, that the substitute of hard labor in public, was tried (I believe it was in Pennsylvania) without success. Exhibited as a public spectacle, with shaved heads and mean clothing, working on the high roads, produced in the criminals such a prostration of character, such an abandonment of self-respect, as, instead of reforming, plunged them into the most desperate and hardened depravity of morals and character. To pursue the subject of this law.—I was written to in 1785 (being then in Paris) by directors appointed to superintend the building of a Capitol in Richmond, to advise them as to a plan, and to add to it one of a Prison. Thinking it a favorable opportunity of introducing into the State an example of architecture, in the classic style of antiquity, and the Maison quarrée of Nismes, an ancient Roman temple, being considered as the most perfect model existing of what may be called Cubic architecture, I applied to M. Clerissault, who had published drawings of the Antiquities of Nismes, to

have me a model of the building made in stucco, only changing the order from Corinthian to Ionic, on account of the difficulty of the Corinthian capitals. I yielded, with reluctance, to the taste of Clerissault, in his preference of the modern capital of Scamozzi to the more noble capital of antiquity. This was executed by the artist whom Choiseul Gouffier had carried with him to Constantinople, and employed, while Ambassador there, in making those beautiful models of the remains of Grecian architecture which are to be seen at Paris. To adapt the exterior to our use, I drew a plan for the interior, with the apartments necessary for legislative, executive, and judiciary purposes; and accommodated in their size and distribution to the form and dimensions of the building. These were forwarded to the Directors, in 1786, and were carried into execution, with some variations, not for the better, the most important of which, however, admit of future correction. With respect to the plan of a Prison, requested at the same time, I had heard of a benevolent society, in England, which had been indulged by the government, in an experiment of the effect of labor, in *solitary confinement*, on some of their criminals; which experiment had succeeded beyond expectation. The same idea had been suggested in France, and an Architect of Lyons had proposed a plan of a well-contrived edifice, on the principle of solitary confinement. I procured a copy, and as it was too large for our purposes, I drew one on a scale less extensive, but susceptible of additions as they should be wanting. This I sent to the Directors, instead of a plan of a common prison, in the hope that it would suggest the idea of labor in solitary confinement, instead of that on the public works, which we had adopted in our Revised Code. Its principle, accordingly, but not its exact form, was adopted by Latrobe in carrying the plan into execution, by the erection of what is now called the Penitentiary, built under his direction. In the meanwhile, the public opinion was ripening, by time, by reflection, and by the example of Pennsylvania, where labor on the highways had been tried, without approbation, from 1786 to '89, and had been followed by their Penitentiary system on the principle of confinement and labor, which was proceeding auspiciously. In 1796, our legislature resumed the subject, and passed the law for amending the Penal laws of the commonwealth. They adopted solitary, instead of public, labor, established a gradation in the duration of the confinement, approximated the style of the law more to the modern usage, and, instead of the settled distinctions of murder and manslaughter, preserved in my bill, they introduced the new terms of murder in the first and second degree. Whether these have produced more or fewer questions of definition, I am not sufficiently informed of our judiciary transactions to say. I will here, however, insert the text of my bill, with the notes I made in the course of my researches into the subject.*

The acts of Assembly concerning the College of William and Mary,

---

* In both the *Autobiography* and *The Anas* we have omitted bills and other papers mentioned by the author but not germane to the purpose of this volume.

were properly within Mr. Pendleton's portion of our work; but these related chiefly to its revenue, while its constitution, organization and scope of science, were derived from its charter. We thought that on this subject, a systematical plan of general education should be proposed, and I was requested to undertake it. I accordingly prepared three bills for the Revisal, proposing three distinct grades of education, reaching all classes. 1st. Elementary schools, for all children generally, rich and poor. 2d. Colleges, for a middle degree of instruction, calculated for the common purposes of life, and such as would be desirable for all who were in easy circumstances. And, 3d, an ultimate grade for teaching the sciences generally, and in their highest degree. The first bill proposed to lay off every county into Hundreds, or Wards, of a proper size and population for a school, in which reading, writing, and common arithmetic should be taught; and that the whole State should be divided into twenty-four districts, in each of which should be a school for classical learning, grammar, geography, and the higher branches of numerical arithmetic. The second bill proposed to amend the constitution of William and Mary College, to enlarge its sphere of science, and to make it in fact a University. The third was for the establishment of a library. These bills were not acted on until the same year, '96, and then only so much of the first as provided for elementary schools. The College of William and Mary was an establishment purely of the Church of England; the Visitors were required to be all of that Church; the Professors to subscribe its thirty-nine Articles; its Students to learn its Catechism; and one of its fundamental objects was declared to be, to raise up Ministers for that church. The religious jealousies, therefore, of all the dissenters, took alarm lest this might give an ascendancy to the Anglican sect, and refused acting on that bill. Its local eccentricity, too, and unhealthy autumnal climate, lessened the general inclination towards it. And in the Elementary bill, they inserted a provision which completely defeated it; for they left it to the court of each county to determine for itself, when this act should be carried into execution, within their county. One provision of the bill was, that the expenses of these schools should be borne by the inhabitants of the county, every one in proportion to his general tax rate. This would throw on wealth the education of the poor; and the justices, being generally of the more wealthy class, were unwilling to incur that burden, and I believe it was not suffered to commence in a single county. I shall recur again to this subject, towards the close of my story, if I should have life and resolution enough to reach that term; for I am already tired of talking about myself.

The bill on the subject of slaves, was a mere digest of the existing laws respecting them, without any intimation of a plan for a future and general emancipation. It was thought better that this should be kept back, and attempted only by way of amendment, whenever the bill should be brought on. The principles of the amendment, however, were agreed on, that is to say, the freedom of all born after a certain day, and deportation at a proper age. But it was found that the public mind would not yet bear the proposition, nor will it bear it even at this day. Yet the day is not distant when it must bear and adopt it, or worse will follow. Nothing is more certainly written in the book of fate, than that these people are to be free; nor is it less certain that the two races, equally free, cannot live in the same government. Nature, habit, opinion have drawn indelible lines of distinction between them. It is still in our power to direct the process of emancipation and deportation, peaceably, and in such slow degree, as that the evil will wear off insensibly, and their place be, *pari passu*, filled up by free white laborers. If, on the contrary, it is left to force itself on, human nature must shudder at the prospect held up. We should in vain look for an example in the Spanish deportation or deletion of the Moors. This precedent would fall far short of our case.

I considered four of these bills, passed or reported, as forming a system by which every fibre would be eradicated of ancient or future aristocracy; and a foundation laid for a government truly republican. The repeal of the laws of entail would prevent the accumulation and perpetuation of wealth, in select families, and preserve the soil of the country from being daily more and more absorbed in mortmain. The abolition of primogeniture, and equal partition of inheritances, removed the feudal and unnatural distinctions which made one member of every family rich, and all the rest poor, substituting equal partition, the best of all Agrarian laws. The restoration of the rights of conscience re-lieved the people from taxation for the support of a religion not theirs; for the establishment was truly of the religion of the rich, the dissenting sects being entirely composed of the less wealthy people; and these, by the bill for a general education, would be qualified to understand their rights, to maintain them, and to exercise with intelligence their parts in self-government; and all this would be effected, without the violation of a single natural right of any one individual citizen. To these, too, might be added, as a further security, the introduction of the trial by jury, into the Chancery courts, which have already ingulfed, and continue to ingulf, so great a proportion of the jurisdiction over our property.

On the 1st of June, 1779, I was appointed Governor of the Common-wealth, and retired from the legislature. Being elected, also, one of the Visitors of William and Mary college, a self-electing body, I effected, during my residence in Williamsburg that year, a change in the organ-ization of that institution, by abolishing the Grammar school, and the two professorships of Divinity and Oriental languages, and substituting a professorship of Law and Police, one of Anatomy, Medicine and Chemistry, and one of Modern languages; and the charter confining us to six professorships, we added the Law of Nature and Nations, and the Fine Arts to the duties of the Moral professor, and Natural History to those of the professor of Mathematics and Natural Philosophy.

Being now, as it were, identified with the Commonwealth itself, to write my own history, during the two years of my administration, would be to write the public history of that portion of the revolution within this State. This has been done by others, and particularly by Mr. Girardin, who wrote his Continuation of Burke's History of Vir-ginia, while at Milton, in this neighborhood, had free access to all my papers while composing it, and has given as faithful an account as I could myself. For this portion, therefore, of my own life, I refer altogether to his history. From a belief that, under the pressure of the invasion under which we were then laboring, the public would have more con-fidence in a Military chief, and that the Military commander, being invested with the Civil power also, both might be wielded with more energy, promptitude and effect for the defence of the State, I resigned the administration at the end of my second year, and General Nelson was appointed to succeed me.

Soon after my leaving Congress, in September, '76, to wit, on the last day of that month, I had been appointed, with Dr. Franklin, to go to France, as a Commissioner, to negotiate treaties of alliance and commerce with that government. Silas Deane, then in France, acting as agent for procuring military stores, was joined with us in commission. But such was the state of my family that I could not leave it, nor could I expose it to the dangers of the sea, and of capture by the British ships, then covering the ocean. I saw, too, that the laboring oar was really at home, where much was to be done, of the most permanent interest, in new modelling our governments, and much to defend our fanes and fire-sides from the desolations of an invading enemy, pressing on our country in every point. I declined, therefore, and Dr. Lee was appointed in my place. On the 15th of June, 1781, I had been appointed, with Mr. Adams, Dr. Franklin, Mr. Jay, and Mr. Laurens, a Minister Plenipotentiary for negotiating peace, then expected to be effected through the mediation of the Empress of Russia. The same reasons obliged me still to decline; and the negotiation was in fact never entered on. But, in the autumn of the next year, 1782, Congress receiving assurances that a general peace would be concluded in the winter and spring, they renewed my appointment on the 13th of November of that year. I had, two months before that, lost the cherished companion of my life, in whose affections, unabated on both sides, I had lived the last ten years in unchequered happiness. With the public interests, the state of my mind concurred in recommending the change of scene proposed; and I accepted the appointment, and left Monticello on the 19th of December, 1782, for Philadelphia, where I arrived on the 27th. The Minister of France, Luzerne, offered me a passage in the Romulus frigate, which I accepted; but she was then lying a few miles below Baltimore, blocked up in the ice. I remained, therefore, a month in Philadelphia, looking over the papers in the office of State, in order to possess myself of the general state of our foreign relations, and then went to Baltimore, to await the liberation of the frigate from the ice.

After waiting there nearly a month, we received information that a Provisional treaty of peace had been signed by our Commissioners on the 3d of September, 1782, to become absolute, on the conclusion of peace between France and Great Britain. Considering my proceeding to Europe as now of no utility to the public, I returned immediately to Philadelphia, to take the orders of Congress, and was excused by them from further proceeding. I, therefore, returned home, where I arrived on the 15th of May, 1783.

On the 6th of the following month, I was appointed by the legislature a delegate to Congress, the appointment to take place on the 1st of November ensuing, when that of the existing delegation would expire. I, accordingly, left home on the 16th of October, arrived at Trenton, where Congress was sitting, on the 3d of November, and took my seat on the 4th, on which day Congress adjourned, to meet at Annapolis on the 26th.

Congress had now become a very small body, and the members very remiss in their attendance on its duties, insomuch, that a majority of the States, necessary by the Confederation to constitute a House even for minor business, did not assemble until the 13th of December.

They, as early as January 7, 1782, had turned their attention to the moneys current in the several States, and had directed the Financier, Robert Morris, to report to them a table of rates, at which the foreign coins should be received at the treasury. That officer, or rather his assistant, Gouverneur Morris, answered them on the 15th, in an able and elaborate statement of the denominations of money current in the several States, and of the comparative value of the foreign coins chiefly in circulation with us. He went into the consideration of the necessity of establishing a standard of value with us, and of the adoption of a money Unit. He proposed for that Unit, such a fraction of pure silver as would be a common measure of the penny of every State, without leaving a fraction. This common divisor he found to be 1-1440 of a dollar, or 1-1600 of the crown sterling. The value of a dollar was, therefore, to be expressed by 1,440 units, and of a crown by 1,600; each Unit containing a quarter of a grain of fine silver. Congress turning again their attention to this subject the following year, the Financier, by a letter of April 30, 1783, further explained and urged the Unit he had proposed; but nothing more was done on it until the ensuing year, when it was again taken up, and referred to a committee, of which I was a member. The general views of the Financier were sound, and the principle was ingenious on which he proposed to found his Unit; but it was too minute for ordinary use, too laborious for computation, either by the head or in figures. The price of a loaf of bread, 1/20 of a dollar, would be 72 units.

A pound of butter, 1/5 of a dollar, 288 units.

A horse or bullock, of eighty dollars value, would require a notation of six figures, to wit, 115,200, and the public debt, suppose of eighty millions, would require twelve figures, to wit, 115,200,000,000 units. Such a system of money-arithmetic would be entirely unmanageable for the common purposes of society. I proposed, therefore, instead of this, to adopt the Dollar as our Unit of account and payment, and that its divisions and sub-divisions should be in the decimal ratio. I wrote some Notes on the subject, which I submitted to the consideration of the Financier. I received his answer and adherence to his general system, only agreeing to take for his Unit one hundred of those he first proposed, so that a Dollar should be 14 40/100, and a crown 16 units. I replied to this, and printed my notes and reply on a flying sheet, which I put into the hands of the members of Congress for consideration, and the Committee agreed to report on my principle. This was adopted the ensuing year, and is the system which now prevails. I insert, here, the Notes and Reply, as showing the different views on which the adoption of our money system hung.* The divisions into dimes, cents, and mills is now so well understood, that it would be easy of introduction into the kindred branches of weights and measures. I use, when I travel, an Odometer of Clarke's invention, which divides the mile into cents, and I find every one comprehends a distance readily, when stated to him in miles and cents; so he would in feet and cents, pounds and cents, &c.

The remissness of Congress, and their permanent session, began to be a subject of uneasiness; and even some of the legislatures had recom-

* The Notes and Reply are omitted, as they are purely technical.

mended to them intermissions, and periodical sessions. As the Confederation had made no provision for a visible head of the government, during vacations of Congress, and such a one was necessary to superintend the executive business, to receive and communicate with foreign ministers and nations, and to assemble Congress on sudden and extraordinary emergencies, I proposed, early in April, the appointment of a committee, to be called the "Committee of the States," to consist of a member from each State, who should remain in session during the recess of Congress: that the functions of Congress should be divided into executive and legislative, the latter to be reserved, and the former, by a general resolution, to be delegated to that Committee. This proposition was afterwards agreed to; a Committee appointed, who entered on duty on the subsequent adjournment of Congress, quarrelled very soon, split into two parties, abandoned their post, and left the government without any visible head, until the next meeting in Congress. We have since seen the same thing take place in the Directory of France; and I believe it will forever take place in any Executive consisting of a plurality. Our plan, best, I believe, combines wisdom and practicability, by providing a plurality of Counsellors, but a single Arbiter for ultimate decision. I was in France when we heard of this schism, and separation of our Committee, and, speaking with Dr. Franklin of this singular disposition of men to quarrel, and divide into parties, he gave his sentiments, as usual, by way of Apologue. He mentioned the Eddystone lighthouse, in the British channel, as being built on a rock, in the mid-channel, totally inaccessible in winter, from the boisterous character of that sea, in that season; that, therefore, for the two keepers employed to keep up the lights, all provisions for the winter were necessarily carried to them in autumn, as they could never be visited again till the return of the milder season; that, on the first practicable day in the spring, a boat put off to them with fresh supplies. The boatmen met at the door one of the keepers, and accosted him with a "How goes it, friend? Very well. How is your companion? I do not know. Don't know? Is not he here? I can't tell. Have not you seen him today? No. When did you see him? Not since last fall. You have killed him? Not I, indeed." They were about to lay hold of him, as having certainly murdered his companion; but he desired them to go up stairs and examine for themselves. They went up, and there found the other keeper. They had quarrelled, it seems, soon after being left there, had divided into two parties, assigned the cares below to one, and those above to the other, and had never spoken to, or seen, one another since.

But to return to our Congress at Annapolis. The definitive treaty of peace which had been signed at Paris on the 3d of September, 1783, and received here, could not be ratified without a House of nine States. On the 23d of December, therefore, we addressed letters to the several Governors, stating the receipt of the definitive treaty; that seven States only were in attendance, while nine were necessary to its ratification; and urging them to press on their delegates the necessity of their immediate attendance. And on the 26th, to save time, I moved that the Agent of Marine (Robert Morris) should be instructed to have ready a vessel at this place, at New York, and at some Eastern port, to carry over the ratification of the treaty when agreed to. It met the general sense of the House, but was opposed by Dr. Lee, on the ground of expense, which it would authorize the Agent to incur for us; and, he said, it would be better to ratify at once, and send on the ratification. Some members had before suggested, that seven States were competent to the ratification. My motion was therefore postponed, and another brought forward by Mr. Read, of South Carolina, for an immediate ratification. This was debated the 26th and 27th. Reed, Lee, Williamson and Jeremiah Chase, urged that ratification was a mere matter of form, that the treaty was conclusive from the moment it was signed by the ministers; that, although the Confederation requires the assent of *nine States* to *enter into* a treaty, yet, that its conclusion could not be called *entrance into it*; that supposing nine States requisite, it would be in the power of five States to keep us always at war; that nine States had virtually authorized the ratification, having ratified the provisional treaty, and instructed their ministers to agree to a definitive one in the same terms, and the present one was, in fact, substantially, and almost verbatim, the same; that there now remain but sixty-seven days for the ratification, for its passage across the Atlantic, and its exchange; that there was no hope of our soon having nine States present; in fact, that this was the ultimate point of time to which we could venture to wait; that if the ratification was not in Paris by the time stipulated, the treaty would become void; that if ratified by seven States, it would go under our seal, without its being known to Great Britain that only seven had concurred; that it was a question of which they had no right to take cognizance, and we were only answerable for it to our constituents; that it was like the ratification which Great Britain had received from the Dutch, by the negotiations of Sir William Temple.

On the contrary, it was argued by Monroe, Gerry, Howel, Ellery and myself, that by the modern usage of Europe, the ratification was considered as the act which gave validity to a treaty, until which, it was not obligatory. That the commission to the ministers reserved the ratification to Congress; that the treaty itself stipulated that it should be ratified; that it became a second question, who were competent to the ratification? That the Confederation expressly required nine States to enter into any treaty; that, by this, that instrument must have intended, that the assent of nine States should be necessary, as well to the *completion* as to the *commencement* of the treaty, its object having been to guard the rights of the Union in all those important cases where nine States are called for; that by the contrary construction, seven States, containing less than one-third of our whole citizens, might rivet on us a treaty, commenced indeed under commission and instructions from nine States, but formed by the minister in express contradiction to such instructions, and in direct sacrifice of the interests of so great a majority; that the definitive treaty was admitted not to be a verbal copy of the provisional one, and whether the departures from it were of substance, or not, was a question on which nine States alone were competent to decide; that the circumstances of the ratification of the provisional articles by nine States, the instructions to our ministers to form a definitive one by them, and their actual agreement in substance, do not render us competent to ratify in the present instance; if these circumstances are in themselves a ratification, nothing further is requisite than to give attested copies of them, in exchange for the British ratification; if they are not, we remain where we were, without a ratification by nine States, and incompetent ourselves to ratify; that it was but four days since the seven States, now present, unanimously concurred in a resolution, to be forwarded to the Governors of the absent States, in which they stated, as a cause for urging on their delegates, that nine States were necessary to ratify the treaty; that in the case of the Dutch ratification, Great Britain had courted it, and therefore was glad to accept it as it was; that they knew our Constitution, and would object to a ratification by seven; that, if that circumstance was kept back, it would be known hereafter, and would give them ground to deny the validity of a ratification, into which they should have been surprised and cheated, and it would be a dishonorable prostitution of our seal; that there is a hope of nine States; that if the treaty would become null, if not ratified in time, it would not be saved by an imperfect ratification; but that, in fact, it would not be null, and would be placed on better ground, going in unexceptionable form, though a few days too late, and rested on the small importance of this circumstance, and the physical impossibilities which had prevented a punctual compliance in point of time; that this would be approved by all nations, and by Great Britain herself, if not determined to renew the war, and if so determined, she would never want excuses, were this out of the way. Mr. Read gave notice, he should call for the yeas and nays; whereon those in opposition, prepared a resolution, expressing pointedly the reasons of their dissent from his motion. It appearing, however, that his proposition could not be carried, it was thought better to make no entry at all. Massachusetts alone would have been for it; Rhode Island, Pennsylvania and Virginia against it, Delaware, Maryland and North Carolina, would have been divided.

Our body was little numerous, but very contentious. Day after day was wasted on the most unimportant questions. A member, one of those afflicted with the morbid rage of debate, of an ardent mind, prompt imagination, and copious flow of words, who heard with impatience any logic which was not his own, sitting near me on some occasion of a trifling but wordy debate, asked me how I could sit in silence, hearing so much false reasoning, which a word should refute? I observed to him, that to refute indeed was easy, but to silence was impossible; that in measures brought forward by myself, I took the laboring oar, as was incumbent on me; but that in general, I was willing to listen; that if every sound argument or objection was used by some one or other of the numerous debaters, it was enough; if not, I thought it sufficient to suggest the omission, without going into a repetition of what had been already said by others: that this was a waste and abuse of the time and patience of the House, which could not be justified. And I believe, that if the members of deliberate bodies were to observe this course generally, they would do in a day, what takes them a week; and it is really more questionable, than may at first be thought, whether Bonaparte's dumb legislature, which said nothing, and did much, may not

be preferable to one which talks much, and does nothing. I served with General Washington in the legislature of Virginia, before the revolution, and, during it, with Dr. Franklin in Congress. I never heard either of them speak ten minutes at a time, nor to any but the main point, which was to decide the question. They laid their shoulders to the great points, knowing that the little ones would follow of themselves. If the present Congress errs in too much talking, how can it be otherwise, in a body to which the people send one hundred and fifty lawyers, whose trade it is to question everything, yield nothing, and talk by the hour? That one hundred and fifty lawyers should do business together, ought not to be expected. But to return again to our subject.

Those who thought seven States competent to the ratification, being very restless under the loss of their motion, I proposed, on the third of January, to meet them on middle ground, and therefore moved a resolution, which premised, that there were but seven States present, who were unanimous for the ratification, but that they differed in opinion on the question of competency; that those however in the negative were unwilling that any powers which it might be supposed they possessed, should remain unexercised for the restoration of peace, provided it could be done, saving their good faith, and without importing any opinion of Congress, that seven States were competent, and resolving that the treaty be ratified so far as they had power; that it should be transmitted to our ministers, with instructions to keep it uncommunicated; to endeavor to obtain three months longer for exchange of ratifications; that they should be informed, that so soon as nine States shall be present, a ratification by nine shall be sent them: if this should get to them before the ultimate point of time for exchange, they were to use it, and not the other; if not, they were to offer the act of the seven States in exchange, informing them the treaty had come to hand while Congress was not in session; that but seven States were as yet assembled, and these had unanimously concurred in the ratification. This was debated on the third and fourth; and on the fifth, a vessel being to sail for England, from this port (Annapolis), the House directed the President to write to our ministers accordingly.

January 14. Delegates from Connecticut having attended yesterday, and another from South Carolina coming in this day, the treaty was ratified without a dissenting voice; and three instruments of ratification were ordered to be made out, one of which was sent by Colonel Harmer, another by Colonel Franks, and the third transmitted to the Agent of Marine, to be forwarded by any good opportunity.

Congress soon took up the consideration of their foreign relations. They deemed it necessary to get their commerce placed with every nation, on a footing as favorable as that of other nations; and for this purpose, to propose to each a distinct treaty of commerce. This act too would amount to an acknowledgment, by each, of our independence, and of our reception into the fraternity of nations; which, although as possessing our station of right, and in fact we would not condescend to ask, we were not unwilling to furnish opportunities for receiving their friendly salutations and welcome. With France, the United Netherlands, and Sweden, we had already treaties of commerce; but commissions were given for these countries also, should any amendments be thought necessary. The other States to which treaties were to be proposed, were England, Hamburg, Saxony, Prussia, Denmark, Russia, Austria, Venice, Rome, Naples, Tuscany, Sardinia, Genoa, Spain, Portugal, the Porte, Algiers, Tripoli, Tunis, and Morocco.

On the 7th of May Congress resolved that a Minister Plenipotentiary should be appointed, in addition to Mr. Adams and Dr. Franklin, for negotiating treaties of commerce with foreign nations, and I was elected to that duty. I accordingly left Annapolis on the 11th, took with me my eldest daughter, then at Philadelphia (the two others being too young for the voyage), and proceeded to Boston, in quest of a passage. While passing through the different States, I made a point of informing myself of the state of the commerce of each; went on to New Hampshire with the same view, and returned to Boston. Thence I sailed on the 5th of July, in the Ceres, a merchant ship of Mr. Nathaniel Tracey, bound to Cowes. He was himself a passenger, and, after a pleasant voyage of nineteen days, from land to land, we arrived at Cowes on the 26th. I was detained there a few days by the indisposition of my daughter. On the 30th, we embarked for Havre, arrived there on the 31st, left it on the 3d of August, and arrived at Paris on the 6th. I called immediately on Dr. Franklin, at Passy, communicated to him our charge, and we wrote to Mr. Adams, then at the Hague, to join us at Paris.

Before I had left America, that is to say, in the year 1781, I had received a letter from M. de Marbois, of the French legation in Philadelphia, informing me, he had been instructed by his government to obtain such statistical accounts of the different States of our Union, as might be useful for their information; and addressing to me a number of queries relative to the State of Virginia. I had always made it a practice, whenever an opportunity occurred, of obtaining any information of our country, which might be of use to me in any station, public or private, to commit it to writing. These memoranda were on loose papers, bundled up without order, and difficult of recurrence, when I had occasion for a particular one. I thought this a good occasion to embody their substance, which I did in the order of Mr. Marbois' queries, so as to answer his wish, and to arrange them for my own use. Some friends, to whom they were occasionally communicated, wished for copies; but their volume rendering this too laborious by hand, I proposed to get a few printed, for their gratification. I was asked such a price, however, as exceeded the importance of the object. On my arrival at Paris, I found it could be done for a fourth of what I had been asked here. I therefore corrected and enlarged them, and had two hundred copies printed, under the title of "Notes on Virginia." I gave a very few copies to some particular friends in Europe, and sent the rest to my friends in America. An European copy, by the death of the owner, got into the hands of a bookseller, who engaged its translation, and when ready for the press, communicated his intentions and manuscript to me, suggesting that I should correct it, without asking any other permission for the publication. I never had seen so wretched an attempt at translation. Interverted, abridged, mutilated, and often reversing the sense of the original, I found it a blotch of errors, from beginning to end. I corrected some of the most material, and, in that form, it was printed in French. A London bookseller, on seeing the translation, requested me to permit him to print the English original. I thought it best to do so, to let the world see that it was not really so bad as the French translation had made it appear. And this is the true history of that publication.

Mr. Adams soon joined us at Paris, and our first employment was to prepare a general form, to be proposed to such nations as were disposed to treat with us. During the negotiations for peace with the British Commissioner, David Hartley, our Commissioners had proposed, on the suggestion of Dr. Franklin, to insert an article, exempting from capture by the public or private armed ships, of either belligerent, when at war, all merchant vessels and their cargoes, employed merely in carrying on the commerce between nations. It was refused by England, and unwisely, in my opinion. For, in the case of a war with us, their superior commerce places infinitely more at hazard on the ocean, than ours; and, as hawks abound in proportion to game, so our privateers would swarm, in proportion to the wealth exposed to their prize, while theirs would be few, for want of subjects of capture. We inserted this article in our form, with a provision against the molestation of fishermen, husbandmen, citizens unarmed, and following their occupations in unfortified places, for the humane treatment of prisoners of war, the abolition of contraband of war, which exposes merchant vessels to such vexatious and ruinous detentions and abuses; and for the principle of free bottoms, free goods.

In a conference with the Count de Vergennes, it was thought better to leave to legislative regulation, on both sides, such modifications of our commercial intercourse, as would voluntarily flow from amicable dispositions. Without urging, we sounded the ministers of several European nations, at the court of Versailles, on their dispositions towards mutual commerce, and the expediency of encouraging it by the protection of a treaty. Old Frederic, of Prussia, met us cordially, and without hesitation, and appointing the Baron de Thulemeyer, his minister at the Hague, to negotiate with us, we communicated to him our Projét, which, with little alteration by the King, was soon concluded. Denmark and Tuscany entered also into negotiations with us. Other powers appearing indifferent, we did not think it proper to press them. They seemed, in fact, to know little about us, but as rebels, who had been successful in throwing off the yoke of the mother country. They were ignorant of our commerce, which had been always monopolized by England, and of the exchange of articles it might offer advantageously to both parties. They were inclined, therefore, to stand aloof, until they could see better what relations might be usefully instituted with us. The negotiations, therefore, begun with Denmark and Tuscany, we protracted designedly, until our powers had expired; and abstained from making new propositions to others having no colonies; because our commerce being an exchange of raw for wrought materials, is a competent price for admission into the colonies of those possessing them; but were we to give it, without price, to others, all would claim it, without price, on the ordinary ground of *gentis amicissimae.**

* Most favored nation.

Mr. Adams being appointed Minister Plenipotentiary of the United States, to London, left us in June, and in July, 1785, Dr. Franklin returned to America, and I was appointed his successor at Paris. In February, 1786, Mr. Adams wrote to me, pressingly, to join him in London immediately, as he thought he discovered there some symptoms of better disposition towards us. Colonel Smith, his secretary of legation, was the bearer of his urgencies for my immediate attendance. I, accordingly, left Paris on the 1st of March, and, on my arrival in London, we agreed on a very summary form of treaty, proposing an exchange of citizenship for our citizens, our ships, and our productions generally, except as to office. On my presentation, as usual, to the King and Queen, at their levées, it was impossible for anything to be more ungracious, than their notice of Mr. Adams and myself. I saw, at once, that the ulcerations of mind in that quarter, left nothing to be expected on the subject of my attendance; and, on the first conference with the Marquis of Caermarthen, the Minister for foreign affairs, the distance and disinclination which he betrayed in his conversation, the vagueness and evasions of his answers to us, confirmed me in the belief of their aversion to have anything to do with us. We delivered him, however, our Projét, Mr. Adams not despairing as much as I did, of its effect. We afterwards, by one or more notes, requested his appointment of an interview and conference, which, without directly declining, he evaded, by pretences of other pressing occupations for the moment. After staying there seven weeks, till within a few days of the expiration of our commission, I informed the minister, by note, that my duties at Paris required my return to that place, and that I should, with pleasure, be the bearer of any commands to his Ambassador there. He answered, that he had none, and, wishing me a pleasant journey, I left London the 26th, and arrived at Paris the 30th of April.

While in London, we entered into negotiations with the Chevalier Pinto, Ambassador of Portugal, at that place. The only article of difficulty between us was, a stipulation that our bread stuff should be received in Portugal, in the form of flour as well as of grain. He approved of it himself, but observed that several Nobles, of great influence at their court, were the owners of wind-mills in the neighborhood of Lisbon, which depended much for their profits on manufacturing our wheat, and that this stipulation would endanger the whole treaty. He signed it, however, and its fate was what he had candidly portended.

My duties, at Paris, were confined to a few objects; the receipt of our whale-oils, salted fish, and salted meats, on favorable terms; the admission of our rice on equal terms with that of Piedmont, Egypt and the Levant; a mitigation of the monopolies of our tobacco by the Farmers-general, and a free admission of our productions into their islands, were the principal commercial objects which required attention; and, on these occasions, I was powerfully aided by all the influence and the energies of the Marquis de La Fayette, who proved himself equally zealous for the friendship and welfare of both nations; and, in justice, I must also say, that I found the government entirely disposed to befriend us on all occasions, and to yield us every indulgence, not absolutely injurious to themselves. The Count de Vergennes had the reputation, with the diplomatic corps, of being wary and slippery in his diplomatic intercourse; and so he might be with those whom he knew to be slippery, and double-faced themselves. As he saw that I had no indirect views, practised no subtleties, meddled in no intrigues, pursued no concealed object, I found him as frank, as honorable, as easy of access to reason, as any man with whom I had ever done business; and I must say the same for his successor, Montmorin, one of the most honest and worthy of human beings.

Our commerce, in the Mediterranean, was placed under early alarm, by the capture of two of our vessels and crews by the Barbary cruisers. I was very unwilling that we should acquiesce in the European humiliation, of paying a tribute to those lawless pirates, and endeavored to form an association of the powers subject to habitual depredations from them. I accordingly prepared, and proposed to their Ministers at Paris, for consultation with their governments, articles of a special confederation, in the following form:

"Proposals for concerted operation among the powers at war with the piratical States of Barbary.

1. "It is proposed, that the several powers at war with the piratical States of Barbary, or any two or more of them who shall be willing,

shall enter into a convention to carry on their operations against those States, in concert, beginning with the Algerines.

2. "This convention shall remain open to any other powers, who shall, at any future time, wish to accede to it; the parties reserving the right to prescribe the conditions of such accession, according to the circumstances existing at the time it shall be proposed.

3. "The object of the convention shall be, to compel the piratical States to perpetual peace, without price, and to guarantee that peace to each other.

4. "The operations for obtaining this peace shall be constant cruises on their coast, with a naval force now to be agreed on. It is not proposed that this force shall be so considerable as to be inconvenient to any party. It is believed that half a dozen frigates, with as many Tenders or Xebecs, one half of which shall be in cruise, while the other half is at rest, will suffice.

5. "The force agreed to be necessary, shall be furnished by the parties, in certain quotas, now to be fixed; it being expected, that each will be willing to contribute, in such proportion as circumstances may render reasonable.

6. "As miscarriages often proceed from the want of harmony among

officers of different nations, the parties shall now consider and decide, whether it will not be better to contribute their quotas in money, to be employed in fitting out and keeping on duty, a single fleet of the force agreed on.

7. "The difficulties and delays, too, which will attend the management of these operations, if conducted by the parties themselves separately, distant as their courts may be from one another, and incapable of meeting in consultation, suggest a question, whether it will not be better for them to give full powers, for that purpose, to their Ambassadors, or other Ministers resident at some one court of Europe, who shall form a Committee, or Council, for carrying this convention into effect; wherein, the vote of each member shall be computed in proportion to the quota of his sovereign, and the majority so computed, shall prevail in all questions within the view of this convention. The court of Versailles is proposed, on account of its neighborhood to the Mediterranean, and because all those powers are represented there, who are likely to become parties to this convention.

8. "To save to that Council the embarrassment of personal solicitations for office, and to assure the parties that their contributions will be applied solely to the object for which they are destined, there shall be no establishment of officers for the said Council, such as Commissioners, Secretaries, or any other kind, with either salaries or perquisites, nor any other lucrative appointments but such whose functions are to be exercised on board the said vessels.

9. "Should war arise between any two of the parties to this convention, it shall not extend to this enterprise, nor interrupt it; but as to this they shall be reputed at peace.

10. "When Algiers shall be reduced to peace, the other piratical States, if they refuse to discontinue their piracies, shall become the objects of this convention, either successively or together, as shall seem best.

11. "Where this convention would interfere with treaties actually existing between any of the parties and the States of Barbary, the treaty shall prevail, and such party shall be allowed to withdraw from the operations against that State."

Spain had just concluded a treaty with Algiers, at the expense of three millions of dollars, and did not like to relinquish the benefit of that, until the other party should fail in their observance of it. Portugal, Naples, the two Sicilies, Venice, Malta, Denmark and Sweden, were favorably disposed to support such an association; but their representatives at Paris expressed apprehensions that France would interfere, and, either openly or secretly, support the Barbary powers; and they required, that I should ascertain the dispositions of the Count de Vergennes on the subject. I had before taken occasion to inform him of what we were proposing, and, therefore, did not think it proper to insinuate any doubt of the fair conduct of his government; but, stating our propositions, I mentioned the apprehensions entertained by us, that England would interfere in behalf of those piratical governments. "She dares not do it," said he. I pressed it no further. The other Agents were satisfied with this indication of his sentiments, and nothing was now wanting to bring it into direct and formal consideration, but the assent of our government, and their authority to make the formal proposition. I communicated to them the favorable prospect of protecting our commerce from the Barbary depredations, and for such a continuance of time, as, by an exclusion of them from the sea, to change their habits and characters, from a predatory to an agricultural people: towards which, however, it was expected they would contribute a frigate, and its expenses, to be in constant cruise. But they were in no condition to make any such engagement. Their recommendatory powers for obtaining contributions were so openly neglected by the several States, that they declined an engagement which they were conscious they could not fulfil with punctuality; and so it fell through.

In 1786, while at Paris, I became acquainted with John Ledyard, of Connecticut, a man of genius, of some science, and of fearless courage and enterprise. He had accompanied Captain Cook in his voyage to the Pacific, had distinguished himself on several occasions by an unrivalled intrepidity, and published an account of that voyage, with details unfavorable to Cook's deportment towards the savages, and lessening our regrets at his fate. Ledyard had come to Paris, in the hope of forming a company to engage in the fur trade of the Western coast of

America. He was disappointed in this, and, being out of business, and of a roaming, restless character, I suggested to him the enterprise of exploring the Western part of our continent, by passing through St. Petersburg to Kamschatka, and procuring a passage thence in some of the Russian vessels to Nootka Sound, whence he might make his way across the continent to the United States; and I undertook to have the permission of the Empress of Russia solicited. He eagerly embraced the proposition, and M. de Sémoulin, the Russian Ambassador, and more particularly Baron Grimm, the special correspondent of the Empress, solicited her permission for him to pass through her dominions, to the Western coast of America. And here I must correct a material error, which I have committed in another place, to the prejudice of the Empress. In writing some notes of the life of Captain Lewis, prefixed to his "Expedition to the Pacific," I stated that the Empress gave the permission asked, and afterwards retracted it. This idea, after a lapse of twenty-six years, had so insinuated itself into my mind, that I committed it to paper, without the least suspicion of error. Yet I find, on recurring to my letters of that date, that the Empress refused permission at once, considering the enterprise as entirely chimerical. But Ledyard would not relinquish it, persuading himself that, by proceeding to St. Petersburg, he could satisfy the Empress of its practicability, and obtain her permission. He went accordingly, but she was absent on a visit to some distant part of her dominions, and he pursued his course to within two hundred miles of Kamschatka, where he was overtaken by an arrest from the Empress, brought back to Poland, and there dismissed. I must therefore, in justice, acquit the Empress of ever having for a moment countenanced, even by the indulgence of an innocent passage through her territories, this interesting enterprise.

The pecuniary distresses of France produced this year a measure of which there had been no example for near two centuries, and the consequences of which, good and evil, are not yet calculable. For its remote causes, we must go a little back.

Celebrated writers of France and England had already sketched good principles on the subject of government; yet the American Revolution seems first to have awakened the thinking part of the French nation in general, from the sleep of despotism in which they were sunk. The officers too, who had been to America, were mostly young men, less shackled by habit and prejudice, and more ready to assent to the suggestions of common sense, and feeling of common rights, than others. They came back with new ideas and impressions. The press, notwithstanding its shackles, began to disseminate them; conversation assumed new freedoms; Politics became the theme of all societies, male and female, and a very extensive and zealous party was formed, which acquired the appellation of the Patriotic party, who, sensible of the abusive government under which they lived, sighed for occasions of reforming it. The party comprehended all the honesty of the kingdom, sufficiently at leisure to think, the men of letters, the easy Bourgeois, the young nobility, partly from reflection, partly from mode; for these sentiments became matter of mode, and as such, united most of the young women to the party. Happily for the nation, it happened, at the same moment, that the dissipations of the Queen and court, the abuses of the pension-list, and dilapidations in the administration of every branch of the finances, had exhausted the treasures and credit of the nation, insomuch that its most necessary functions were paralyzed. To reform these abuses would have overset the Minister; to impose new taxes by the authority of the King, was known to be impossible, from the determined opposition of the Parliament to their enregistry. No resource remained then, but to appeal to the nation. He advised, therefore, the call of an Assembly of the most distinguished characters of the nation, in the hope that, by promises of various and valuable improvements in the organization and regimen of the government, they would be induced to authorize new taxes, to control the opposition of the Parliament, and to raise the annual revenue to the level of expenditures. An Assembly of Notables therefore, about one hundred and fifty in number, named by the King, convened on the 22d of February. The Minister (Calonne) stated to them, that the annual excess of expenses beyond the revenue, when Louis XVI came to the throne, was thirty-seven millions of livres; that four hundred and forty millions had been borrowed to re-establish the navy; that the American war had cost them fourteen hundred and forty millions (two hundred and fifty-six millions of dollars), and that the interest of these sums, with other increased expenses, had added forty millions more to the annual deficit. (But a subsequent and more candid estimate made it fifty-six millions.) He proffered them an universal redress of grievances, laid open those grievances fully, pointed out sound remedies, and, covering his canvas with objects of this magnitude, the deficit dwindled to a little accessory, scarcely attracting attention. The persons chosen were the most able and independent characters in the kingdom, and their support, if it could be obtained, would be enough for him. They improved the occasion for redressing their grievances, and agreed that the public wants should be relieved; but went into an examination of the causes of them. It was supposed that Calonne was conscious that his accounts could not bear examination; and it was said, and believed, that he asked of the King, to send four members to the Bastille, of whom the Marquis de La Fayette was one, to banish twenty others, and two of his Ministers. The King found it shorter to banish him. His successor went on in full concert with the Assembly. The result was an augmentation of the revenue, a promise of economies in its expenditure, of an annual settlement of the public accounts before a council, which the Comptroller, having been heretofore obliged to settle only with the King in person, of course never settled at all; an acknowledgment that the King could not lay a new tax, a reformation of the Criminal laws, abolition of torture, suppression of corvees, reformation of the gabelles, removal of the interior Custom Houses, free commerce of grain, internal and external, and the establishment of Provincial Assemblies; which, altogether, constituted a great mass of improvement in the condition of the nation. The establishment of the Provincial Assemblies was, in itself, a fundamental improvement. They would be of the choice of the people, one-third renewed every year, in those provinces where there are no States, that is to say, over about three-fourths of the kingdom. They would be partly an Executive themselves, and partly an Executive Council to the Intendant, to whom the Executive power, in his province, had been heretofore entirely delegated. Chosen by the people, they would soften the execution of hard laws, and, having a right of representation to the King, they would censure bad laws, suggest good ones, expose abuses, and their representations, when united, would command respect. To the other advantages, might be added the precedent itself of calling the Assemblée des Notables, which would perhaps grow into habit. The hope was, that the improvements thus promised would be carried into effect; that they would be maintained during the present reign, and that that would be long enough for them to take some root in the constitution, so that they might come to be considered as a part of that, and be protected by time, and the attachment of the nation.

The Count de Vergennes had died a few days before the meeting of the Assembly, and the Count de Montmorin had been named Minister of Foreign Affairs, in his place. Villedeuil succeeded Calonne, as Comptroller General, and Loménie de Brienne, Archbishop of Toulouse, afterwards of Sens, and ultimately Cardinal Loménie, was named Minister principal, with whom the other Ministers were to transact the business of their departments, heretofore done with the King in person; and the Duke de Nivernois, and M. de Malesherbes, were called to the Council. On the nomination of the Minister principal, the Marshals de Ségur and de Castries retired from the departments of War and Marine, unwilling to act subordinately, or to share the blame of proceedings taken out of their direction. They were succeeded by the Count de Brienne, brother of the Prime Minister, and the Marquis de La Luzerne, brother to him who had been Minister in the United States.

A dislocated wrist, unsuccessfully set, occasioned advice from my surgeon, to try the mineral waters of Aix, in Provence, as a corroborant. I left Paris for that place therefore, on the 28th of February, and proceeded up the Seine, through Champagne and Burgundy, and down the Rhone through the Beaujolais by Lyons, Avignon, Nismes to Aix; where, finding on trial no benefit from the waters, I concluded to visit the rice country of Piedmont, to see if anything might be learned there, to benefit the rivalship of our Carolina rice with that, and thence to make a tour of the seaport towns of France, along its Southern and Western coast, to inform myself, if anything could be done to favor our commerce with them. From Aix, therefore, I took my route by Marseilles, Toulon, Hieres, Nice, across the Col de Tende, by Coni, Turin, Vercelli, Novara, Milan, Pavia, Novi, Genoa. Thence, returning along the coast of Savona, Noli, Albenga, Oneglia, Monaco, Nice, Antibes, Frejus, Aix, Marseilles, Avignon, Nismes, Montpellier, Frontignan, Cette, Agde, and along the canal of Languedoc, by Bezieres, Narbonne, Carcassonne, Castelnaudari, through the Souterrain of St. Feriol, and back by Castelnaudari, to Toulouse; thence to Montauban, and down the Garonne by Langon to Bordeaux. Thence to Rochefort, la Rochelle, Nantes, L'Orient; then back by Rennes to Nantes, and up the Loire by Angers, Tours, Amboise, Blois to Orleans, thence direct to Paris, where I arrived on the 10th of June. Soon after my return from this journey, to wit, about the latter part of July, I received my younger daughter, Maria, from Virginia, by the way of London, the youngest having died some time before.

The treasonable perfidy of the Prince of Orange, Stadtholder and Captain General of the United Netherlands, in the war which England waged against them, for entering into a treaty of commerce with the United States, is known to all. As their Executive officer, charged with the conduct of the war, he contrived to baffle all the measures of the States General, to dislocate all their military plans, and played false into the hands of England against his own country, on every possible occasion, confident in her protection, and in that of the King of Prussia, brother to his Princess. The States General, indignant at this patricidal conduct, applied to France for aid, according to the stipulations of the treaty concluded with her in '85. It was assured to them readily, and in cordial terms, in a letter from the Count de Vergennes, to the Marquis de Verac, Ambassador of France at the Hague, of which the following is an extract:

Extrait de la dépêche de Monsieur le Comte de Vergennes à Monsieur le Marquis de Verac, Ambassadeur de France à la Haye, du 1er Mars, 1786:

Le Roi concourrera, autant qu'il sera en son pouvoir, au succès de la chose, et vous in-viterez, de sa part, les patriotes de lui communiquer leurs vues, leurs plans, et leurs envieux. Vous les assurerez, que le roi prend un interet véritable à leurs personnes comme à leur cause, et qu'ils peuvent compter sur sa protection. Ils doivent y compter d'autant plus, Monsieur, que nous ne dissimulons pas, que si Monsieur le Stadhoulder reprend son ancienne influence, le système Anglois ne tardera pas de prévaloir, et que notre alliance deviendroit un être de *raison. Les Patriotes sentiront facilement, que cette position seroit incompatible avec la dignité, comme avec la considération de sa majesté. Mais dans le cas, Monsieur, ou les chefs des Patriotes auroient à craindre une scission, ils auroient le temps suffisant pour ramener ceux de leurs amis, que les Anglomanes ont égarés, et préparer les choses de manière que la question de nouveau mise en délibération, soit decidée selon leurs désirs. Dans cette hypothèse, le roi vous autorise à agir de concert avec eux, de suivre la direction qu'ils jugeront devoir vous donner, et d'employer tous les moyens pour augmenter le nombre des partisans de la bonne cause. Il me reste, Monsieur, de vous parler de la sureté personnelle des Patriotes. Vous les assurerez, que dans tout état de cause, le roi les prend sous sa protection immédiate, et vous ferez connoitre, partout ou vous le jugerez nécessaire, que sa Majesté regarderoit comme une offense personelle, tout ce qu'on entreprenderoit contre leur liberté. Il est à presumer que ce langage, tenu avec énergie, en imposera à l'audace des Anglomanes, et que Monsieur le Prince de Nassau croira courir quelque risque en provoquant le ressentiment de sa Majesté.**

This letter was communicated by the Patriots to me, when at Amsterdam, in 1788, and a copy sent by me to Mr. Jay, in my letter to him of March 16, 1788.

The object of the Patriots was, to establish a representative and republican government. The majority of the States General were with them, but the majority of the populace of the towns was with the Prince of Orange; and that populace was played off with great effect, by the triumvirate of . . . Harris, the English Ambassador, afterwards

---

* The following translation appeared in the Memorial Edition of Jefferson's Writings (Washington, 1903):

Extract from the despatch of the Count de Vergennes, to the Marquis de Verac, Ambassador from France, at the Hague, dated March 1, 1786:

"The King will give his aid, as far as may be in his power, towards the success of the affair, and will, on his part, invite the Patriots to communicate to him their views, their plans, and their discontents. You may assure them that the King takes a real interest in themselves as well as their cause, and that they may rely upon his protection. On this they may place the greater dependence, as we do not conceal, that if the Stadtholder resumes his former influence, the English System will soon prevail, and our alliance become a mere affair of the imagination. The Patriots will readily feel, that this position would be incompatible both with the dignity and consideration of his Majesty. But in case the Chief of the Patriots should have to fear a division, they would have time sufficient to reclaim those whom the Anglomaniacs had misled, and to prepare matters in such a manner, that the question when again agitated, might be decided according to their wishes. In such a hypothetical case, the King authorizes you to act in concert with them, to pursue the direction which they may think proper to give you, and to employ every means to augment the number of the partisans of the good cause. It remains for me to speak of the personal security of the Patriots. You may assure them, that under every circumstance, the King will take them under his immediate protection, and you will make known wherever you may judge necessary, that his Majesty will regard as a personal offence every undertaking against their liberty. It is to be presumed that this language, energetically maintained, may have some effect on the audacity of the Anglomaniacs, and that the Prince de Nassau will feel that he runs some risk in provoking the resentment of his Majesty."

Lord Malmesbury, the Prince of Orange, a stupid man, and the Princess as much a man as either of her colleagues, in audaciousness, in enterprise, and in the thirst of domination. By these, the mobs of the Hague were excited against the members of the States General; their persons were insulted and endangered in the streets; the sanctuary of their houses was violated; and the Prince, whose function and duty it was to repress and punish these violations of order, took no steps for that purpose. The States General, for their own protection, were therefore obliged to place their militia under the command of a Committee. The Prince filled the courts of London and Berlin with complaints at this usurpation of his prerogatives, and, forgetting that he was but the first servant of a Republic, marched his regular troops against the city of Utrecht, where the States were in session. They were repulsed by the militia. His interests now became marshalled with those of the public enemy, and against his own country. The States, therefore, exercising their rights of sovereignty, deprived him of all his powers. The great Frederic had died in August, '86. He had never intended to break with France in support of the Prince of Orange. During the illness of which he died, he had, through the Duke of Brunswick, declared to the Marquis de La Fayette, who was then at Berlin, that he meant not to support the English interest in Holland: that he might assure the government of France, his only wish was, that some honorable place in the Constitution should be reserved for the Stadtholder and his children, and that he would take no part in the quarrel, unless an entire abolition of the Stadtholderate should be attempted. But his place was now occupied by Frederic William, his great-nephew, a man of little understanding, much caprice, and very inconsiderate; and the Princess, his sister, although her husband was in arms against the legitimate authorities of the country, attempting to go to Amsterdam, for the purpose of exciting the mobs of that place, and being refused permission to pass a military post on the way, he put the Duke of Brunswick at the head of twenty thousand men, and made demonstrations of marching on Holland. The King of France hereupon declared, by his Chargé des Affaires in Holland, that if the Prussian troops continued to menace Holland with an invasion, his Majesty, in quality of Ally, was determined to succor that province. In answer to this, Eden gave official information to Count Montmorin, that England must consider as at an end its convention with France relative to giving notice of its naval armaments, and that she was arming generally. War being now imminent, Eden, since Lord Aukland, questioned me on the effect of our treaty with France, in the case of a war, and what might be our dispositions. I told him frankly, and without hesitation, that our dispositions would be neutral, and that I thought it would be the interest of both these powers that we should be so; because, it would relieve both from all anxiety as to feeding their West India islands; that England, too, by suffering us to remain so, would avoid a heavy land war on our Continent, which might very much cripple her proceedings elsewhere; that our treaty, indeed, obliged us to receive into our ports the armed vessels of France, with their prizes, and to refuse admission to the prizes made on her by her enemies: that there was a clause, also, by which we guaranteed to France her American possessions, which might perhaps force us into the war, if these were attacked. "Then it will be war," said he, "for they will assuredly be attacked." Liston, at Madrid, about the same time, made the same inquiries of Carmichael. The Government of France then declared a determination to form a camp of observation at Givet, commenced arming her marine, and named the Bailli de Suffrein their Generalissimo on the Ocean. She secretly engaged, also, in negotiations with Russia, Austria, and Spain, to form a quadruple alliance. The Duke of Brunswick having advanced to the confines of Holland, sent some of his officers to Givet, to reconnoitre the state of things there, and report them to him. He said afterwards, that "if there had been only a few tents at that place, he should not have advanced further, for that the King would not, merely for the interest of his sister, engage in a war with France." But, finding that there was not a single company there, he boldly entered the country, took their towns as fast as he presented himself before them, and advanced on Utrecht. The States had appointed the Rhingrave of Salm their Commander-in-Chief; a Prince without talents, without courage, and without principle. He might have held out in Utrecht for a considerable time, but he surrendered the place without firing a gun, literally ran away and hid himself, so that for months it was not known what had become of him. Amsterdam was then attacked, and capitulated. In the meantime, the negotiations for the quadruple alliance were proceeding favorably; but the secrecy with which they were attempted to be conducted, was penetrated by Fraser, Chargé des Affaires of England at St. Petersburg, who instantly notified his court, and gave the alarm to Prussia. The King saw at once what would be his situation, between the jaws of France, Austria, and Russia. In great dismay, he besought the court of London not to abandon him, sent Alvensleben to Paris to explain and soothe; and England, through the Duke of Dorset and Eden, renewed her conferences for accommodation. The Archbishop, who shuddered at the idea of war, and preferred a peaceful surrender of right to an armed vindication of it, received them with open arms, entered into cordial conferences, and a declaration, and counter-declaration, were cooked up at Versailles, and sent to London for approbation. They were approved there, reached Paris at one o'clock of the 27th, and were signed that night at Versailles. It was said and believed at Paris, that M. de Montmorin, literally *"pleuroit comme un enfant,"* when obliged to sign this counter-declaration; so distressed was he by the dishonor of sacrificing the Patriots, after assurances so solemn of protection, and absolute encouragement to proceed. The Prince of Orange was reinstated in all his powers, now become regal. A great emigration of the Patriots took place; all were deprived of office, many exiled, and their property confiscated. They were received in France, and subsisted, for some time, on her bounty. Thus fell Holland, by the treachery of her Chief, from her honorable independence, to become a province of England; and so, also, her Stadtholder, from the high station of the first citizen of a free Republic, to be the servile Viceroy of a foreign Sovereign. And this was effected by a mere scene of bullying and demonstration; not one of the parties, France, England, or Prussia, having ever really meant to encounter actual war for the interest of the Prince of Orange. But it had all the effect of a real and decisive war.

Our first essay, in America, to establish a federative government had fallen, on trial, very short of its object. During the war of Independence, while the pressure of an external enemy hooped us together, and their enterprises kept us necessarily on the alert, the spirit of the people, excited by danger, was a supplement to the Confederation, and urged them to zealous exertions, whether claimed by that instrument or not; but, when peace and safety were restored, and every man became engaged in useful and profitable occupation, less attention was paid to the calls of Congress. The fundamental defect of the Confederation was, that Congress was not authorized to act immediately on the people, and by its own officers. Their power was only requisitory, and these requisitions were addressed to the several Legislatures, to be by them carried into execution, without other coercion than the moral principle of duty. This allowed, in fact, a negative to every Legislature, on every measure proposed by Congress; a negative so frequently exercised in practice, as to benumb the action of the Federal government, and to render it inefficient in its general objects, and more especially in pecuniary and foreign concerns. The want, too, of a separation of the Legislative, Executive, and Judiciary functions, worked disadvantageously in practice. Yet this state of things afforded a happy augury of the future march of our Confederacy, when it was seen that the good sense and good dispositions of the people, as soon as they perceived the incompetence of their first compact, instead of leaving its correction to insurrection and civil war, agreed, with one voice, to elect deputies to a general Convention, who should peaceably meet and agree on such a Constitution as "would ensure peace, justice, liberty, the common defence and general welfare."

This Convention met at Philadelphia on the 25th of May, '87. It sat with closed doors, and kept all its proceedings secret, until its dissolution on the 17th of September, when the results of its labors were published all together. I received a copy, early in November, and read and contemplated its provisions with great satisfaction. As not a member of the Convention, however, nor probably a single citizen of the Union, had approved it in all its parts, so I, too, found articles which I thought objectionable. The absence of express declarations ensuring freedom of religion, freedom of the press, freedom of the person under the uninterrupted protection of the Habeas corpus, and trial by jury in

Civil as well as in Criminal cases, excited my jealousy; and the re-eligibility of the President for life, I quite disapproved. I expressed freely, in letters to my friends, and most particularly to Mr. Madison and General Washington, my approbations and objections. How the good should be secured and the ill brought to rights, was the difficulty. To refer it back to a new Convention might endanger the loss of the

whole. My first idea was, that the nine States first acting, should accept it unconditionally, and thus secure what in it was good, and that the four last should accept on the previous condition, that certain amendments should be agreed to; but a better course was devised, of accepting the whole, and trusting that the good sense and honest intentions of our citizens would make the alterations which should be deemed necessary. Accordingly, all accepted, six without objection, and seven with recommendations of specified amendments. Those respecting the press, religion, and juries, with several others, of great value, were accordingly made; but the Habeas corpus was left to the discretion of Congress, and the amendment against the re-eligibility of the President was not proposed. My fears of that feature were founded on the importance of the office, on the fierce contentions it might excite among ourselves, if continuable for life, and the dangers of interference, either with money or arms, by foreign nations, to whom the choice of an American President might become interesting. Examples of this abounded in history; in the case of the Roman Emperors, for instance; of the Popes, while of any significance; of the German Emperors; the Kings of Poland, and the Deys of Barbary. I had observed, too, in the feudal history, and in the recent instance, particularly, of the Stadtholder of Holland, how easily offices, or tenures for life, slide into inheritances. My wish, therefore, was, that the President should be elected for seven years, and be ineligible afterwards. This term I thought sufficient to enable him, with the concurrence of the Legislature, to carry through and establish any system of improvement he should propose for the general good. But the practice adopted, I think, is better, allowing his continuance for eight years, with a liability to be dropped at half way of the term, making that a period of probation. That his continuance should be restrained to seven years, was the opinion of the Convention at an earlier stage of its session, when it voted that term, by a majority of eight against two, and by a simple majority that he should be ineligible a second time. This opinion was confirmed by the House so late as July 26, referred to the Committee of detail, reported favorably by them, and changed to the present form by final vote, on the last day but one only of their session. Of this change, three States expressed their disapprobation; New York, by recommending an amendment, that the President should not be eligible a third time, and Virginia and North Carolina that he should not be capable of serving more than eight, in any term of sixteen years; and though this amendment has not been made in form, yet practice seems to have established it. The example of four Presidents voluntarily retiring at the end of their eighth year, and the progress of public opinion, that the principle is salutary, have given it in practice the force of precedent and usage; insomuch, that, should a President consent to be a candidate for a third election, I trust he would be rejected, on this demonstration of ambitious views.

But there was another amendment, of which none of us thought at the time, and in the omission of which, lurks the germ that is to destroy this happy combination of National powers in the General government, for matters of National concern, and independent powers in the States, for what concerns the States severally. In England, it was a great point gained at the Revolution, that the commissions of the Judges, which had hitherto been during pleasure, should thenceforth be made during good behavior. A Judiciary, dependent on the will of the King, had proved itself the most oppressive of all tools, in the hands of that Magistrate. Nothing, then, could be more salutary, than a change there, to the tenure of good behavior; and the question of good behavior, left to the vote of a simple majority in the two Houses of Parliament. Before the Revolution, we were all good English Whigs, cordial in their free principles, and in their jealousies of their Executive Magistrate. These jealousies are very apparent, in all our state Constitutions; and, in the General government in this instance, we have gone even beyond the English caution, by requiring a vote of two-thirds, in one of the Houses, for removing a Judge; a vote so impossible, where any defence is made, before men of ordinary prejudices and passions, that our Judges are effectually independent of the nation. But this ought not to be. I would not, indeed, make them dependent on the Executive authority, as they formerly were in England; but I deem it indispensable to the continuance of this government, that they should be submitted to some practical and impartial control; and that this, to be imparted, must be compounded of a mixture of State and Federal authorities. It is not enough that honest men are appointed Judges. All know the influence of interest on the mind of man, and how unconsciously his judgment is warped by that influence. To this bias add that of the *esprit de corps*, of their peculiar maxim and creed, that "it is the office of a good Judge to enlarge his jurisdiction," and the absence of responsibility; and how can we expect impartial decision between the General government, of which they are themselves so eminent a part, and an individual State, from which they have nothing to hope or fear? We have seen, too, that contrary to all correct example, they are in the habit of going out of the question before them, to throw an anchor ahead, and grapple further hold for future advances of power. They are then, in fact, the corps of sappers and miners, steadily working to undermine the independent rights of the States, and to consolidate all power in the hands of that government in which they have so important a freehold estate. But it is not by the consolidation, or concentration of powers, but by their distribution, that good government is effected. Were not this great country already divided into States, that division must be made, that each might do for itself what concerns itself directly, and what it can so much better do than a distant authority. Every State again is divided into counties, each to take care of what lies within its local bounds; each county again into townships or wards, to manage minuter details; and every ward into farms, to be governed each by its individual proprietor. Were we directed from Washington when to sow, and when to reap, we should soon want bread. It is by this partition of cares, descending in gradation from general to particular, that the mass of human affairs may be best managed, for the good and prosperity of all. I repeat, that I do not charge the Judges with wilful and ill-intentioned error; but honest error must be arrested, where its toleration leads to public ruin. As, for the safety of society, we commit honest maniacs to Bedlam, so judges should be withdrawn from their bench, whose erroneous biases are leading us to dissolution. It may, indeed, injure them in fame or in fortune; but it saves the Republic, which is the first and supreme law.

Among the debilities of the government of the Confederation, no one was more distinguished or more distressing, than the utter impossibility of obtaining, from the States, the moneys necessary for the payment of debts, or even for the ordinary expenses of the government. Some contributed a little, some less, and some nothing; and the last furnished at length an excuse for the first to do nothing also. Mr. Adams, while residing at the Hague, had a general authority to borrow what sums might be requisite, for ordinary and necessary expenses. Interest on the public debt, and the maintenance of the diplomatic establishment in Europe, had been habitually provided in this way. He was now elected Vice-President of the United States, was soon to return to America, and had referred our bankers to me for future counsel, on our affairs in their hands. But I had no powers, no instructions, no means, and no familiarity with the subject. It had always been exclusively under his management, except as to occasional and partial deposits in the hands of Mr. Grand, banker in Paris, for special and local purposes. These last had been exhausted for some time, and I had fervently pressed the Treasury board to replenish this particular deposit, as Mr. Grand now refused to make further advances. They answered candidly, that no funds could be obtained until the new government should get into action, and have time to make its arrangements. Mr. Adams had received his appointment to the court of London, while engaged at Paris, with Dr. Franklin and myself, in the negotiations under our joint commissions. He had repaired thence to London, without returning to the Hague, to take leave of that government. He thought it necessary, however, to do so now, before he should leave Europe, and accordingly went there. I learned his departure from London, by a letter from Mrs. Adams, received on the very day on which he would arrive at the Hague. A consultation with him, and some provision for the future, was indispensable, while we could yet avail ourselves of his powers; for when they would be gone, we should be without resource. I was daily dunned by a Company who had formerly made a small loan to the United States, the principal of which was now become due; and our bankers in Amsterdam, had notified me that the interest on our general debt would be expected in June; that if we failed to pay it, it would be deemed an act of bankruptcy, and would effectually destroy the credit of the United States, and all future prospect of obtaining money there; that the loan they had been authorized to open, of which a third only was filled, had now ceased to get forward, and rendered desperate that hope of resource. I saw that there was not a moment to lose, and set out for the Hague on the second morning after receiving the information of Mr. Adams's journey. I went the direct road by Louvres, Senlis, Roye, Pont St. Maxence, Bois le duc, Gournay, Peronne, Cambray, Bouchain, Valenciennes, Mons, Bruxelles, Malines, Antwerp, Mordick, and Rotterdam, to the Hague, where I happily found Mr. Adams. He concurred with me at once in opinion, that something must be done, and that we ought to risk ourselves on doing it without instructions, to save the credit of the United States. We foresaw, that before the new government could be adopted, assembled, establish its financial system, get the money into the Treasury, and place it in Europe, considerable time would elapse; that, therefore, we had better provide at once, for the years '88, '89, and '90, in order to place our government at its ease, and our credit in security, during that trying interval. We set out, therefore, by the way of Leyden, for Amsterdam, where we arrived on the 10th. I had prepared an estimate, showing that

		Florins.
There would be necessary for the year '88		531,937–10
'89		538,540
'90		473,540
Total		1,544,017–10
		Florins.
To meet this, the bankers had in hand .	79,268–2–8	
and the unsold bonds would yield ...	542,800	
		622,068–2–8
Leaving a deficit of		921,949–7–4
We proposed then to borrow a million, yielding		920,000
Which would leave a small deficiency of		1,949–7–4

Mr. Adams accordingly executed 1000 bonds, for 1000 florins each, and deposited them in the hands of our bankers, with instructions, however, not to issue them until Congress should ratify the measure. This done, he returned to London, and I set out for Paris; and, as nothing urgent forbade it, I determined to return along the banks of the Rhine, to Strasburg, and thence strike off to Paris. I accordingly left Amsterdam on the 30th of March, and proceeded by Utrecht, Nimeguen, Cleves, Duysberg, Dusseldorf, Cologne, Bonn, Coblentz, Nassau, Hocheim, Frankfort, and made an excursion to Hanau, thence to Mayence, and another excursion to Rudesheim, and Johansberg; then by Oppenheim, Worms, and Mannheim, making an excursion to Heidelberg, then by Spire, Carlsruh, Rastadt and Kehl, to Strasburg, where I arrived the 16th, and proceeded again on the 18th, by Phalsbourg, Fenestrange, Dieuze, Moyenvie, Nancy, Toul, Ligny, Barleduc, St. Diziers, Vitry, Châlons sur Marne, Epernay, Château Thierry, Meaux, to Paris, where I arrived on the 23d of April; and I had the satisfaction to reflect, that by this journey our credit was secured, the new government was placed at ease for two years to come, and that, as well as myself, relieved from the torment of incessant duns, whose just complaints could not be silenced by any means within our power.

A Consular Convention had been agreed on in '84, between Dr. Franklin and the French government, containing several articles, so entirely inconsistent with the laws of the several States, and the general spirit of our citizens, that Congress withheld their ratification, and sent it back to me, with instructions to get these articles expunged, or modified so as to render them compatible with our laws. The Minister unwillingly released us from these concessions, which, indeed, authorized the exercise of powers very offensive in a free State. After much discussion, the Convention was reformed in a considerable degree, and was signed by the Count Montmorin and myself, on the 14th of November, '88; not, indeed, such as I would have wished, but such as could be obtained with good humor and friendship.

On my return from Holland, I found Paris as I had left it, still in high fermentation. Had the Archbishop, on the close of the Assembly of Notables, immediately carried into operation the measures contemplated, it was believed they would all have been registered by the Parliament; but he was slow, presented his edicts, one after another, and at considerable intervals, which gave time for the feelings excited by the proceedings of the Notables to cool off, new claims to be advanced, and a pressure to arise for a fixed constitution, not subject to changes at the will of the King. Nor should we wonder at this pressure, when we consider the monstrous abuses of power under which this people were ground to powder; when we pass in review the weight of their taxes, and the inequality of their distribution; the oppressions of the tithes, the tailles, the corvees, the gabelles, the farms and the barriers; the shackles on commerce by monopolies; on industry by guilds and corporations; on the freedom of conscience, of thought, and of speech; on the freedom of the press by the Censure; and of the person by Lettres de Cachet; the cruelty of the Criminal code generally; the atrocities of the Rack; the venality of the Judges, and their partialities to the rich; the monopoly of Military honors by the Noblesse; the enormous expenses of the Queen, the Princes and the Court; the prodigalities of pensions; and the riches, luxury, indolence and immorality of the Clergy. Surely under such a mass of misrule and oppression, a people might justly press for a thorough reformation, and might even dismount their rough-shod riders, and leave them to walk on their own legs. The edicts, relative to the corvees and free circulation of grain, were first presented to the Parliament and registered; but those for the impôt territorial, and stamp tax, offered some time after, were refused by the Parliament, which proposed a call of the States General, as alone competent to their authorization. Their refusal produced a Bed of justice, and their exile to Troyes. The Advocates, however, refusing to attend them, a suspension in the administration of justice took place. The Parliament held out for awhile, but the ennui of their exile and absence from Paris, began at length to be felt, and some dispositions for compromise to appear. On their consent, therefore, to prolong some of the former taxes, they were recalled from exile; the King met them in session, November 19, '87, promised to call the States General in the year '92, and a majority expressed their assent to register an edict for successive and annual loans from 1788 to '92; but a protest being entered by the Duke of Orleans, and this encouraging others in a disposition to retract, the King ordered peremptorily the registry of the edict, and left the assembly abruptly. The Parliament immediately protested, that the votes for the enregistry had not been legally taken, and that they gave no sanction to the loans proposed. This was enough to discredit and defeat them. Hereupon issued another edict, for the establishment of a cour plenière, and the suspension of all the Parliaments in the kingdom. This being opposed, as might be expected, by reclamations from all the Parliaments and Provinces, the King gave way, and by an edict of July 5th, '88, renounced his cour plenière, and promised the States General for the 1st of May, of the ensuing year; and the Archbishop, finding the times beyond his faculties, accepted the promise of a Cardinal's hat, was removed [September '88] from the Ministry, and M. Necker was called to the department of finance. The innocent rejoicings of the people of Paris on this change provoked the interference of an officer of the city guards, whose order for their dispersion not being obeyed, he charged them with fixed bayonets, killed two or three, and wounded many. This dispersed them for the moment, but they collected the next day in great numbers, burnt ten or twelve guardhouses, killed two or three of the guards, and lost six or eight more of their own number. The city was hereupon put under Martial law, and after awhile the tumult subsided. The effect of this change of ministers, and the promise of the States General at an early day, tranquillized the nation. But two great questions now occurred. 1st. What proportion shall the number of deputies of the Tiers état bear to those of the Nobles and Clergy? And 2d, shall they sit in the same or in distinct apartments? M. Necker, desirous of avoiding himself these knotty questions, proposed a second call of the same Notables, and that their advice should be asked on the subject. They met, November 9, '88; and, by five bureaux against one, they recommended the forms of the States General of 1614; wherein the Houses were separate, and voted by orders, not by persons. But the whole nation declaring at once against this, and that the Tiers état should be, in numbers, equal to both the other orders, and the Parliament deciding for the same proportion, it was determined so to be, by a declaration of December 27th, '88. A Report of M. Necker, to the King, of about the same date, contained other very important concessions. 1. That the King could neither lay a new tax, nor prolong an old one. 2. It expressed a readiness to agree on the periodical meeting of the States. 3. To consult on the necessary restriction on Lettres de Cachet; and 4. How far the press might be made free. 5. It admits that the States are to appropriate the public money; and 6. That Ministers shall be responsible for public expenditures. And these concessions came from the very heart of the King. He had not a wish but for the good of the nation; and for that object, no personal sacrifice would ever have cost him a moment's regret; but his mind was weakness itself, his constitution timid, his judgment null, and without sufficient firmness even to stand by the faith of his word. His Queen, too, haughty and bearing no contradiction, had an absolute ascendency over him; and around her were rallied the King's brother d'Artois, the court generally, and the aristocratic part of his Ministers, particularly Breteuil, Broglie, Vauguyon, Foulon, Luzerne, men whose principles of government were those of the age of Louis XIV. Against this host, the good counsels of Necker, Montmorin, St. Priest, although in unison with the wishes of the King himself, were of little avail. The resolutions of the morning, formed under their advice, would be reversed in the evening, by the influence of the Queen and court. But the hand of heaven weighed heavily indeed on the machinations of this junto; producing collateral incidents, not arising out of the case, yet powerfully co-exciting the nation to force a regeneration of its government, and overwhelming with accumulated difficulties, this liberticide resistance. For, while laboring under the want of money for even ordinary purposes, in a government which required a million of livres a day, and driven to the last ditch by the universal call for liberty, there came on a winter of such severe cold, as was without example in the memory of man, or in the written records of history. The Mercury was at times 50° below the freezing point of Fahrenheit, and 22° below that of Reaumur. All outdoor labor was suspended, and the poor, without the wages of labor, were, of course, without either bread or fuel. The government found its necessities aggravated by that of procuring immense quantities of fire-wood, and of keeping great fires at all the cross streets, around which the people gathered in crowds, to avoid perishing with cold. Bread, too, was to be bought, and distributed daily, gratis, until a relaxation of the season should enable the people to work; and the slender stock of bread stuff had for some time threatened famine, and had raised that article to an enormous price. So great, indeed, was the scarcity of bread, that, from the highest to the lowest citizen, the bakers were permitted to deal but a scanty allowance per head, even to those who paid for it; and, in cards of invitation to dine in the richest houses, the guest was notified to bring his own bread. To eke out the existence of the people, every person who had the means, was called on for a weekly subscription, which the Curés collected, and employed in providing messes for the nourishment of the poor, and vied with each

other in devising such economical compositions of food, as would subsist the greatest number with the smallest means. This want of bread
had been foreseen for some time past, and M. de Montmorin had desired me to notify it in America, and that, in addition to the market
price, a premium should be given on what should be brought from the
United States. Notice was accordingly given, and produced considerable supplies. Subsequent information made the importations from
America, during the months of March, April and May, into the Atlantic ports of France, amount to about twenty-one thousand barrels
of flour, besides what went to other ports, and in other months; while

our supplies to their West Indian islands relieved them also from that
drain. This distress for bread continued till July.

Hitherto no acts of popular violence had been produced by the struggle for political reformation. Little riots, on ordinary incidents, had
taken place as at other times, in different parts of the kingdom, in
which some lives, perhaps a dozen or twenty, had been lost; but in the
month of April, a more serious one occurred in Paris, unconnected,
indeed, with the Revolutionary principle, but making part of the history
of the day. The Fauxbourg St. Antoine is a quarter of the city inhabited
entirely by the class of day laborers and journeymen in every line. A
rumor was spread among them, that a great paper manufacturer, of the
name of Reveillon, had proposed, on some occasion, that their wages
should be lowered to fifteen sous a day. Inflamed at once into rage, and

without inquiring into its truth, they flew to his house in vast numbers, destroyed everything in it, and in his magazines and work-shops, without secreting, however, a pin's worth to themselves, and were continuing this work of devastation, when the regular troops were called in. Admonitions being disregarded, they were of necessity fired on, and a regular action ensued, in which about one hundred of them were killed, before the rest would disperse. There had rarely passed a year without such a riot, in some part or other of the Kingdom; and this is distinguished only as cotemporary with the Revolution, although not produced by it.

The States General were opened on the 5th of May, '89, by speeches from the King, the Garde des Sceaux, Lamoignon, and M. Necker. The last was thought to trip too lightly over the constitutional reformations which were expected. His notices of them in his speech, were not as full as in his previous "Rapport au Roi." This was observed, to his disadvantage; but much allowance should have been made for the situation in which he was placed, between his own counsels, and those of the ministers and party of the court. Overruled in his own opinions, compelled to deliver, and to gloss over those of his opponents, and even to keep their secrets, he could not come forward in his own attitude.

The composition of the Assembly, although equivalent, on the whole, to what had been expected, was something different in its elements. It had been supposed, that a superior education would carry into the scale of the Commons a respectable portion of the Noblesse. It did so as to those of Paris, of its vicinity, and of the other considerable cities, whose greater intercourse with enlightened society had liberalized their minds, and prepared them to advance up to the measure of the times. But the Noblesse of the country, which constituted two-thirds of that body, were far in their rear. Residing constantly on their patrimonial feuds, and familiarized, by daily habit, with Seigneurial powers and practices, they had not yet learned to suspect their inconsistence with reason and right. They were willing to submit to equality of taxation, but not to descend from their rank and prerogatives to be incorporated in session with the Tiers état. Among the Clergy, on the other hand, it had been apprehended that the higher orders of the Hierarchy, by their wealth and connections, would have carried the elections generally; but it turned out, that in most cases, the lower clergy had obtained the popular majorities. These consisted of the Curés, sons of the peasantry, who had been employed to do all the drudgery of parochial services for ten, twenty, or thirty Louis a year; while their superiors were consuming their princely revenues in palaces of luxury and indolence.

The objects for which this body was convened, being of the first order of importance, I felt it very interesting to understand the views of the parties of which it was composed, and especially the ideas prevalent as to the organization contemplated for their government. I went, therefore, daily from Paris to Versailles, and attended their debates, generally till the hour of adjournment. Those of the Noblesse were impassioned and tempestuous. They had some able men on both sides, actuated by equal zeal. The debates of the Commons were temperate, rational, and inflexibly firm. As preliminary to all other business, the awful questions came on, shall the States sit in one, or in distinct apartments? And shall they vote by heads or houses? The opposition was soon found to consist of the Episcopal order among the clergy, and two-thirds of the Noblesse; while the Tiers état were, to a man, united and determined. After various propositions of compromise had failed, the Commons undertook to cut the Gordian knot. The Abbé Siéyès, the most logical head of the nation (author of the pamphlet "Qu'est ce que le Tiers état?" which had electrified that country, as Paine's Common Sense did us), after an impressive speech on the 10th of June, moved that a last invitation should be sent to the Noblesse and Clergy, to attend in the hall of the States, collectively or individually, for the verification of powers, to which the Commons would proceed immediately, either in their presence or absence. This verification being finished, a motion was made, on the 15th, that they should constitute themselves a National Assembly; which was decided on the 17th, by a majority of four-fifths. During the debates on this question, about twenty of the Curés had joined them, and a proposition was made, in the chamber of the Clergy, that their whole body should join. This was rejected, at first, by a small majority only; but, being afterwards somewhat modified, it was decided affirmatively, by a majority of eleven.

While this was under debate, and unknown to the court, to wit, on the 19th, a council was held in the afternoon, at Marly, wherein it was proposed that the King should interpose, by a declaration of his sentiments, in a *séance royale*. A form of declaration was proposed by Necker, which, while it censured, in general, the proceedings, both of the Nobles and Commons, announced the King's views, such as substantially to coincide with the Commons. It was agreed to in Council, the *séance* was fixed for the 22d, the meetings of the States were till then to be suspended, and everything, in the meantime, kept secret. The members, the next morning (the 20th) repairing to their house, as usual, found the doors shut and guarded, a proclamation posted up for a *séance royale* on the 22d, and a suspension of their meetings in the meantime. Concluding that their dissolution was now to take place, they repaired to a building called the "Jeu de paume" (or Tennis court) and there bound themselves by oath to each other, never to separate, of their own accord, till they had settled a constitution for the nation, on a solid basis, and, if separated by force, that they would reassemble in some other place. The next day they met in the church of St. Louis, and were joined by a majority of the clergy. The heads of the Aristocracy saw that all was lost without some bold exertion. The King was still at Marly. Nobody was permitted to approach him but their friends. He was assailed by falsehoods in all shapes. He was made to believe that the Commons were about to absolve the army from their oath of fidelity to him, and to raise their pay. The court party were now all rage and desperation. They procured a committee to be held, consisting of the King and his Ministers, to which Monsieur and the Count d'Artois should be admitted. At this committee, the latter attacked M. Necker personally, arraigned his declaration, and proposed one which some of his prompters had put into his hands. M. Necker was brow-beaten and intimidated, and the King shaken. He determined that the two plans should be deliberated on the next day, and the *séance royale* put off a day longer. This encouraged a fiercer attack on M. Necker the next day. His draught of a declaration was entirely broken up, and that of the Count d'Artois inserted into it. Himself and Montmorin offered their resignation, which was refused; the Count d'Artois saying to M.

Necker, "No sir, you must be kept as the hostage; we hold you responsible for all the ill which shall happen." This change of plan was immediately whispered without doors. The Noblesse were in triumph; the people in consternation. I was quite alarmed at this state of things. The soldiery had not yet indicated which side they should take, and that which they should support would be sure to prevail. I considered a successful reformation of government in France, as insuring a general reformation through Europe, and the resurrection, to a new life, of their people, now ground to dust by the abuses of the governing powers. I was much acquainted with the leading patriots of the Assembly. Being from a country which had successfully passed through a similar reformation, they were disposed to my acquaintance, and had some confidence in me. I urged, most strenuously, an immediate compromise; to secure what the government was now ready to yield, and trust to future occasions for what might still be wanting. It was well understood that the King would grant, at this time, 1. Freedom of the person by Habeas corpus: 2. Freedom of conscience: 3. Freedom of the press: 4. Trial by jury: 5. A representative Legislature: 6. Annual meetings: 7. The origination of laws: 8. The exclusive right of taxation and appropriation: and 9. The responsibility of Ministers; and with the exercise of these powers they could obtain, in future, whatever might be further necessary to improve and preserve their constitution. They thought otherwise, however, and events have proved their lamentable error. For, after thirty years of war, foreign and domestic, the loss of millions of lives, the prostration of private happiness, and the foreign subjugation of their own country for a time, they have obtained no more, nor even that securely. They were unconscious of (for who could foresee?) the melancholy sequel of their well-meant perseverance; that their physical force would be usurped by a first tyrant to trample on the independence, and even the existence, of other nations: that this would afford a fatal example for the atrocious conspiracy of Kings against their people; would generate their unholy and homicide alliance to make common cause among themselves, and to crush, by the power of the whole, the efforts of any part to moderate their abuses and oppressions.

When the King passed, the next day, through the lane formed from the Château to the "Hotel des états," there was a dead silence. He was about an hour in the House, delivering his speech and declaration. On his coming out, a feeble cry of "vive le Roi" was raised by some children, but the people remained silent and sullen. In the close of his speech, he had ordered that the members should follow him, and resume their deliberations the next day. The Noblesse followed him, and so did the Clergy, except about thirty, who, with the Tiers, remained in the room, and entered into deliberation. They protested against what the King had done, adhered to all their former proceedings, and resolved the inviolability of their own persons. An officer came, to order them out of the room in the King's name. "Tell those who sent you," said Mirabeau, "that we shall not move hence but at our own will, or the point of the bayonet." In the afternoon, the people, uneasy, began to assemble in great numbers in the courts, and vicinities of the palace. This produced alarm. The Queen sent for M. Necker. He was conducted, amidst the shouts and acclamations of the multitude, who filled all the apartments of the palace. He was a few minutes only with the Queen, and what passed between them did not transpire. The King went out to ride. He passed through the crowd to his carriage, and into it, without being in the least noticed. As M. Necker followed him, universal acclamations were raised of "vive Monsieur Necker, vive le sauveur de la France opprimée." He was conducted back to his house with the same demonstrations of affection and anxiety. About two hundred deputies of the Tiers, catching the enthusiasm of the moment, went to his house, and extorted from him a promise that he would not resign. On the 25th, forty-eight of the Nobles joined the Tiers, and among them the Duke of Orleans. There were then with them one hundred and sixty-four members of the Clergy, although the minority of that body still sat apart, and called themselves the Chamber of the Clergy. On the 26th, the Archbishop of Paris joined the Tiers, as did some others of the Clergy and of the Noblesse.

These proceedings had thrown the people into violent ferment. It gained the soldiery, first of the French guards, extended to those of every other denomination, except the Swiss, and even to the body guards of the King. They began to quit their barracks, to assemble in squads, to declare they would defend the life of the King, but would not be the murderers of their fellow-citizens. They called themselves the soldiers *of the nation*, and left now no doubt on which side they would be, in case of rupture. Similar accounts came in from the troops in other parts of the kingdom, giving good reason to believe they would side with their fathers and brothers, rather than with their officers. The operation of this medicine at Versailles was as sudden as it was powerful. The alarm there was so complete, that in the afternoon of the 27th, the King wrote, with his own hand, letters to the Presidents of the Clergy and Nobles, engaging them immediately to join the Tiers. These two bodies were debating, and hesitating, when notes from the Count d'Artois decided their compliance. They went in a body, and took their seats with the Tiers, and thus rendered the union of the orders in one chamber complete.

The Assembly now entered on the business of their mission, and first proceeded to arrange the order in which they would take up the heads of their constitution, as follows:

First, and as Preliminary to the whole, a general Declaration of the Rights of Man. Then, specifically, the Principles of the Monarchy; Rights of the Nation; rights of the King; rights of the Citizens; organization and rights of the National Assembly; forms necessary for the enactment of Laws; organization and functions of the Provincial and Municipal Assemblies; duties and limits of the Judiciary power; functions and duties of the Military power.

A Declaration of the Rights of Man, as the preliminary of their work, was accordingly prepared and proposed by the Marquis de La Fayette.

But the quiet of their march was soon disturbed by information that troops, and particularly the foreign troops, were advancing on Paris from various quarters. The King had probably been advised to this, on the pretext of preserving peace in Paris. But his advisers were believed to have other things in contemplation. The Marshal de Broglie was appointed to their command, a high-flying aristocrat, cool and capable of everything. Some of the French guards were soon arrested, under other pretexts, but really, on account of their dispositions, in favor of the National cause. The people of Paris forced their prison, liberated them, and sent a deputation to the Assembly to solicit a pardon. The Assembly recommended peace and order to the people of Paris, the prisoners to the King, and asked from him the removal of the troops. His answer was negative and dry, saying they might remove themselves, if they pleased, to Noyons or Soissons. In the meantime, these troops, to the number of twenty or thirty thousand, had arrived, and were posted in, and between Paris and Versailles. The bridges and passes were guarded. At three o'clock in the afternoon of the 11th of July, the Count de La Luzerne was sent to notify M. Necker of his dismission, and to enjoin him to retire instantly, without saying a word of it to anybody. He went home, dined, and proposed to his wife a visit to a friend, but went in fact to his country house at St. Ouen, and at midnight set out for Brussels. This was not known till the next day (the 12th), when the whole Ministry was changed, except Villedeuil, of the domestic department, and Barenton, Garde des sceaux. The changes were as follows:

The Baron de Breteuil, President of the Council of Finance; de la Galaisière, Comptroller General, in the room of M. Necker; the Marshal de Broglie, Minister of War, and Foulon under him, in the room of Puy-Ségur; the Duke de la Vauguyon, Minister of Foreign Affairs, instead of the Count de Montmorin; de La Porte, Minister of Marine, in place of the Count de La Luzerne; St. Priest was also removed from the Council. Luzerne and Puy-Ségur had been strongly of the Aristocratic party in the Council, but they were not considered equal to the work now to be done. The King was now completely in the hands of men, the principal among whom had been noted, through their lives, for the Turkish despotism of their characters, and who were associated around the King, as proper instruments for what was to be executed. The news of this change began to be known at Paris, about one or two o'clock. In the afternoon, a body of about one hundred German cavalry were advanced, and drawn up in the Place Louis XV, and about two hundred Swiss posted at a little distance in their rear. This drew people to the spot, who thus accidentally found themselves in front of the troops, merely at first as spectators; but, as their numbers increased, their indignation rose. They retired a few steps, and posted themselves on and behind large piles of stones, large and small, collected in that place for a bridge, which was to be built adjacent to it. In this position, happening to be in my carriage on a visit, I passed through the lane they had formed, without interruption. But the moment after I had passed, the people attacked the cavalry with stones. They charged, but the advantageous position of the people, and the showers of stones, obliged the horse to retire, and quit the field altogether, leaving one

of their number on the ground, and the Swiss in the rear not moving to their aid. This was the signal for universal insurrection, and this body of cavalry, to avoid being massacred, retired towards Versailles. The people now armed themselves with such weapons as they could find in armorers, shops, and private houses, and with bludgeons; and were roaming all night, through all parts of the city, without any decided object. The next day (the 13th), the Assembly pressed on the King to send away the troops, to permit the Bourgeoisie of Paris to arm for the preservation of order in the city, and offered to send a deputation from their body to tranquillize them; but their propositions were refused. A committee of magistrates and electors of the city were appointed by those bodies, to take upon them its government. The people, now openly joined by the French guards, forced the prison of St. Lazare, released all the prisoners, and took a great store of corn, which they carried to the corn-market. Here they got some arms, and the French guards began to form and train them. The city-committee determined to raise forty-eight thousand Bourgeois, or rather to restrain their numbers to forty-eight thousand. On the 14th, they sent one of their members (Monsieur de Corny) to the Hotel des Invalides, to ask arms for their Garde Bourgeoise. He was followed by, and he found there, a great collection of people. The Governor of the Invalids came out, and represented the impossibility of his delivering arms, without the orders of those from whom he received them. De Corny advised the people then to retire, and retired himself; but the people took possession of the arms. It was remarkable, that not only the Invalids themselves made no opposition, but that a body of five thousand foreign troops, within four hundred yards, never stirred. M. de Corny, and five others, were then sent to ask arms of M. de Launay, Governor of the Bastille. They found a great collection of people already before the place, and they immediately planted a flag of truce, which was answered by a like flag hoisted on the parapet. The deputation prevailed on the people to fall back a little, advanced themselves to make their demand of the Governor, and in that instant, a discharge from the Bastille killed four persons of those nearest to the deputies. The deputies retired. I happened to be at the house of M. de Corny, when he returned to it, and received from him a narrative of these transactions. On the retirement of the deputies, the people rushed forward, and almost in an instant, were in possession of a fortification of infinite strength, defended by one hundred men, which in other times had stood several regular sieges, and had never been taken. How they forced their entrance has never been explained. They took all the arms, discharged the prisoners, and such of the garrison as were not killed in the first moment of fury; carried the Governor and Lieutenant Governor to the Place de Grève (the place of public execution), cut off their heads, and sent them through the city, in triumph, to the Palais royal. About the same instant, a treacherous correspondence having been discovered in M. de Flesselles, Prevôt des Marchands, they seized him in the Hotel de Ville, where he was in the execution of his office, and cut off his head. These events, carried imperfectly to Versailles, were the subject of two successive deputations from the Assembly to the King, to both of which he gave dry and hard answers; for nobody had as yet been permitted to inform him, truly and fully, of what had passed at Paris. But at night, the Duke de Liancourt forced his way into the King's bed chamber, and obliged him to hear a full and animated detail of the disasters of the day in Paris. He went to bed fearfully impressed. The decapitation of de Launay worked powerfully through the night on the whole Aristocratic party; insomuch, that in the morning, those of the greatest influence on the Count d'Artois, represented to him the absolute necessity that the King should give up everything to the Assembly. This according with the dispositions of the King, he went about eleven o'clock, accompanied only by his brothers, to the Assembly, and there read to them a speech, in which he asked their interposition to re-establish order. Although couched in terms of some caution, yet the manner in which it was delivered, made it evident that it was meant as a surrender at discretion. He returned to the Château a foot, accompanied by the Assembly. They sent off a deputation to quiet Paris, at the head of which was the Marquis de La Fayette, who had, the same morning, been named Commandant en chef of the Milice Bourgeoise; and Monsieur Bailly, former President of the States General, was called for as Prevôt des Marchands. The demolition of the Bastille was now ordered and begun. A body of the Swiss guards, of the regiment of Ventimille, and the city horse guards joined the people. The alarm at Versailles increased. The foreign troops were ordered off instantly. Every Minister resigned. The King confirmed Bailly as Prevôt des Marchands, wrote to M. Necker, to recall him, sent his letter open to the Assembly, to be forwarded by them, and invited them to go with him to Paris the next day, to satisfy the city of his dispositions; and that night, and the next morning, the Count d'Artois, and M. de Montesson, a deputy connected with him, Madame de Polignac, Madame de Guiche, and the Count de Vaudreuil, favorites of the Queen, the Abbé de Vermont her confessor, the Prince of Conde, and Duke of Bourbon fled. The King came to Paris, leaving the Queen in consternation for his return. Omitting the less important figures of the procession, the King's carriage was in the centre; on each side of it, the Assembly, in two ranks a foot; at their head the Marquis de La Fayette, as Commander-in-chief, on horseback, and Bourgeois guards before and behind. About sixty thousand citizens, of all forms and conditions, armed with the conquests of the Bastille and Invalids, as far as they would go, the rest with pistols, swords, pikes, pruning-hooks, scythes, &c., lined all the streets through which the procession passed, and with the crowds of people in the streets, doors, and windows, saluted them everywhere with the cries of "vive la nation," but not a single "vive le Roi" was heard. The King stopped at the Hotel de Ville. There M. Bailly presented and put into his hat, the popular cockade, and addressed him. The King being unprepared, and unable to answer, Bailly went to him, gathered from him some scraps of sentences, and made out an answer, which he delivered to the audience, as from the King. On their return, the popular cries were "vive le Roi et la nation." He was conducted by a Garde Bourgeoise to his palace at Versailles, and thus concluded an "amende honorable," as no sovereign ever made, and no people ever received.

And here, again, was lost another precious occasion of sparing to France the crimes and cruelties through which she has since passed, and to Europe, and finally America, the evils which flowed on them also from this mortal source. The King was now become a passive machine in the hands of the National Assembly, and had he been left to himself, he would have willingly acquiesced in whatever they should devise as best for the nation. A wise constitution would have been formed, hereditary in his line, himself placed at its head, with powers so large as to enable him to do all the good of his station, and so limited, as to restrain him from its abuse. This he would have faithfully administered, and more than this, I do not believe, he ever wished. But he had a Queen of absolute sway over his weak mind and timid virtue, and of a character the reverse of his in all points. This angel, as gaudily painted in the rhapsodies of Burke, with some smartness of fancy, but no sound sense, was proud, disdainful of restraint, indignant at all obstacles to her will, eager in the pursuit of pleasure, and firm enough to hold to her desires, or perish in their wreck. Her inordinate gambling and dissipations, with those of the Count d'Artois, and others of her *clique*, had been a sensible item in the exhaustion of the treasury, which called into action the reforming hand of the nation; and her opposition to it, her inflexible perverseness, and dauntless spirit, led herself to the Guillotine, drew the King on with her, and plunged the world into crimes and calamities which will forever stain the pages of modern history. I have ever believed, that had there been no Queen, there would have been no revolution. No force would have been provoked, nor exercised. The King would have gone hand in hand with the wisdom of his sounder counsellors, who, guided by the increased lights of the age, wished only, with the same pace, to advance the principles of their social constitution. The deed which closed the mortal course of these sovereigns, I shall neither approve nor condemn. I am not prepared to say, that the first magistrate of a nation cannot commit treason against his country, or is unamenable to its punishment; nor yet, that where there is no written law, no regulated tribunal, there is not a law in our hearts, and a power in our hands, given for righteous employment in maintaining right, and redressing wrong. Of those who judged the King many thought him wilfully criminal; many, that his existence would keep the nation in perpetual conflict with the horde of Kings who would war against a generation which might come home to themselves, and that it were better that one should die than all. I should not have voted with this portion of the legislature. I should have shut up the Queen in a convent, putting harm out of her power, and placed the King in his station, investing him with limited powers, which, I verily believe, he would have honestly exercised, according to the measure of his understanding. In this way, no void would have been created, courting the usurpation of a military adventurer, nor occasion given for those enormities which demoralized the nations of the world, and destroyed, and is yet to destroy, millions and millions of its inhabitants. There are three epochs in history, signalized by the total extinction of national morality. The first was of the successors of Alexander, not omitting himself: The next, the successors of the first Cæsar: The third, our own age. This was begun by the partition of Poland, followed by that of the treaty of Pillnitz; next the conflagration of Copenhagen; then the enormities of Bonaparte, partitioning the earth at his will, and devastating it with fire and sword; now the conspiracy of Kings, the successors of Bonaparte, blasphemously calling themselves the Holy Alliance, and treading in the footsteps of their incarcerated leader; not yet, indeed, usurping the government of other nations, avowedly and in detail, but controlling by their armies the forms in which they will permit them to be governed; and reserving, *in petto*, the order and extent of the usurpations further meditated. But I will return from a digression, anticipated, too, in time, into which I have been led by reflection on the criminal passions which refused to the world a favorable occasion of saving it from the afflictions it has since suffered.

M. Necker had reached Basle before he was overtaken by the letter of the King, inviting him back to resume the office he had recently left. He returned immediately, and all the other Ministers having resigned, a new administration was named, to wit: St. Priest and Montmorin were restored; the Archbishop of Bordeaux was appointed Garde des sceaux, La Tour du Pin, Minister of War; La Luzerne, Minister of Marine. This last was believed to have been effected by the friendship of Montmorin; for although differing in politics, they continued firm in friendship, and Luzerne, although not an able man, was thought an honest one. And the Prince of Bauvau was taken into the Council.

Seven Princes of the blood Royal, six ex-Ministers, and many of the high Noblesse, having fled, and the present Ministers, except Luzerne, being all of the popular party, all the functionaries of government moved, for the present, in perfect harmony.

In the evening of August the 4th, and on the motion of the Viscount de Noailles, brother in law of La Fayette, the Assembly abolished all titles of rank, all the abusive privileges of feudalism, the tithes and casuals of the Clergy, all Provincial privileges, and, in fine, the Feudal regimen generally. To the suppression of tithes, the Abbé Siéyès was vehemently opposed; but his learned and logical arguments were unheeded, and his estimation lessened by a contrast of his egoism (for he was beneficed on them), with the generous abandonment of rights by the other members of the Assembly. Many days were employed in putting into the form of laws, the numerous demolitions of ancient abuses; which done, they proceeded to the preliminary work of a Declaration of rights. There being much concord of sentiment on the elements of this instrument, it was liberally framed, and passed with a very general approbation. They then appointed a Committee for the "reduction of a projet" of a constitution, at the head of which was the Archbishop of Bordeaux. I received from him, as chairman of the Committee, a letter of July 20th, requesting me to attend and assist at their deliberations; but I excused myself, on the obvious considerations, that my mission was to the King as Chief Magistrate of the nation, that my duties were limited to the concerns of my own country, and forbade me to intermeddle with the internal transactions of that, in which I had been received under a specific character only. Their plan of a constitution was discussed in sections, and so reported from time to time, as agreed to by the Committee. The first respected the general frame of the government; and that this should be formed into three departments, Executive, Legislative and Judiciary, was generally agreed. But when they proceeded to subordinate developments, many and various shades of opinion came into conflict, and schism, strongly marked, broke the Patriots into fragments of very discordant principles. The first question, Whether there should be a King? met with no open opposition; and it was readily agreed, that the government of France should be monarchical and hereditary. Shall the King have a negative on the laws? shall that negative be absolute, or suspensive only? Shall there be two Chambers of Legislation? or one only? If two, shall one of them be hereditary? or for life? or for a fixed term? and named by the King? or elected by the people? These questions found strong differences of opinion, and produced repulsive combinations among the Patriots. The Aristocracy was cemented by a common principle, of preserving the ancient regime, or whatever should be nearest to it. Making this their polar star, they moved in phalanx, gave preponderance on every question to the minorities of the Patriots, and always to those who advocated the least change. The features of the new constitution were thus assuming a fearful aspect, and great alarm was produced among the honest Patriots by these dissensions in their ranks. In this uneasy state of things, I received one day a note from the Marquis de La Fayette, informing me that he should bring a party of six or eight friends to ask a dinner of me the next day. I assured him of their welcome. When they arrived, they were La Fayette himself, Duport, Barnave, Alexander la Meth, Blacon, Mounier, Maubourg, and Dagout. These were leading Patriots, of honest but differing opinions, sensible of the necessity of effecting a coalition by mutual sacrifices, knowing each other, and not afraid, therefore, to unbosom themselves mutually. This last was a material principle in the selection. With this view, the Marquis had invited the conference, and had fixed the time and place inadvertently, as to the embarrassment under which it might place me. The cloth being removed, and wine set on the table, after the American manner, the Marquis introduced the objects of the conference, by summarily reminding them of the state of things in the Assembly, the course which the principles of the Constitution were taking, and the inevitable result, unless checked by more concord among the Patriots themselves. He observed, that although he also had his opinion, he was ready to sacrifice it to that of his brethren of the same cause; but that a common opinion must now be formed, or the Aristocracy would carry everything, and that, whatever they should now agree on, he, at the head of the National force, would maintain. The discussions began at the hour of four, and were continued till ten o'clock in the evening; during which time, I was a silent witness to a coolness and candor of argument, unusual in the conflicts of political opinion; to a logical reasoning, and chaste eloquence, disfigured by no gaudy tinsel of rhetoric or declamation, and truly worthy of being placed in parallel with the finest dialogues of antiquity, as handed to us by Xenophon, by Plato and Cicero. The result was, that the King should have a suspensive veto on the laws, that the legislature should be composed of a single body only, and that to be chosen by the people. This Concordate decided the fate of the constitution. The Patriots all rallied to the principles thus settled, carried every question agreeably to them, and reduced the Aristocracy to insignificance and impotence. But duties of exculpation were now incumbent on me. I waited on Count Montmorin the next morning, and explained to him, with truth and candor, how it had happened that my house had been made the scene of conferences of such a character. He told me, he already knew everything which had passed, that so far from taking umbrage at the use made of my house on that occasion, he earnestly wished I would habitually assist at such conferences, being sure I should be useful in moderating the warmer spirits, and promoting a wholesome and practicable reformation only. I told him, I knew too well the duties I owed to the King, to the nation, and to my own country, to take any part in councils concerning their internal government, and that I should persevere, with care, in the character of a neutral and passive spectator, with wishes only, and very sincere ones, that those measures might prevail which would be for the greatest good of the nation. I have no doubts, indeed, that this conference was previously known and approved by this honest Minister, who was in confidence and communication with the Patriots, and wished for a reasonable reform of the Constitution.

Here I discontinue my relation of the French Revolution. The minuteness with which I have so far given its details, is disproportioned to the general scale of my narrative. But I have thought it justified by the interest which the whole world must take in this Revolution. As yet, we are but in the first chapter of its history. The appeal to the rights of man, which had been made in the United States, was taken up by France, first of the European nations. From her, the spirit has spread over those of the South. The tyrants of the North have allied indeed against it; but it is irresistible. Their opposition will only multiply its millions of human victims; their own satellites will catch it, and the condition of man through the civilized world will be greatly ameliorated. This is a wonderful instance of great events from small causes. So inscrutable is the arrangement of causes and consequences in this world, that a two-penny duty on tea, unjustly imposed in a sequestered part of it, changes the condition of all its inhabitants. I have been more minute in relating the early transactions of this regeneration, because I was in circumstances peculiarly favorable for a knowledge of the truth. Possessing the confidence and intimacy of the leading Patriots, and more than all, of the Marquis Fayette, their head and Atlas, who had no secrets from me, I learned with correctness the views and proceedings of that party; while my intercourse with the diplomatic missionaries of Europe at Paris, all of them with the court, and eager in prying into its councils and proceedings, gave me a knowledge of these also. My information was always, and immediately committed to writing, in letters to Mr. Jay, and often to my friends, and a recurrence to these letters now insures me against errors of memory.

These opportunities of information ceased at this period, with my retirement from this interesting scene of action. I had been more than a year soliciting leave to go home, with a view to place my daughters in the society and care of their friends, and to return for a short time to my station at Paris. But the metamorphosis through which our government was then passing from its Chrysalid to its Organic form suspended its action in a great degree; and it was not till the last of August, that I received the permission I had asked. And here, I cannot leave this great and good country, without expressing my sense of its pre-eminence of character among the nations of the earth. A more benevolent people I have never known, nor greater warmth and devotedness in their select friendships. Their kindness and accommodation to strangers is unparalleled, and the hospitality of Paris is beyond anything I had conceived to be practicable in a large city. Their eminence, too, in science, the communicative dispositions of their scientific men, the politeness of the general manners, the ease and vivacity of their conversation, give a charm to their society, to be found nowhere else. In a comparison of this, with other countries, we have the proof of primacy, which was given to Themistocles, after the battle of Salamis. Every general voted to himself the first reward of valor, and the second to Themistocles. So, asked the travelled inhabitant of any nation, in what country on earth would you rather live?—Certainly, in my own, where are all my friends, my relations, and the earliest and sweetest affections and recollections of my life. Which would be your second choice? France.

On the 26th of September I left Paris for Havre, where I was detained by contrary winds until the 8th of October. On that day, and the 9th, I crossed over to Cowes, where I had engaged the Clermont,

Capt. Colley, to touch for me. She did so; but here again we were detained by contrary winds, until the 22d, when we embarked, and landed at Norfolk on the 23d of November. On my way home, I passed some days at Eppington, in Chesterfield, the residence of my friend and connection, Mr. Eppes; and, while there, I received a letter from the President, General Washington, by express, covering an appointment to be Secretary of State. I received it with real regret. My wish had been to return to Paris, where I had left my household establishment, as if there myself, and to see the end of the Revolution, which I then thought would be certainly and happily closed in less than a year. I then meant to return home, to withdraw from political life, into which I had been impressed by the circumstances of the times, to sink into the bosom of my family and friends, and devote myself to studies more congenial to my mind. In my answer of December 15th, I expressed these dispositions candidly to the President, and my preference of a return to Paris; but assured him, that if it was believed I could be more useful in the administration of the government, I would sacrifice my own inclinations without hesitation, and repair to that destination; this I left to his decision. I arrived at Monticello on the 23d of December, where I received a second letter from the President, expressing his continued wish that I should take my station there, but leaving me still at liberty to continue in my former office, if I could not reconcile myself to that now proposed. This silenced my reluctance, and I accepted the new appointment.

In the interval of my stay at home, my eldest daughter had been happily married to the eldest son of the Tuckahoe branch of Randolphs, a young gentleman of genius, science, and honorable mind, who afterwards filled a dignified station in the General Government, and the most dignified in his own State. I left Monticello on the first of March, 1790, for New York. At Philadelphia I called on the venerable and beloved Franklin. He was then on the bed of sickness from which he never rose. My recent return from a country in which he had left so many friends, and the perilous convulsions to which they had been exposed, revived all his anxieties to know what part they had taken, what had been their course, and what their fate. He went over all in succession, with a rapidity and animation almost too much for his strength. When all his inquiries were satisfied, and a pause took place, I told him I had learned with much pleasure that, since his return to America, he had been occupied in preparing for the world the history of his own life. I cannot say much of that, said he; but I will give you a sample of what I shall leave; and he directed his little grandson (William Bache) who was standing by the bedside, to hand him a paper from the table, to which he pointed. He did so; and the Doctor putting it into my hands, desired me to take it and read it at my leisure. It was about a quire of folio paper, written in a large and running hand, very like his own. I looked into it slightly, then shut it, and said I would accept his permission to read it, and would carefully return it. He said, "No, keep it." Not certain of his meaning, I again looked into it, folded it for my pocket, and said again, I would certainly return it. "No," said he, "keep it." I put it into my pocket, and shortly after took leave of him. He died on the 17th of the ensuing month of April; and as I understood that he had bequeathed all his papers to his grandson, William Temple Franklin, I immediately wrote to Mr. Franklin, to inform him I possessed this paper, which I should consider as his property, and would deliver to his order. He came on immediately to New York, called on me for it, and I delivered it to him. As he put it into his pocket, he said carelessly, he had either the original, or another copy of it, I do not recollect which. This last expression struck my attention forcibly, and for the first time suggested to me the thought that Dr. Franklin had meant it as a confidential deposit in my hands, and that I had done wrong in parting from it. I have not yet seen the collection he published of Dr. Franklin's works, and, therefore, know not if this is among them. I have been told it is not. It contained a narrative of the negotiations between Dr. Franklin and the British Ministry, when he was endeavoring to prevent the contest of arms which followed. The negotiation was brought about by the intervention of Lord Howe and his sister, who, I believe, was called Lady Howe, but I may misremember her title. Lord Howe seems to have been friendly to America, and exceedingly anxious to prevent a rupture. His intimacy with Dr. Franklin, and his position with the Ministry, induced him to undertake a mediation between them; in which his sister seemed to have been associated. They carried from one to the other, backwards and forwards, the several propositions and answers which passed, and seconded with their own intercessions, the importance of mutual sacrifices, to preserve the peace and connection of the two countries. I remember that Lord North's answers were dry, unyielding, in the spirit of unconditional submission, and betrayed an absolute indifference to the occurrence of a rupture; and he said to the mediators distinctly, at last, that "a rebellion was not to be deprecated on the part of Great Britain; that the confiscations it would produce would provide for many of their friends." This expression was reported by the mediators to Dr. Franklin, and indicated so cool and calculated a purpose in the Ministry, as to render compromise hopeless, and the negotiation was discontinued. If this is not among the papers published, we ask, what has become of it? I delivered it with my own hands, into those of Temple Franklin. It certainly established views so atrocious in the British government, that its suppression would, to them, be worth a great price. But could the grandson of Dr. Franklin be, in such degree, an accomplice in the parricide of the memory of his immortal grandfather? The suspension for more than twenty years of the general publication, bequeathed and confided to him, produced, for awhile, hard suspicions against him; and if, at last, all are not published, a part of these suspicions may remain with some.

I arrived at New York on the 21st of March, where Congress was in session.

So far July 29, 1821.

The Anas

EXPLANATIONS OF THE THREE VOLUMES
BOUND IN MARBLED PAPER

February 4, 1818

IN THESE three volumes will be found copies of the official opinions given in writing by me to General Washington, while I was Secretary of State, with sometimes the documents belonging to the case. Some of these are the rough draughts, some press-copies, some fair ones. In the earlier part of my acting in that office, I took no other note of the passing transactions: but after awhile, I saw the importance of doing it, in aid of my memory. Very often therefore I made memorandums on loose scraps of paper, taken out of my pocket in the moment, and laid by to be copied fair at leisure, which however they hardly ever were. These scraps therefore, ragged, rubbed, and scribbled as they were, I had bound with the others by a binder who came into my cabinet, did it under my own eye, and without the opportunity of reading a single paper.

At this day, after the lapse of 25 years, or more, from their dates, I have given the whole a calm revisal, when the passions of the time are passed away, and the reasons of the transactions act alone on the judgment. Some of the informations I had recorded are now cut out from the rest, because I have seen that they were incorrect, or doubtful, or merely personal or private, with which we have nothing to do. I should perhaps have thought the rest not worth preserving, but for their testimony against the only history of that period which pretends to have been compiled from authentic and unpublished documents. Could these documents, all, be laid open to the public eye, they might be compared, contrasted, weighed, and the truth fairly sifted out of them, for we are not to suppose that every thing found among General Washington's papers is to be taken as gospel truth. Facts indeed of his own writing and inditing, must be believed by all who knew him; and opinions, which were his own, merit veneration and respect; for few men have lived whose opinions were more unbiassed and correct. Not that it is pretended he never felt bias. His passions were naturally strong; but his reason, generally, stronger. But the materials from his own pen make probably an almost insensible part of the mass of papers which fill his presses. He possessed the love, the veneration, and confidence of all. With him were deposited suspicions and certainties, rumors and realities, facts and falsehoods, by all those who were, or who wished to be thought, in correspondence with him, and by the many Anonymi who were ashamed to put their names to their slanders. From such a Congeries history may be made to wear any hue, with which the passions of the compiler, royalist or republican, may chuse to tinge it. Had General Washington himself written from these materials a history of the period they embrace, it would have been a conspicuous monument of the integrity of his mind, the soundness of his judgment, and its powers of discernment between truth and falsehood; principles and pretensions.

But the party feelings of his biographer, to whom after his death the collection was confided, has culled from it a composition as different from what General Washington would have offered, as was the candor of the two characters during the period of the war. The partiality of this pen is displayed in lavishments of praise on certain military characters, who had done nothing military, but who afterwards, and before he wrote, had become heroes in party, although not in war; and in his reserve on the merits of others, who rendered signal services indeed, but did not earn his praise by apostatising in peace from the republican principles for which they had fought in war. It shews itself too in the cold indifference with which a struggle for the most animating of human objects is narrated. No act of heroism ever kindles in the mind of this writer a single aspiration in favor of the holy cause which inspired the bosom, and nerved the arm of the patriot warrior. No gloom of events, no lowering of prospects ever excites a fear for the issue of a contest which was to change the condition of man over the civilized globe. The sufferings inflicted on endeavors to vindicate the rights of humanity are related with all the frigid insensibility with which a monk would have contemplated the victims of an auto da fé. Let no man believe that General Washington ever intended that his papers should be used for the suicide of the cause, for which he had lived, and for which there never was a moment in which he would not have died. The abuse of these materials is chiefly however manifested in the history of the period immediately following the establishment of the present constitution; and nearly with that my memorandums begin. Were a reader of this period to form his idea of it from this history alone, he would suppose the republican party (who were in truth endeavoring to keep the government within the line of the Constitution, and prevent its being monarchised in practice) were a mere set of grumblers, and disorganisers, satisfied with no government, without fixed principles of any, and, like a British parliamentary opposition, gaping after loaves and fishes, and ready to change principles, as well as position, at any time, with their adversaries.

But a short review of facts omitted, or uncandidly stated in this history will shew that the contests of that day were contests of principle, between the advocates of republican, and those of kingly government, and that, had not the former made the efforts they did, our government would have been, even at this early day, a very different thing from what the successful issue of those efforts have made it.

The alliance between the States under the old Articles of Confederation, for the purpose of joint defence against the aggression of Great Britain, was found insufficient, as treaties of alliance generally are, to enforce compliance with their mutual stipulations; and these, once fulfilled, that bond was to expire of itself, and each State to become sovereign and independent in all things. Yet it could not but occur to everyone, that these separate independencies, like the petty States of Greece, would be eternally at war with each other, and would become at length the mere partisans and satellites of the leading powers of Europe. All then must have looked forward to some further bond of union, which would insure eternal peace, and a political system of our own, independent of that of Europe. Whether all should be consolidated into a single government, or each remain independent as to internal matters, and the whole form a single nation as to what was foreign only, and whether that national government should be a monarchy or republic, would of course divide opinions, according to the constitutions, the habits, and the circumstances of each individual. Some officers of the army, as it has always been said and believed (and Steuben and Knox have ever been named as the leading agents), trained to monarchy by military habits, are understood to have proposed to General Washington to decide this great question by the army before its disbandment, and to assume himself the crown on the assurance of their support. The indignation with which he is said to have scouted this parricide proposition was equally worthy of his virtue and wisdom. The next effort was (on suggestion of the same individuals, in the moment of their separation), the establishment of an hereditary order under the name of the Cincinnati, ready prepared by that distinction to be ingrafted into the future frame of government, and placing General Washington still at their head. The General wrote to me on this subject, while I was in Congress at Annapolis, and an extract from my letter is inserted in 5th Marshall's history, page 28. He afterwards called on me at that place on his way to a meeting of the society, and after a whole evening of consultation, he left that place fully determined to use all his endeavors for its total suppression. But he found it so firmly riveted in the affections of the members, that, strengthened as they happened to be by an adventitious occurrence of the moment, he could effect no more than the abolition of its hereditary principle. He called again on his return, and explained to me fully the opposition which had been made, the effect of the occurrence from France, and the difficulty with which its duration had been limited to the lives of the present members. Further details will be found among my papers, in his and my letters, and some in the *Encyclopédie Méthodique et Dictionnaire d'Économie Politique*, communicated by myself to M. Meusnier, its author, who had made the establishment of this society the ground, in that work, of a libel on our country.

The want of some authority which should procure justice to the public creditors, and an observance of treaties with foreign nations, produced, some time after, the call of a convention of the States at Annapolis. Although, at this meeting, a difference of opinion was evident on the question of a republican or kingly government, yet, so general through the States was the sentiment in favor of the former, that the friends of the latter confined themselves to a course of obstruction only, and delay, to everything proposed; they hoped, that nothing being done, and all things going from bad to worse, a kingly government might be usurped, and submitted to by the people, as better than anarchy and wars internal and external, the certain consequences of the present want of a general government. The effect of their manœuvres, with the defective attendance of Deputies from the States, resulted in the measure of calling a more general convention, to be held at Philadelphia. At this, the same party exhibited the same practices, and with the same views of preventing a government of concord, which they foresaw would be republican, and of forcing through anarchy their way to monarchy. But the mass of that convention was too honest, too wise, and too steady, to be baffled and misled by their manœuvres. One of these was a form of government proposed by Colonel Hamilton, which would have been in fact a compromise between the two parties of royalism and republicanism. According to this, the executive and one branch of the legislature were to be during good behavior, *i.e.*, for life, and the governors of the States were to be named by these two permanent organs. This, however, was rejected; on which Hamilton left the convention, as desperate, and never returned again until near its final conclusion. These opinions and efforts, secret or avowed, of the advocates for monarchy, had begotten great jealousy through the States generally; and this jealousy it was which excited the strong opposition to the conventional constitution; a jealousy which yielded at last only to a general determination to establish certain amendments as barriers against a government either monarchical or consolidated. In what passed through the whole period of these conventions, I have gone on the information of those who were members of them, being absent myself on my mission to France.

I returned from that mission in the first year of the new government, having landed in Virginia in December, 1789, and proceeded to New York in March, 1790, to enter on the office of Secretary of State. Here, certainly, I found a state of things which, of all I had ever contemplated, I the least expected. I had left France in the first year of her revolution, in the fervor of natural rights, and zeal for reformation. My conscientious devotion to these rights could not be heightened, but it had been aroused and excited by daily exercise. The President received me cordially, and my colleagues and the circle of principal citizens apparently with welcome. The courtesies of dinner parties given me, as a stranger newly arrived among them, placed me at once in their familiar society. But I cannot describe the wonder and mortification with which the table conversation filled me. Politics were the chief topic, and a preference of kingly over republican government was evidently the favorite sentiment. An apostate I could not be, nor yet a hypocrite; and I found myself, for the most part, the only advocate on the republican side of the question, unless among the guests there chanced to be some member of that party from the legislative Houses. Hamilton's financial system had then passed. It had two objects; 1st, as a puzzle, to exclude popular understanding and inquiry; 2d, as a machine for the corruption of the legislature; for he avowed the opinion, that man could be governed by one of two motives only, force or interest; force, he observed, in this country was out of the question, and the interests, therefore, of the members must be laid hold of, to keep the legislative in unison with the executive. And with grief and shame it must be acknowledged that his machine was not without effect; that even in this, the birth of our government, some members were found sordid enough to bend their duty to their interests, and to look after personal rather than public good.

It is well known that during the war the greatest difficulty we encountered was the want of money or means to pay our soldiers who fought, or our farmers, manufacturers and merchants, who furnished the necessary supplies of food and clothing for them. After the expedient of paper money had exhausted itself, certificates of debt were given to the individual creditors, with assurance of payment so soon as the United States should be able. But the distresses of these people often obliged them to part with these for the half, the fifth, and even a tenth of their value; and the speculators had made a trade of cozening them from the holders by the most fraudulent practices, and persuasions that they would never be paid. In the bill for funding and paying these, Hamilton made no difference between the original holders and the fraudulent purchasers of this paper. Great and just repugnance arose at putting these two classes of creditors on the same footing, and great exertions were used to pay the former the full value, and to the latter, the price only which they had paid, with interest. But this would have prevented the game which was to be played, and for which the minds of greedy members were already tutored and prepared. When the trial of strength on these several efforts had indicated the form in which the bill would finally pass, this being known within doors sooner than without, and especially, than to those who were in distant parts of the Union, the base scramble began. Couriers and relay horses by land, and swift sailing pilot boats by sea, were flying in all directions. Active partners and agents were associated and employed in every State, town, and country neighborhood, and this paper was bought up at five shillings, and even as low as two shillings in the pound, before the holder knew that Congress had already provided for its redemption at par. Immense sums were thus filched from the poor and ignorant, and fortunes accumulated by those who had themselves been poor enough before. Men thus enriched by the dexterity of a leader, would follow of course the chief who was leading them to fortune, and become the zealous instruments of all his enterprises.

This game was over, and another was on the carpet at the moment of my arrival; and to this I was most ignorantly and innocently made to hold the candle. This fiscal manœuvre is well known by the name of the Assumption. Independently of the debts of Congress, the States had during the war contracted separate and heavy debts; and Massachusetts particularly, in an absurd attempt, absurdly conducted, on the British post of Penobscott: and the more debt Hamilton could rake up, the

more plunder for his mercenaries. This money, whether wisely or fool-
ishly spent, was pretended to have been spent for general purposes,
and ought, therefore, to be paid from the general purse. But it was
objected, that nobody knew what these debts were, what their amount,
or what their proofs. No matter; we will guess them to be twenty
millions. But of these twenty millions, we do not know how much
should be reimbursed to one State, or how much to another. No matter;
we will guess. And so another scramble was set on foot among the
several States, and some got much, some little, some nothing. But the
main object was obtained, the phalanx of the Treasury was reinforced
by additional recruits. This measure produced the most bitter and angry contest ever known in Congress, before or since the Union of the
States. I arrived in the midst of it. But a stranger to the ground, a
stranger to the actors on it, so long absent as to have lost all familiarity
with the subject, and as yet unaware of its object, I took no concern in
it. The great and trying question, however, was lost in the House of
Representatives. So high were the feuds excited by this subject, that on
its rejection business was suspended. Congress met and adjourned from
day to day without doing any thing, the parties being too much out of
temper to do business together. The eastern members particularly,
who, with Smith from South Carolina, were the principal gamblers in
these scenes, threatened a secession and dissolution. Hamilton was in
despair. As I was going to the President's one day, I met him in the
street. He walked me backwards and forwards before the President's
door for half an hour. He painted pathetically the temper into which
the legislature had been wrought; the disgust of those who were called
the creditor States; the danger of the *secession* of their members, and
the separation of the States. He observed that the members of the administration ought to act in concert; that though this question was not
of my department, yet a common duty should make it a common concern; that the President was the centre on which all administrative
questions ultimately rested, and that all of us should rally around him,
and support, with joint efforts, measures approved by him; and that the
question having been lost by a majority only, it was probable that an
appeal from me to the judgment and discretion of some of my friends,

might effect a change in the vote, and the machine of government, now suspended, might be again set into motion. I told him that I was really a stranger to the whole subject; that not having yet informed myself of the system of finances adopted, I knew not how far this was a necessary sequence; that undoubtedly, if its rejection endangered a dissolution of our Union at this incipient stage, I should deem that the most unfortunate of all consequences, to avert which all partial and temporary evils should be yielded. I proposed to him, however, to dine with me the next day, and I would invite another friend or two, bring them into conference together, and I thought it impossible that reasonable men, consulting together coolly, could fail, by some mutual sacrifices of opinion, to form a compromise which was to save the Union. The discussion took place. I could take no part in it but an exhortatory one, because I was a stranger to the circumstances which should govern it. But it was finally agreed, that whatever importance had been attached to the rejection of this proposition, the preservation of the Union and of concord among the States was more important, and that therefore it would be better that the vote of rejection should be rescinded, to effect which, some members should change their votes. But it was observed that this pill would be peculiarly bitter to the southern States, and that some concomitant measure should be adopted, to sweeten it a little to them. There had before been propositions to fix the seat of government either at Philadelphia, or at Georgetown on the Potomac; and it was thought that by giving it to Philadelphia for ten years, and to Georgetown permanently afterwards, this might, as an anodyne, calm in some degree the ferment which might be excited by the other measure alone. So two of the Potomac members (White and Lee, but White with a revulsion of stomach almost convulsive), agreed to change their votes, and Hamilton undertook to carry the other point. In doing this, the influence he had established over the eastern members, with the agency of Robert Morris with those of the middle States, effected his side of the engagement; and so the Assumption was passed, and twenty millions of stock divided among favored States, and thrown in as a pabulum to the stock-jobbing herd. This added to the number of votaries to the Treasury, and made its chief the master of every vote in the legislature, which might give to the government the direction suited to his political views.

I know well, and so must be understood, that nothing like a majority in Congress had yielded to this corruption. Far from it. But a division, not very unequal, had already taken place in the honest part of that body, between the parties styled republican and federal. The latter being monarchists in principle, adhered to Hamilton of course, as their leader in that principle, and this mercenary phalanx added to them, insured him always a majority in both Houses: so that the whole action of legislature was now under the direction of the Treasury. Still the machine was not complete. The effect of the funding system, and of the Assumption, would be temporary; it would be lost with the loss of the individual members whom it has enriched, and some engine of influence more permanent must be contrived, while these myrmidons were yet in place to carry it through all opposition. This engine was the Bank of the United States. All that history is known, so I shall say nothing about it. While the government remained at Philadelphia, a selection of members of both Houses were constantly kept as directors who, on every question interesting to that institution, or to the views of the federal head, voted at the will of that head; and, together with the stockholding members, could always make the federal vote that of the majority. By this combination, legislative expositions were given to the constitution, and all the administrative laws were shaped on the model of England, and so passed. And from this influence we were not relieved, until the removal from the precincts of the bank, to Washington.

Here then was the real ground of the opposition which was made to the course of administration. Its object was to preserve the legislature pure and independent of the executive, to restrain the administration to republican forms and principles, and not permit the constitution to be construed into a monarchy, and be warped, in practice, into all the principles and pollutions of their favorite English model. Nor was this an opposition to General Washington. He was true to the republican charge confided to him; and has solemnly and repeatedly protested to me, in our conversations, that he would lose the last drop of his blood in support of it; and he did this the oftener and with the more earnestness, because he knew my suspicions of Hamilton's designs against it, and wished to quiet them. For he was not aware of the drift, or of the effect of Hamilton's schemes. Unversed in financial projects and calculations and budgets, his approbation of them was bottomed on his confidence in the man.

But Hamilton was not only a monarchist, but for a monarchy bottomed on corruption. In proof of this, I will relate an anecdote, for the truth of which I attest the God who made me. Before the President set out on his southern tour in April, 1791, he addressed a letter of the fourth of that month, from Mount Vernon, to the Secretaries of State, Treasury and War, desiring that if any serious and important cases should arise during his absence, they would consult and act on them. And he requested that the Vice-President should also be consulted. This was the only occasion on which that officer was ever requested to take part in a cabinet question. Some occasion for consultation arising, I invited those gentlemen (and the Attorney General, as well as I remember), to dine with me, in order to confer on the subject. After the cloth was removed, and our question agreed and dismissed, conversation began on other matters, and by some circumstance, was led to the British constitution, on which Mr. Adams observed, "Purge that constitution of its corruption, and give to its popular branch equality of representation, and it would be the most perfect constitution ever devised by the wit of man." Hamilton paused and said, "Purge it of its corruption, and give to its popular branch equality of representation, and it would become an *impracticable* government: as it stands at present, with all its supposed defects, it is the most perfect government which ever existed." And this was assuredly the exact line which separated the political creeds of these two gentlemen. The one was for two hereditary branches and an honest elective one: the other, for an hereditary King, with a House of Lords and Commons corrupted to his will, and standing between him and the people. Hamilton was, indeed, a singular character. Of acute understanding, disinterested, honest, and honorable in all private transactions, amiable in society, and duly valuing virtue in private life, yet so bewitched and perverted by the British example, as to be under thorough conviction that corruption was essential to the government of a nation. Mr. Adams had originally been a republican. The glare of royalty and nobility, during his mission to England, had made him believe their fascination a necessary ingredient in government; and Shays's rebellion, not sufficiently understood where he then was, seemed to prove that the absence of want and oppression was not a sufficient guarantee of order. His book on the American constitutions having made known his political bias, he was taken up by the monarchical federalists in his absence, and on his return to the United States, he was by them made to believe that the general disposition of our citizens was favorable to monarchy. He here wrote his Davila, as a supplement to a former work, and his election to the Presidency confirmed him in his errors. Innumerable addresses, too, artfully and industriously poured in upon him, deceived him into a confidence that he was on the pinnacle of popularity, when the gulf was yawning at his feet, which was to swallow up him and his deceivers. For when General Washington was withdrawn, these *energumeni* of royalism, kept in check hitherto by the dread of his honesty, his firmness, his patriotism, and the authority of his name, now mounted on the car of State and free from control, like Phaeton on that of the sun, drove headlong and wild, looking neither to right nor left, nor regarding anything but the objects they were driving at; until, displaying these fully, the eyes of the nation were opened, and a general disbandment of them from the public councils took place.

Mr. Adams, I am sure, has been long since convinced of the treacheries with which he was surrounded during his administration. He has since thoroughly seen, that his constituents were devoted to republican government, and whether his judgment is re-settled on its ancient basis, or not, he is conformed as a good citizen to the will of the majority, and would now, I am persuaded, maintain its republican structure with the zeal and fidelity belonging to his character. For even an enemy has said, "He is always an honest man, and often a great one." But in the fervor of the fury and the follies of those who made him their stalking horse, no man who did not witness it can form an idea of their unbridled madness, and the terrorism with which they surrounded themselves.

The horrors of the French revolution, then raging, aided them mainly, and using that as a raw head and bloody bones, they were enabled by their stratagems of X. Y. Z. in which . . . was a leading mountebank, their tales of tub-plots, ocean massacres, bloody buoys, and pulpit lyings and slanderings, and maniacal ravings of their Gardeners, their Osgoods and parishes, to spread alarm into all but the firmest breasts. Their Attorney General had the impudence to say to a republican member, that deportation must be resorted to, of which, said he, "you re-

publicans have set the example"; thus daring to identify us with the murderous Jacobins of France. These transactions, now recollected but as dreams of the night, were then sad realities; and nothing rescued us from their liberticide effect, but the unyielding opposition to those firm spirits who sternly maintained their post in defiance of terror, until their fellow citizens could be aroused to their own danger, and rally and rescue the standard of the constitution. This has been happily done. Federalism and monarchism have languished from that moment, until their treasonable combinations with the enemies of their country during the late war, their plots of dismembering the Union, and their Hartford convention, have consigned them to the tomb of the dead; and I fondly hope, "we may now truly say, we are all republicans, all federalists," and that the motto of the standard to which our country will forever rally, will be, "federal union, and republican government"; and sure I am we may say, that we are indebted for the preservation of this point of ralliance, to that opposition of which so injurious an idea is so artfully insinuated and excited in this history.

Much of this relation is notorious to the world; and many intimate proofs of it will be found in these notes. From the moment where they end, of my retiring from the administration, the federalists* got unchecked hold of General Washington. His memory was already sensibly impaired by age, the firm tone of mind for which he had been remarkable, was beginning to relax, its energy was abated, a listlessness of labor, a desire for tranquillity had crept on him, and a willingness to let others act, and even think for him. Like the rest of mankind, he was disgusted with atrocities of the French revolution, and was not sufficiently aware of the difference between the rabble who were used as instruments of their perpetration, and the steady and rational character of the American people, in which he had not sufficient confidence. The opposition too of the republicans to the British treaty, and the zealous support of the federalists in that unpopular but favorite measure of theirs, had made him all their own. Understanding, moreover, that I disapproved of that treaty, and copiously nourished with falsehoods by a malignant neighbor of mine, who ambitioned to be his correspondent, he had become alienated from myself personally, as from the republican body generally of his fellow citizens; and he wrote the letters to Mr. Adams and Mr. Carroll, over which, in devotion to his imperishable fame, we must forever weep as monuments of mortal decay.

* See conversation with General Washington, October 1, 1792, pp. 141–145.

The Anas

═══

1791–1806

≫ AUGUST THE 13TH, 1791. Notes of a conversation between Alexander Hamilton and Thomas Jefferson. Th: Jefferson mentioned to him a letter received from John Adams, disavowing Publicola, and denying that he ever entertained a wish to bring this country under an hereditary executive, or introduce an hereditary branch of Legislature, &c. See his letter. Alexander Hamilton condemning Mr. Adams' writings, and most particularly Davila, as having a tendency to weaken the present government, declared in substance as follows: "I own it is my own opinion, though I do not publish it in Dan or Beersheba, that the present government is not that which will answer the ends of society, by giving stability and protection to its rights, and that it will probably be found expedient to go into the British form. However, since we have undertaken the experiment, I am for giving it a fair course, whatever my expectations may be. The success, indeed, so far, is greater than I had expected, and therefore, at present, success seems more possible than it had done heretofore, and there are still other and other stages of improvement which, if the present does not succeed, may be tried, and ought to be tried, before we give up the republican form altogether; for that mind must be really depraved, which would not prefer the equality of political rights, which is the foundation of pure republicanism, if it can be obtained consistently with order. Therefore, whoever by his writings disturbs the present order of things, is really blameable, however pure his intentions may be, and he was sure Mr. Adams' were pure." This is the substance of a declaration made in much more lengthy terms, and which seemed to be more formal than usual for a private conversation between two, and as if intended to qualify some less guard-ed expressions which had been dropped on former occasions. Th: Jeffer-son has committed it to writing in the moment of A. Hamilton's leaving the room.

❧ December the 25th, 1791. Colonel Gunn (of Georgia) dining the other day with Colonel Hamilton, said to him, with that plain freedom he is known to use, "I wish, Sir, you would advise your friend King, to observe some kind of consistency in his votes. There has been scarcely a question before the Senate on which he has not voted both ways. On the representation bill, for instance, he first voted for the proposition of the Representatives, and ultimately voted against it." "Why," says Colonel Hamilton, "I'll tell you as to that, Colonel Gunn, that it never was intended that bill should pass." Gunn told this to Butler, who told it to Th: Jefferson.

❧ Conversations with the President, February the 28th, 1792. I was to have been with him long enough before three o'clock (which was the hour and day he received visits), to have opened to him a proposition for doubling the velocity of the post riders, who now travel about fifty miles a day, and might, without difficulty, go one hundred, and for taking measures (by way bills) to know where the delay is, when there is any. I was delayed by business, so as to have scarcely time to give him the outlines. I run over them rapidly, and observed afterwards, that I had hitherto never spoken to him on the subject of the post office, not knowing whether it was considered as a revenue law, or a law for the general accommodation of the citizens: that the law just passed seemed to have removed the doubt, by declaring that the whole profits of the office should be applied to extending the posts, and that even the past profits should be refunded by the treasury for the same purpose: that I therefore conceive it was now in the department of the Secretary of State: that I thought it would be advantageous so to declare it for another reason, to wit: that the department of the Treasury possessed already such an influence as to swallow up the whole executive powers, and that even the future Presidents (not supported by the weight of character which himself possessed), would not be able to make head against this department. That in urging this measure I had certainly no personal interest, since, if I was supposed to have any appetite for power, yet as my career would certainly be exactly as short as his own, the intervening time was too short to be an object. My real wish was to avail the public of every occasion, during the residue of the President's period, to place things on a safe footing. He was now called on to attend his company, and he desired me to come and breakfast with him the next morning.

February the 29th. I did so; and after breakfast we retired to his room, and I unfolded my plan for the post office, and after such an approbation of it as he usually permitted himself on the first presentment of any idea, and desiring me to commit it to writing, he, during that pause of conversation which follows a business closed, said in an affectionate tone, that he had felt much concern at an expression which dropped from me yesterday, and which marked my intention of retiring when he should. That as to himself, many motives obliged him to it. He had, through the whole course of the war, and most particularly at the close of it, uniformly declared his resolution to retire from public affairs, and never to act in any public office; that he had retired under that firm resolution: that the government, however, which had been formed, being found evidently too inefficacious, and it being supposed that his aid was of some consequence towards bringing the people to consent to one of sufficient efficacy for their own good, he consented to come into the convention, and on the same motive, after much pressing, to take a part in the new government, and get it under way. That were he to continue longer, it might give room to say, that having tasted the sweets of office, he could not do without them: that he really felt himself growing old, his bodily health less firm, his memory, always bad, becoming worse, and perhaps the other faculties of his mind showing a decay to others of which he was insensible himself; that this apprehension particularly oppressed him: that he found, moreover, his activity lessened, business therefore more irksome, and tranquillity and retirement become an irresistible passion. That however he felt himself obliged, for these reasons, to retire from the government, yet he should consider it as unfortunate, if that should bring on the retirement of the great officers of the government, and that this might produce a shock on the public mind of dangerous consequence.

I told him that no man had ever had less desire of entering into public offices than myself; that the circumstance of a perilous war, which brought every thing into danger, and called for all the services which every citizen could render, had induced me to undertake the administration of the government of Virginia; that I had both before and after refused repeated appointments of Congress to go abroad in that sort of office, which, if I had consulted my own gratification, would almost have been the most agreeable to me; that at the end of two years, I resigned the government of Virginia, and retired with a firm resolution never more to appear in public life; that a domestic loss, however, happened, and made me fancy that absence and a change of scene for a time might be expedient for me; that I therefore accepted a foreign appointment, limited to two years; that at the close of that, Doctor Franklin having left France, I was appointed to supply his place, which I had accepted, and though I continued in it three or four years, it was under the constant idea of remaining only a year or two longer; that the revolution in France coming on, I had so interested myself in the event of that, that when obliged to bring my family home, I had still an idea of returning and awaiting the close of that, to fix the era of my final retirement; that on my arrival here I found he had appointed me to my present office; that he knew I had not come into it without some reluctance; that it was, on my part, a sacrifice of inclination to the opinion that I might be more serviceable here than in France, and with a firm resolution in my mind, to indulge my constant wish for retirement at no very distant day; that when, therefore, I had received his letter, written from Mount Vernon, on his way to Carolina and Georgia (April the 1st, 1791), and discovered, from an expression in that, that he meant to retire from the government ere long, and as to the precise epoch there could be no doubt, my mind was immediately made up, to make that the epoch of my own retirement from those labors of which I was heartily tired. That, however, I did not believe there was any idea in any of my brethren in the administration of retiring; that on the contrary, I had perceived at a late meeting of the trustees of the sinking fund, that the Secretary of the Treasury had developed the plan he intended to pursue, and that it embraced years in its view.

He said, that he considered the Treasury department as a much more limited one, going only to the single object of revenue, while that of the Secretary of State, embracing nearly all the objects of administration, was much more important, and the retirement of the officer therefore, would be more noticed: that though the government had set out with a pretty general good will of the public, yet that symptoms of dissatisfaction had lately shown themselves far beyond what he could have expected, and to what height these might arise, in case of too great a change in the administration, could not be foreseen.

I told him, that in my opinion, there was only a single source of these discontents. Though they had indeed appeared to spread themselves over the War department also, yet I considered that as an overflowing only from their real channel, which would never have taken place, if they had not first been generated in another department, to wit, that of the Treasury. That a system had there been contrived, for deluging the States with paper money instead of gold and silver, for withdrawing our citizens from the pursuits of commerce, manufactures, buildings, and other branches of useful industry, to occupy themselves and their capitals in a species of gambling, destructive of morality, and which had introduced its poison into the government itself. That it was a fact, as certainly known as that he and I were then conversing, that particular members of the legislature, while those laws were on the carpet, had feathered their nests with paper, had then voted for the laws, and constantly since lent all the energy of their talents, and instrumentality of their offices, to the establishment and enlargement of this system; that they had chained it about our necks for a great length of time, and in order to keep the game in their hands had, from time to time, aided in making such legislative constructions of the constitution, as made it a very different thing from what the people thought they had submitted to; that they had now brought forward a proposition far beyond any one ever yet advanced, and to which the eyes of many were turned, as the decision which was to let us know, whether we live under a limited or an unlimited government. He asked me to what proposition I alluded? I answered, to that in the report on manufactures, which, under color of giving *bounties* for the encouragement of particular manufactures, meant to establish the doctrine, that the power given by the constitution to collect taxes to provide for the *general welfare* of the United States, permitted Congress to take everything under their management which *they* should deem for the *public welfare*, and which is susceptible of the application of money; consequently, that the subsequent enumeration of their powers was not the description to which resort must be had, and did not at all constitute the limits of their authority; that this was a very different question from that of the bank, which was thought an incident to an enumerated power; that, therefore, this decision was expected with great anxiety; that, indeed, I hoped the proposition would be rejected, believing there was a majority in both Houses against it, and that if it should be, it would be considered as a proof that things were returning into their true channel; and that, at any rate, I looked forward to the broad representation which would shortly take place, for keeping the general constitution on its true ground; and that this would remove a great deal of the discontent which had shown itself. The conversation ended with this last topic. It is here stated nearly as much at length as it really was; the expressions preserved where I could recollect them, and their substance always faithfully stated.

March 1, 1792.

≫ On the 2d of January, 1792, Messrs. Fitzsimmons and Gerry (among others) dined with me. These two staid, with a Mr. Larned of Connecticut, after the company was gone. We got on the subject of references by the legislature to the Heads of departments, considering their mischief in every direction. Gerry and Fitzsimmons clearly opposed to them.

Two days afterwards (January the 4th), Mr. Bourne from Rhode Island presented a memorial from his State, complaining of inequality in the Assumption, and moved to refer it to the Secretary of the Treasury. Fitzsimmons, Gerry and others opposed it; but it was carried.

January the 19th. Fitzsimmons moved, that the *President of the United States* be requested to direct the Secretary of the Treasury, to lay before the House information to enable the legislature to judge of the additional revenue necessary on the increase of the military establishment. The House, on debate, struck out the words, "President of the United States."

March the 7th. The subject resumed. An animated debate took place on the tendency of references to the Heads of departments; and it seemed that a great majority would be against it; the House adjourned. Treasury greatly alarmed, and much industry supposed to be used before next morning, when it was brought on again, and debated through the day, and on the question, the Treasury carried it by thirty-one to twenty-seven; but deeply wounded, since it was seen that all Pennsylvania, except Jacobs, voted against the reference; that Tucker of South Carolina voted for it, and Sumpter absented himself, debauched for the moment only, because of the connection of the question with a further Assumption which South Carolina favored; but showing that they never were to be counted on among the Treasury votes. Some others absented themselves. Gerry changed sides. On the whole, it showed that Treasury influence was tottering.

Committed to writing this 10th of March, 1792.

⇾ March the 11th, 1792. Consulted verbally by the President, on whom a committee of the Senate (Izard, Morris, and King) are to wait tomorrow morning, to know whether he will think it proper to redeem our Algerine captives, and make a treaty with the Algerines, on the single vote of the Senate, without taking that of the Representatives.

My opinions run on the following heads:

We must go to Algiers with cash in our hands. Where shall we get it? By loan? By converting money now in the treasury?

Probably a loan might be obtained on the President's authority; but as this could not be repaid without a subsequent act of legislature, the Representatives might refuse it. So if money in the treasury be converted, they may refuse to sanction it.

The subsequent approbation of the Senate being necessary to validate a treaty, they expect to be consulted beforehand, if the case admits.

So the subsequent act of the Representatives being necessary where money is given, why should not they expect to be consulted in like manner, when the case admits. A treaty is a law of the land. But prudence will point out this difference to be attended to in making them; *viz.*, where a treaty contains such articles only as will go into execution of themselves, or be carried into execution by the judges, they may be safely made; but where there are articles which require a law to be passed afterwards by the legislature, great caution is requisite.

For example; the consular convention with France required a very small legislative regulation. This convention was unanimously ratified by the Senate. Yet the same identical men threw by the law to enforce it at the last session, and the Representatives at this session have placed it among the laws which they may take up or not, at their own convenience, as if that was a higher motive than the public faith.

Therefore, against hazarding this transaction without the sanction of both Houses.

The President concurred. The Senate express the motive for this proposition, to be a fear that the Representatives would not keep the secret. He has no opinion of the secrecy of the Senate. In this very case, Mr. Izard made the communication to him, sitting next to him at table, on one hand, while a lady (Mrs. McLane) was on his other hand, and the French minister next to her; and as Mr. Izard got on with his communication, his voice kept rising, and his stutter bolting the words out loudly at intervals, so that the minister might hear if he would. He said he had a great mind at one time to have got up, in order to put a stop to Mr. Izard.

≫ March the 11th, 1792. Mr. Sterret tells me, that sitting round a fire the other day with four or five others [Mr. Smith of South Carolina was one], somebody mentioned that the murderers of Hogeboom, sheriff of Columbia county, New York, were acquitted. "Aye," says Smith, "this is what comes of your damned *trial by jury*."

≫ 1791. Towards the latter end of November, Hamilton had drawn Ternant into a conversation on the subject of the treaty of commerce recommended by the National Assembly of France to be negotiated with us, and, as he had no ready instructions on the subject, he led him into a proposal that Ternant should take the thing up as a volunteer with me, that we should arrange conditions, and let them go for confirmation or refusal. Hamilton communicated this to the President, who came into it, and proposed it to me. I disapproved of it, observing, that such a volunteer project would be binding on us, and not them; that it would enable them to find out how far we would go, and avail themselves of it. However, the President thought it worth trying, and I acquiesced. I prepared a plan of treaty for exchanging the privileges of native subjects, and fixing all duties forever as they now stood. Hamilton did not like this way of fixing the duties, because, he said, many articles here would bear to be raised, and therefore, he would prepare a tariff. He did so, raising duties for the French, from twenty-five to fifty per cent. So they were to give us the privileges of native subjects, and we, as a compensation, were to make them pay higher duties. Hamilton, having made his arrangements with Hammond to pretend that though he had no powers to conclude a treaty of commerce, yet his general commission authorized him to enter into the discussion of one, then proposed to the President at one of our meetings, that the business should be taken up with Hammond in the same informal way. I now discovered the trap which he had laid, by first getting the President into that step with Ternant. I opposed the thing warmly. Hamilton observed, if we did it with Ternant we should also with Hammond. The President thought this reasonable. I desired him to recollect, I had been against it with Ternant, and only acquiesced under his opinion. So the matter went off as to both. His scheme evidently was, to get us engaged first with Ternant, merely that he might have a pretext to engage us on the same ground with Hammond, taking care, at the same time, by an extravagant tariff, to render it impossible we should come to any conclusion with Ternant: probably meaning, at the same time, to propose terms so favorable to Great Britain, as would attach us to that country by treaty. On one of those occasions he asserted, that our commerce with Great Britain and her colonies was put on a much more favorable footing than with France and her colonies. I therefore prepared the tabular comparative view of the footing of our commerce with those nations, which see among my papers. See also my project of a treaty and Hamilton's tariff.   *Committed to writing March the 11th, 1792.*

⇛ It was observable, that whenever, at any of our consultations, anything was proposed as to Great Britain, Hamilton had constantly ready something which Mr. Hammond had communicated to him, which suited the subject and proved the intimacy of their communications; insomuch, that I believe he communicated to Hammond all our views, and knew from him, in return, the views of the British court. Many evidences of this occurred; I will state some. I delivered to the President my report of instructions for Carmichael and Short, on the subject of navigation, boundary and commerce, and desired him to submit it to Hamilton. Hamilton made several just criticisms on different parts of it. But where I asserted that the United States had no right to alienate an inch of the territory of any State, he attacked and denied the doctrine. See my report, his note, and my answer. A few days after came to hand Kirkland's letter, informing us that the British, at Niagara, expected to run a new line between themselves and us; and the reports of Pond and Stedman, informing us it was understood at Niagara, that Captain Stevenson had been sent here by Simcoe to settle that plan with Hammond.

Hence Hamilton's attack of the principle I had laid down, in order to prepare the way for this new line. See minute of March the 9th. Another proof. At one of our consultations, about the last of December, I mentioned that I wished to give in my report on commerce, in which I could not avoid recommending a commercial retaliation against Great Britain. Hamilton opposed it violently; and among other arguments, observed, that it was of more importance to us to have the posts than to commence a commercial war; that this, and this alone, would free us from the expense of the Indian wars; that it would therefore be the height of imprudence in us, while treating for the surrender of the posts, to engage in anything which would irritate them; that if we did so, they would naturally say, "These people mean war, let us therefore hold what we have in our hands." This argument struck me forcibly, and I said, "If there is a hope of obtaining the posts, I agree it would be imprudent to risk that hope by a commercial retaliation. I will, therefore, wait till Mr. Hammond gives me in his assignment of breaches, and if that gives a glimmering of hope that they mean to surrender the posts, I will not give in my report till the next session." Now, Hammond had received my assignment of breaches on the 15th of December, and about the 22d or 23d had made me an apology for not having been able to send me his counter-assignment of breaches; but in terms which showed I might expect it in a few days. From the moment it escaped my lips in the presence of Hamilton, that I would not give in my report till I should see Hammond's counter-complaint, and judge if there was a hope of the posts, Hammond never said a word to me on any occasion, as to the time he should be ready. At length the President got out of patience, and insisted I should jog him. This I did on the 21st of February, at the President's assembly: he immediately promised I should have it in a few days, and accordingly, on the 5th of March I received it.

Written March the 11th, 1792.

⇗⇗ March the 12th, 1792. Sent for by the President, and desired to bring the letter he had signed to the King of France. Went. He said the House of Representatives had, on Saturday, taken up the communication he had made of the King's letter to him, and come to a vote in their own name; that he did not expect this when he sent this message and the letter, otherwise he would have sent the message without the letter, as I had proposed. That he apprehended the legislature would be endeavoring to invade the executive. I told him, I had understood the House had resolved to request him to join their congratulations to his on the completion and acceptance of the constitution; on which part of the vote, there were only two dissentients (Barnwell and Benson); that the vote was thirty-five to sixteen on that part which expressed an approbation of the wisdom of the constitution; that in the letter he had signed, I had avoided saying a word in approbation of the constitution, not knowing whether the King, in his heart, approved it. Why, indeed, says he, I begin to doubt very much of the affairs of France; there are papers from London as late as the 10th of January, which represent them as going into confusion. He read over the letter he had signed, found there was not a word which could commit his judgment about the constitution, and gave it to me back again. This is one of many proofs I have had, of his want of confidence in the event of the French revolution. The fact is, that Gouverneur Morris, a high-flying monarchy man, shutting his eyes and his faith to every fact against his wishes, and believing everything he desires to be true, has kept the President's mind constantly poisoned with his forebodings. That the President wishes the revolution may be established, I believe from several indications. I remember, when I received the news of the King's flight and capture, I first told him of it at his assembly. I never saw him so much dejected by any event in my life. He expressed clearly, on this occasion, his disapprobation of the legislature referring things to the Heads of departments. *Written March the 12th.*

*Eodem die.** Ten o'clock, A.M. The preceding was about nine o'clock. The President now sends Lear to me, to ask what answer he shall give to the committee, and particularly, whether he shall add to it, that, "in making the communication, it was not his expectation that the House should give any answer." I told Mr. Lear that I thought the House had a right, independently of legislation, to express sentiments on other

* The same day.

subjects. That when these subjects did not belong to any other branch particularly, they would publish them by their own authority; that in the present case, which respected a foreign nation, the President being the organ of our nation with other nations, the House would satisfy their duty, if, instead of a direct communication, they should pass their sentiments through the President; that if expressing a sentiment were really an invasion of the executive power, it was so faint a one, that it would be difficult to demonstrate it to the public, and to a public partial

to the French revolution, and not disposed to consider the approbation of it from any quarter as improper. That the Senate, indeed, had given many indications of their wish to invade the executive power: the Representatives had done it in one case, which was indeed mischievous and alarming; that of giving orders to the Heads of the executive departments, without consulting the President; but that the late vote for directing the Secretary of the Treasury to report ways and means, though carried, was carried by so small a majority, and with the aid of members so notoriously under a local influence on that question, as to give a hope that the practice would be arrested, and the constitutional course be taken up, of asking the President to have information laid before them. But that in the present instance, it was so far from being clearly an invasion of the executive, and would be so little approved by the general voice, that I could not advise the President to express any dissatisfaction at the vote of the House; and I gave Lear, in writing, what I thought should be his answers. See it.

≫ March the 31st. A meeting at the President's; present, Thomas Jefferson, Alexander Hamilton, Henry Knox and Edmund Randolph. The subject was the resolution of the House of Representatives, of March the 27th, to appoint a committee to inquire into the causes of the failure of the late expedition under Major General St. Clair, with the power to call for such persons, papers and records, as may be necessary to assist their inquiries. The committee had written to Knox for the original letters, instructions, &c. The President had called us to consult, merely because it was the first example, and he wished that so far as it should become a precedent, it should be rightly conducted. He neither acknowledged nor denied, nor even doubted the propriety of what the House were doing, for he had not thought upon it, nor was acquainted with subjects of this kind: he could readily conceive there might be papers of so secret a nature, as that they ought not to be given up. We were not prepared, and wished time to think and inquire.

≫ April the 2d. Met again at the President's, on the same subject. We had all considered, and were of one mind, first, that the House was an inquest, and therefore might institute inquiries. Second, that it might call for papers generally. Third, that the executive ought to communicate such papers as the public good would permit, and ought to refuse those, the disclosure of which would injure the public: consequently were to exercise a discretion. Fourth, that neither the committee nor House had a right to call on the Head of a department, who and whose papers were under the President alone; but that the committee should instruct their chairman to move the House to address the President. We had principally consulted the proceedings of the Commons in the case of Sir Robert Walpole, 13 Chandler's Debates. For the first point, see pages 161, 170, 172, 183, 187, 207; for the second, pages 153, 173, 207; for the third, 81, 173, appendix page 44; fourth, page 246. Note; Hamilton agreed with us in all these points, except as to the power of the House to call on Heads of departments. He observed, that as to his department, the act constituting it had made it subject to Congress in some points, but he thought himself not so far subject, as to be obliged to produce all the papers they might call for. They might demand secrets of a very mischievous nature. [Here I thought he began to fear they would go on to examining how far their own members and other persons in the government had been dabbling in stocks, banks, &c., and that he probably would choose in this case to deny their power; and, in short, he endeavored to place himself subject to the House, when the executive should propose what he did not like, and subject to the executive, when the House should propose anything disagreeable.] I observed here a difference between the British parliament and our Congress; that the former was a legislature, an inquest, and a council (S. C. page 91), for the King. The latter was, by the constitution, a legislature and an inquest, but not a council. Finally agreed, to speak separately to the members of the committee, and bring them by persuasion into the right channel. It was agreed in this case, that there was not a paper which might not be properly produced; that copies only should be sent, with an assurance, that if they should desire it, a clerk should attend with the originals to be verified by themselves. The committee were Fitzsimmons, Steele, Mercer, Clarke, Sedgwick, Giles and Vining.

⇒ April the 9th, 1792. The President had wished to redeem our captives at Algiers, and to make peace with them on paying an annual tribute. The Senate were willing to approve this, but unwilling to have the lower House applied to previously to furnish the money; they wished the President to take the money from the treasury, or open a loan for it. They thought that to consult the Representatives on one occasion, would give them a handle always to claim it, and would let them into a participation of the power of making treaties, which the constitution had given exclusively to the President and Senate. They said too, that if the particular sum was voted by the Representatives, it would not be a secret. The President had no confidence in the secrecy of the Senate, and did not choose to take money from the treasury or to borrow. But he agreed he would enter into provisional treaties with the Algerines, not to be binding on us till ratified here. I prepared questions for consultation with the Senate, and added, that the Senate were to be apprized, that on the return of the provisional treaty, and after they should advise the ratification, he would not have the seal put to it till the two Houses should vote the money. He asked me, if the treaty stipulating a sum and ratified by him, with the advice of the Senate, would not be good under the constitution, and obligatory on the Representatives to furnish the money? I answered it certainly would, and that it would be the duty of the Representatives to raise the money; but that they might decline to do what was their duty, and I thought it might be incautious to commit himself by a ratification with a foreign nation, where he might be left in the lurch in the execution: it was possible too, to conceive a treaty, which it would not be their duty to provide for. He said that he did not like throwing too much into democratic hands, that if they would not do what the constitution called on them to do, the government would be at an end, and must *then assume another form*. He stopped here; and I kept silence to see whether he would say anything more in the same line, or add any qualifying expression to soften what he had said; but he did neither.

I had observed, that wherever the agency of either, or both Houses would be requisite subsequent to a treaty, to carry it into effect, it would be prudent to consult them previously, if the occasion admitted. That thus it was, we were in the habit of consulting the Senate previously, when the occasion permitted, because their subsequent ratification would be necessary. That there was the same reason for consulting the lower House previously, where they were to be called on afterwards, and especially in the case of money, as they held the purse strings, and would be jealous of them. However, he desired me to strike out the intimation that the seal would not be put till both Houses should have voted the money.

➽ April the 6th. The President called on me before breakfast, and first introduced some other matter, then fell on the representation bill, which he had now in his possession for the tenth day. I had before given him my opinion in writing, that the method of apportionment was contrary to the constitution. He agreed that it was contrary to the common understanding of that instrument, and to what was understood at the time by the makers of it; that yet it would bear the construction which the bill put, and he observed that the vote for and against the bill was perfectly geographical, a northern against a southern vote, and he feared he should be thought to be taking side with a southern party. I admitted the motive of delicacy, but that it should not induce him to do wrong; urged the dangers to which the scramble for the fractionary members would always lead. He here expressed his fear that there would, ere long, be a separation of the Union; that the public mind seemed dissatisfied and tending to this. He went home, sent for Randolph, the Attorney General, desired him to get Mr. Madison immediately and come to me, and if we three concurred in opinion that he should negative the bill, he desired to hear nothing more about it, but that we would draw the instrument for him to sign. They came. Our minds had been before made up. We drew the instrument. Randolph carried it to him, and told him we all concurred in it. He walked with him to the door, and as if he still wished to get off, he said, "And you say you approve of this yourself." "Yes, Sir," says Randolph, "I do upon my honor." He sent it to the House of Representatives instantly. A few of the hottest friends of the bill expressed passion, but the majority were satisfied, and both in and out of doors it gave pleasure to have, at length, an instance of the negative being exercised. *Written this the 9th of April.*

➽ July the 10th, 1792. My letter of —— to the President, directed to him at Mount Vernon, had not found him there, but came to him here. He told me of this, and that he would take an occasion of speaking with me on the subject. He did so this day. He began by observing that he had put it off from day to day because the subject was painful, to wit, his remaining in office, which that letter solicited. He said that the declaration he had made when he quitted his military command, of never again entering into public life, was sincere. That, however, when he was called on to come forward to set the present government in motion, it appeared to him that circumstances were so changed as to justify a change in his resolution: he was made to believe that in two years all would be well in motion, and he might retire. At the end of two years he found some things still to be done. At the end of the third year, he thought it was not worth while to disturb the course of things, as in one year more his office would expire, and he was decided then to retire. Now he was told there would still be danger in it. Certainly, if he thought so, he would conquer his longing for retirement. But he feared it would be said his former professions of retirement had been mere affectation, and that he was like other men, when once in office he could not quit it. He was sensible, too, of a decay of his hearing, perhaps his other faculties might fall off and he not be sensible of it. That with respect to the existing causes of uneasiness, he thought there were suspicions against a particular party, which had been carried a great deal too far; there might be *desires*, but he did not believe there were *designs* to change the form of government into a monarchy; that there might be a few who wished it in the higher walks of life, particularly in the great cities, but that the main body of the people in the eastern States were as steadily for republicanism as in the southern. That the pieces lately published, and particularly in Freneau's paper,* seemed to have in view the exciting opposition to the government. That this had taken place in Pennsylvania as to the excise law, according to information he had received from General Hand. That they tended to produce a separation of the Union, the most dreadful of all calamities, and that whatever tended to produce anarchy, tended, of course, to produce a resort to monarchical government. He considered those papers as attacking him directly, for he must be a fool indeed to swallow the little sugar plums here and there thrown out to him. That in condemning the administration of the government, they condemned him, for if they thought there were measures pursued contrary to his sentiments, they must conceive him too careless to attend to them, or too stupid to understand them.

---

* Philip M. Freneau founded the *National Gazette*, a democratic paper rivaling Fenno's *Gazette of the United States*.

That though, indeed, he had signed many acts which he did not approve in all their parts, yet he had never put his name to one which he did not think, on the whole, was eligible. That as to the bank, which had been an act of so much complaint, until there was some infallible criterion of reason, a difference of opinion must be tolerated. He did not believe the discontents extended far from the seat of government. He had seen and spoken with many people in Maryland and Virginia in his late journey. He found the people contented and happy. He wished, however, to be better informed on this head. If the discontents were more extensive than he supposed, it might be that the desire that he should remain in the government was not general.

My observations to him tended principally to enforce the topics of my letter. I will not, therefore, repeat them, except where they produced observations from him. I said that the two great complaints were, that the national debt was unnecessarily increased, and that it had furnished the means of corrupting both branches of the legislature; that he must know, and everybody knew, there was a considerable squadron in both, whose votes were devoted to the paper and stock-jobbing interest, that the names of a weighty number were known, and several others suspected on good grounds. That on examining the votes of these men, they would be found uniformly for every Treasury measure, and that as most of these measures had been carried by small majorities, they were carried by these very votes. That, therefore, it was a cause of just uneasiness, when we saw a legislature legislating for their own interests, in opposition to those of the people. He said not a word on the corruption of the legislature, but took up the other point, defended the Assumption, and argued that it had not increased the debt, for that all of it was honest debt. He justified the excise law, as one of the best laws which could be passed, as nobody would pay the tax who did not choose to do it. With respect to the increase of the debt by the Assumption, I observed to him that what was meant and objected to was, that it increased the debt of the General Government, and carried it beyond the possibility of payment. That if the balances had been settled, and the debtor States directed to pay their deficiencies to the creditor States, they would have done it easily, and by resources of taxation in their power, and acceptable to the people; by a direct tax in the south, and an excise in the north. Still, he said, it would be paid by the people. Finding him decided, I avoided entering into argument with him on those points.

» Sept. the 30th, 1792. The constitution as agreed to till a fortnight before the Convention rose, was such a one as he would have set his hand and heart to. 1st. The President was to be elected for seven years. Then ineligible for seven years more. 2d. Rotation in the Senate. 3d. A vote of two-thirds in the legislature on particular subjects, and expressly on that of navigation. The three New England States were constantly with us in all questions (Rhode Island not there, and New York seldom), so that it was these three States, with the five southern ones, against Pennsylvania, New Jersey, and Delaware.

With respect to the importation of slaves, it was left to Congress. This disturbed the two southernmost States, who knew that Congress would immediately suppress the importation of slaves. These two States, therefore, struck up a bargain with the three New England States. If they would join to admit slaves for some years, the southernmost States would join in changing the clause which required two-thirds of the legislature in any vote. It was done. These articles were changed accordingly, and from that moment the two southernmost States, and the three northern ones, joined Pennsylvania, New Jersey and Delaware, and made the majority eight to three against us, instead of eight to three for us, as it had been through the whole Convention. Under this coalition, the great principles of the constitution were changed in the last days of the Convention.

Anecdote. Yates, Lawsing and Hamilton represented New York. Yates and Lawsing never voted in one single instance with Hamilton, who was so much mortified at it that he went home. When the season for courts came on, Yates, a judge, and Lawsing, a lawyer, went to attend their courts. Then Hamilton returned.

Anecdote. The constitution as agreed at first was, that amendments might be proposed either by Congress or the legislatures. A committee was appointed to digest and redraw. Gouverneur Morris and King were of the committee. One morning Gouverneur Morris moved an instrument for certain alterations (not one-half the members yet come in). In a hurry and without understanding, it was agreed to. The committee reported so that Congress should have the exclusive power of proposing amendments. George Mason observed it on the report, and opposed it. King denied the construction. Mason demonstrated it, and asked the committee by what authority they had varied what had been agreed. Gouverneur Morris then impudently got up, and said, by authority of the Convention, and produced the blind instruction before mentioned, which was unknown by one-half of the House, and not till then understood by the other. They then restored it, as it originally stood.

He said he considered Hamilton as having done us more injury than Great Britain and all her fleets and armies. That his (Mason's) plan of settling our debts would have been something in this way. He would have laid as much tax as could be paid without oppressing the people;—particularly he would have laid an impost of about the amount of the first, laid by Congress, but somewhat different in several of its articles. He would have suspended all application of it one year, during which an office should have been open to register unalienated certificates. At the end of the year he would have appropriated his revenue. 1st. To pay the civil list. 2d. The interest of these certificates. 3d. Instalments of the principal. 4th. A surplus to buy up the alienated certificates, still avoiding to make any other provision for these last. By the time the unalienated certificates should have been all paid, he supposed half the alienated ones would have been bought up at market. He would then have proceeded to redeem the residue of them.

⇛ Bladensburg, October the 1st, 1792. This morning, at Mount Vernon, I had the following conversation with the President. He opened it by expressing his regret at the resolution in which I appeared so fixed, in the letter I had written him, of retiring from public affairs. He said, that he should be extremely sorry that I should do it, as long as he was in office, and that he could not see where he should find another character to fill my office. That, as yet, he was quite undecided whether to retire in March or not. His inclinations led him strongly to do it. Nobody disliked more the ceremonies of his office, and he had not the least taste or gratification in the execution of its functions. That he was happy at home alone, and that his presence there was now peculiarly called for by the situation of Major Washington, whom he thought irrecoverable, and should he get well, he would remove into another part of the country, which might better agree with him. That he did not believe his presence necessary; that there were other characters who would do the business as well or better. Still, however, if his aid was thought necessary to save the cause to which he had devoted his life principally, he would make the sacrifice of a longer continuance. That he therefore reserved himself for future decision, as his declaration would be in time if made a month before the day of election. He had desired Mr. Lear to find out from conversation, without appearing to make the inquiry, whether any other person would be desired by any body. He had informed him, he judged from conversations that it was the universal desire he should continue, and he believed that those who expressed a doubt of his continuance, did it in the language of apprehension, and not of desire. But this, says he, is only from the north; it may be very different in the south. I thought this meant as an opening to me to say what was the sentiment in the south, from which quarter I came. I told him, that as far as I knew, there was but one voice there, which was for his continuance. That as to myself, I had ever preferred the pursuits of private life to those of public, which had nothing in them agreeable to me. I explained to him the circumstances of the war which had first called me into public life, and those following the war, which had called me from a retirement on which I had determined. That I had constantly kept my eye on my own home, and could no longer refrain from returning to it. As to himself, his presence was important; that he was the only man in the United States who possessed the confidence of the whole; that government was founded in opinion and confidence, and that the longer he remained, the stronger would become the habits of the people in submitting to the government, and in thinking it a thing to be maintained; that there was no other person who would be thought anything more than the head of a party. He then expressed his concern at the difference which he found to subsist between the Secretary of the

Treasury and myself, of which he said he had not been aware. He knew, indeed, that there was a marked difference in our political sentiments, but he had never suspected it had gone so far in producing a personal difference, and he wished he could be the mediator to put an end to it. That he thought it important to preserve the check of my opinions in the administration, in order to keep things in their proper channel, and prevent them from going too far. That as to the idea of transforming this government into a monarchy, he did not believe there were ten men in the United States whose opinions were worth attention, who entertained such a thought. I told him there were many more than he imagined. I recalled to his memory a dispute at his own table, a little before we left Philadelphia, between General Schuyler on one side and Pinckney and myself on the other, wherein the former maintained the position, that hereditary descent was as likely to produce good magistrates as election. I told him, that though the people were sound, there were a numerous sect who had monarchy in contemplation; that the Secretary of the Treasury was one of these. That I had heard him say that this constitution was a shilly shally thing, of mere milk and water, which could not last, and was only good as a step to something better. That when we reflected, that he had endeavored in the convention, to make an English constitution of it, and when failing in that, we saw all his measures tending to bring it to the same thing, it was natural for us to be jealous; and particularly, when we saw that these measures had established corruption in the legislature, where there was a squadron devoted to the nod of the Treasury, doing whatever he had directed, and ready to do what he should direct. That if the equilibrium of the three great bodies, legislative, executive and judiciary, could be preserved, if the legislature could be kept independent, I should never fear the result of such a government; but that I could not but be uneasy, when I saw that the executive had swallowed up the legislative branch. He said, that as to that interested spirit in the legislature, it was what could not be avoided in any government, unless we were to exclude particular descriptions of men, such as the holders of the funds, from all office. I told him, there was great difference between the little accidental schemes of self-interest, which would take place in every body

·[143]·

of men, and influence their votes, and a regular system for forming a corps of interested persons, who should be steadily at the orders of the Treasury. He touched on the merits of the funding system, observed there was a difference of opinion about it, some thinking it very bad, others very good; that experience was the only criterion of right which

he knew, and this alone would decide which opinion was right. That for himself, he had seen our affairs desperate and our credit lost, and that this was in a sudden and extraordinary degree raised to the highest pitch. I told him, all that was ever necessary to establish our credit, was an efficient government and an honest one, declaring it would sacredly pay our debts, laying taxes for this purpose, and applying them to it. I avoided going further into the subject. He finished by another exhortation to me not to decide too positively on retirement, and here we were called to breakfast.

≫ October the 31st, 1792. I had sent to the President, Viar and Jaudenes's letter of the 29th instant, whereupon he desired a consultation of Hamilton, Knox, E. Randolph, and myself, on these points: 1. What notice was to be taken hereof to Spain? 2. Whether it should make part of the communication to the legislature? I delivered my opinion, that it ought to be communicated to both Houses, because the communications intended to be made, being to bring on the question, whether they would declare war against any, and which of the nations or parts of the nations of Indians to the south, it would be proper this information should be before them, that they might know how far such a declaration would lead them. There might be some who would be for war against the Indians, if it were to stop there, but who would not be for it, if it were to lead to a war against Spain. I thought it should be laid before both Houses, because it concerned the question of declaring war, which was the function equally of both Houses. I thought a simple acknowledgment of the receipt of the letter should be made by me to the Spanish Chargés, expressing that it contained some things very unexpected to us, but that we should refer the whole, as they had proposed, to the negotiators at Madrid. This would secure to us a continuation of the suspension of Indian hostilities, which the Governor of New Orleans said he had brought about till the result of the negotiation at Madrid should be known; would not commit us as to running or not running the line, or imply any admission of doubt about our territorial right; and would avoid a rupture with Spain, which was much to be desired, while we had similar points to discuss with Great Britain.

Hamilton declared himself the advocate for peace. War would derange our affairs greatly; throw us back many years in the march towards prosperity; be difficult for us to pursue, our countrymen not being disposed to become soldiers; a part of the Union feeling no interest in the war, would with difficulty be brought to exert itself; and we had no navy. He was for everything which would procrastinate the event. A year, even, was a great gain to a nation strengthening as we were. It laid open to us, too, the chapter of accidents, which, in the present state of Europe, was a very pregnant one. That while, however, he was for delaying the event of war, he had no doubt it was to take place between us for the object in question; that jealousy and perseverance were remarkable features in the character of the Spanish government, with respect to their American possessions; that so far from receding as to their claims against us, they had been strengthening themselves in them. He had no doubt the present communication was by authority from the court. Under this impression, he thought we should be looking forward to the day of rupture, and preparing for it. That if we were unequal to the contest ourselves, it behoved us to provide allies for our aid. That in this view, but two nations could be named, France and England. France was too intimately connected with Spain in other points, and of too great mutual value, ever to separate for us. Her affairs, too, were such, that whatever issue they had, she could not be in a situation to make a respectable mediation for us. England alone, then, remained. It would not be easy to affect it with her; however, he was for trying it, and for sounding them on the proposition of a defensive treaty of alliance. The inducements to such a treaty, on their part, might be, 1. The desire of breaking up our former connections, which we knew they had long wished. 2. A continuance of the *status quo* in commerce for ten years, which he believed would be desirable to them. 3. An admission to some navigable part of the Mississippi, by some line drawn from the Lake of the Woods to such navigable part. He had not, he said, examined the map to see how such a line might be run, so as not to make too great a sacrifice. The navigation of the Mississippi being a joint possession, we might then take measures in concert for the joint security of it. He was, therefore, for immediately sounding them on this subject through our ministers at London; yet so as to keep ourselves unengaged as long as possible, in hopes a favorable issue with Spain might be otherwise effected. But he was for sounding immediately, and for not letting slip an opportunity of securing our object.

E. Randolph concurred, in general, with me. He objected that such an alliance could not be effected without pecuniary consideration probably, which we could not give. And what was to be their aid? If men, our citizens would see their armies get foothold in the United States, with great jealousy; it would be difficult to protect them. Even the French, during the distress of the late war, excited some jealous sentiments.

Hamilton said, money was often, but not always demanded, and the aid he should propose to stipulate would be in ships. Knox *non dissentiente.*

The President said the remedy would be worse than the disease, and stated some of the disagreeable circumstances which would attend our making such overtures.

⋙ November, 1792. Hamilton called on me to speak about our furnishing supplies to the French colony of St. Domingo. He expressed his opinion, that we ought to be cautious, and not go too far in our application of money to their use, lest it should not be recognized by the mother country. He did not even think that some kinds of government they might establish could give a sufficient sanction.* I observed, that the National Convention was now met, and would certainly establish a form of government; that as we had recognized the former government because established by authority of the *nation*, so we must recognize any other which should be established by the authority of the nation. He said we had recognized the former, because it contained an important member of the ancient, to wit: the King, and wore the appearance of his consent; but if, in any future form, they should omit the King, he did not know that we could with safety recognize it, or pay money to its order.

---

* There had been a previous consultation at the President's (about the first week in November) on the expediency of suspending payments to France, under her present situation. I had admitted that the late constitution was dissolved by the dethronement of the King; and the management of affairs surviving to the National Assembly only, this was not an integral Legislature, and therefore not competent to give a legitimate discharge for our payments: that I thought, consequently, that none should be made till some legitimate body came into place; and that I should consider the National Convention called, but not met as we had yet heard, to be a legitimate body. Hamilton doubted whether it would be a legitimate body, and whether, if the King should be re-established, he might not disallow such payments on good grounds. Knox, for once, dared to differ from Hamilton, and to express, very submissively, an opinion, that a convention named by the whole body of the nation, would be competent to do anything. It ended by agreeing, that I should write to Gouverneur Morris to suspend payment generally, till further orders.—T.J.

⋙ November the 19th, 1792. Beckley brings me the pamphlet written by Hamilton, before the war, in answer to Common Sense. It is entitled "Plain Truth." Melancthon Smith sends it to Beckley, and in his letter says, it was not printed in New York by Loudon, because prevented by a mob, and was printed in Philadelphia, and that he has these facts from Loudon.

⋙ November the 21st, 1792. Mr. Butler tells me, that he dined last winter with Mr. Campbell from Denmark, in company with Hamilton, Lawrence, Dr. Shippen, T. Shippen, and one other person whom he cannot recollect. That after dinner political principles became the subject of conversation; that Hamilton declared openly, that "there was no stability, no security in any kind of government but a monarchy." That Lawrence took him up, and entered the lists of argument against him; that the dispute continued long, and grew warm, remarkably so as between them; that T. Shippen, at length, joined Lawrence in it; and in fine, that it broke up the company. Butler recommended to the company, that the dispute having probably gone farther than was intended, it ought to be considered as confined to the company.

⋙ December the 10th, 1792. Present: Alexander Hamilton, General Knox, Edmund Randolph, and Th: Jefferson, at the President's.

It was agreed to reject meeting the Indians at the proposed treaty, rather than to admit a *mediation* by Great Britain; but to admit the presence of Governor Simcoe, not as a *party* (if that was insisted on); and that I should make a verbal communication to Mr. Hammond, in substance, as on the back hereof, which I previously read to the President.

⋙ December the 12th. I made the communication to Mr. Hammond. He said the attendance of Governor Simcoe was a circumstance only mentioned by him, but not desired; that he would decline it without difficulty; declared it to be their most ardent wish that peace should take place, for their fur-trade was entirely interrupted; and he urged as decisive proof of the sincerity of their wish,—1st. That they had kept the late Indian council together six weeks at a very great expense, waiting for the Six Nations. 2d. That the Indians at that council were so perfectly satisfied of their desire that they should make peace, that they had not so much as mentioned in council the applying to the British for any supplies. I immediately communicated this to the President.

≫ December the 13th, 1792. The President called on me to see the model and drawings of some mills for sawing stone. After showing them, he in the course of a subsequent conversation asked me if there were not some good manufactories of porcelain in Germany; that he was in want of table china, and had been speaking to Mr. Shaw, who was going to the East Indies to bring him a set, but he found that it would not come till *he should no longer be in a situation to want it*. He took occasion a second time to observe that Shaw said it would be two years, at least, before he could have the china here, before which time he said he should be where he should not need it. I think he asked the question about the manufactories in Germany merely to have an indirect opportunity of telling me he meant to retire, and within the limits of two years.

≫ December the 17th. Hammond says the person is here to whom the Six Nations delivered the invitation for Simcoe to attend, who says they insisted on it, and would consider his non-attendance as an evidence that he does not wish for peace; but he says that Simcoe has not the least idea of attending; that this gentleman says we may procure in Upper Canada any quantity of provisions, which the people will salt up express during winter; and that he will return and carry our request whenever we are ready.

≫ Thursday, December the 27th, 1792. I waited on the President on some current business. After this was over, he observed to me, that he thought it was time to endeavor to effect a stricter connection with France, and that Gouverneur Morris should be written to on this subject. He went into the circumstances of dissatisfaction between Spain and Great Britain, and us, and observed, there was no nation on whom we could rely, at all times, but France; and that, if we did not prepare in time some support, in the event of rupture with Spain and England, we might be charged with a criminal negligence. [I was much pleased with the tone of these observations. It was the very doctrine which had been my polar star, and I did not need the successes of the republican arms in France, lately announced to us, to bring me to these sentiments. For it is to be noted, that on Saturday last (the 22d) I received Mr. Short's letters of October the 9th and 12th, with the Leyden gazettes to October the 13th, giving us the first news of the retreat of the Duke of Brunswick, and the capture of Spires and Worms by Custine, and that of Nice by Anselme.] I therefore expressed to the President my cordial approbation of these ideas; told him I had meant on that day (as an opportunity of writing by the British packet would occur immediately) to take his orders for removing the suspension of payments to France, which had been imposed by my last letter to Gouverneur Morris, but was meant, as I supposed, only for the interval between the abolition of the late constitution by the dethronement of the King, and the meeting of some other body, invested by the will of the nation with powers to transact their affairs; that I considered the National Convention, then assembled, as such a body; and that, therefore, we ought to go on with the payments to them, or to any government they should establish; that, however, I had learned last night, that some clause in the bill for providing reimbursement of the loan made by the bank to the United States, had given rise to a question before the House of Representatives yesterday, which might affect these payments; a clause in that bill proposing, that the money formerly borrowed in Amsterdam, to pay the French debt, and appropriated by law (1690, August 4th, c. 34, s. 2) to that purpose, lying dead as was suggested, should be taken to pay the bank, and the President be authorized to borrow two millions of dollars more, out of which it should be replaced; and if this should be done, the removal of our suspension of payments, as I had been about to propose, would be premature. He expressed his disapprobation of the clause above mentioned; thought it highly improper in the Legislature to change an appropriation once made, and added, that no one could tell in what that would end. I concurred, but observed, that on a division of the House, the ayes for striking out the clause were twenty-seven, the noes twenty-six; whereon the Speaker gave his vote against striking out, which divides the House: the clause for the disappropriation remained of course. I mentioned suspicions, that the whole of this was a trick to serve the bank under a great existing embarrassment; that the debt to the bank was to be repaid by instalments; that the first instalment was of two hundred thousand dollars only, or rather one hundred and sixty thousand dollars (because forty thousand of the two hundred thousand dollars would be the United States' own dividend of the instalment). Yet here were two millions to be paid them at once, and to be taken from a purpose of gratitude and honor, to which it had been appropriated.

December the 30th, 1792. I took the occasion furnished by Pinckney's letter of September the 19th, asking instructions how to conduct himself as to the French revolution, to lay down the catholic principal of republicanism, to wit, that every people may establish what form of government they please, and change it as they please; the will of the nation being the only thing essential. I was induced to do this, in order to extract the President's opinion on the question which divided Hamilton and myself in the conversation of November, 1792, and the previous one of the first week of November, on the suspension of payments to France; and if favorable to mine, to place the principles of record in the letter books of my office. I therefore wrote the letter of December the 30th, to Pinckney, and sent it to the President, and he returned me his approbation in writing, in his note of the same date, which see.

February the 7th, 1793. I waited on the President with letters and papers from Lisbon. After going through these, I told him that I had for some time suspended speaking with him on the subject of my going out of office, because I had understood that the bill for intercourse with foreign nations was likely to be rejected by the Senate, in which case, the remaining business of the department would be too inconsiderable to make it worth while to keep it up. But that the bill being now passed, I was freed from the considerations of propriety which had embarrassed me. That &c. [nearly in the words of a letter to Mr. T. M. Randolph, of a few days ago], and that I should be willing, if he had no arrangements to the contrary, to continue somewhat longer, how long I could not say, perhaps till summer, perhaps autumn. He said, so far from taking arrangements on the subject, he had never mentioned to any mortal the design of retiring which I had expressed to him, till yesterday, when having heard that I had given up my house, and that it was rented by another, he thereupon mentioned it to Mr. E. Randolph, and asked him, as he knew my retirement had been talked of, whether he had heard any persons suggested in conversation to succeed me. He expressed his satisfaction at my change of purpose, and his apprehensions that my retirement would be a new source of uneasiness to the public. He said Governor Lee had that day informed him of the general discontent prevailing in Virginia, of which he never had had any conception, much less sound information. That it appeared to him very alarming. He proceeded to express his earnest wish that Hamilton and myself could coalesce in the measures of the government, and urged here the general reasons for it which he had done to me in two former conversations. He said he had proposed the same thing to Hamilton, who expressed his readiness, and he thought our coalition would secure the general acquiescence of the public. I told him my concurrence was of much less importance than he seemed to imagine; that I kept myself aloof from all cabal and correspondence on the subject of the government, and saw and spoke with as few as I could. That as to a coalition with Mr. Hamilton, if by that was meant that either was to sacrifice his general system to the other, it was impossible. We had both, no doubt, formed our conclusions after the most mature consideration; and principles conscientiously adopted, could not be given up on either side. My wish was, to see both Houses of Congress cleansed of all persons interested in the bank or public stocks; and that a pure legislature being given us, I should always be ready to acquiesce under their determinations, even if contrary to my own opinions; for that I subscribe to the principle, that the will of the majority, honestly expressed, should give law. I confirmed him in the fact of the great discontents to the south; that they were grounded on seeing that their judgments and interests were sacrificed to those of the eastern States on every occasion, and their belief that it was the effect of a corrupt squadron of voters in Congress, at the command of the Treasury; and they see that if the votes of those members who had any interest distinct from, and contrary to the general interest of their constituents, had been withdrawn, as in decency and honesty they should have been, the laws would have been the reverse of what they are on all the great questions. I instanced the new Assumption carried in the House of Representatives by the Speaker's vote. On this subject he made no reply. He explained his remaining in office to have been the effect of strong solicitations after he returned here; declaring that he had never mentioned his purpose of going out but to the Heads of departments and Mr. Madison; he expressed the extreme wretchedness of his existence while in office, and went lengthily into the late attacks on him for levees, &c., and explained to me how he had been led into them by the persons he consulted at New York; and that if he could but know what the sense of the public was, he would most cheerfully conform to it.

»» February the 16th, 1793. E. Randolph tells J. Madison and myself, a curious fact which he had from Lear. When the President went to New York, he resisted for three weeks the efforts to introduce levees. At length he yielded, and left it to Humphreys and some others to settle the forms. Accordingly, an ante-chamber and presence room were provided, and when those who were to pay their court were assembled, the President set out, preceded by Humphreys. After passing through the ante-chamber, the door of the inner room was thrown open, and Humphreys entered first, calling out with a loud voice, "The President of the United States." The President was so much disconcerted with it, that he did not recover from it the whole time of the levee, and when the company was gone, he said to Humphreys, "Well, you have taken me in once, but by God you shall never take me in a second time."

There is reason to believe that the rejection of the late additional Assumption by the Senate, was effected by the President through Lear, operating on Langdon. Beckley knows this.

⧽ February the 20th, 1793. Colonel W. S. Smith called on me to communicate intelligence from France. He had left Paris November the 9th. He says the French ministers are entirely broken with Gouverneur Morris; shut their doors to him, and will never receive another communication from him. They wished Smith to be the bearer of a message from the President, to this effect, but he declined; and they said in that case they would press it through their own minister here. He says they are sending Genet here with full powers to give us all the privileges we can desire in their countries, and particularly in the West Indies; that they even contemplate to set them free the next summer; that they propose to emancipate South America, and will send forty-five ships of the line there next spring, and Miranda at the head of the expedition; that they desire our debt to be paid them in provisions, and have authorized him to negotiate this. In confirmation of this, he delivers a letter to the President from Le Brun, minister for foreign affairs, in which Le Brun says that Colonel Smith will communicate plans worthy of his (the President's) great mind, and he shall be happy to receive his opinion as to the means the most suitable to effect it.

I had, five or six days ago, received from Ternant, extracts from the livres of his ministers, complaining of both Gouverneur Morris and Mr. Short. I sent them this day to the President with an extract from a private letter of Mr. Short, justifying himself, and I called this evening on the President. He said he considered the extracts from Ternant very serious—in short, as decisive; that he saw that Gouverneur Morris could be no longer continued there consistent with the public good; that the moment was critical in our favor, and ought not to be lost; that he was extremely at a loss what arrangement to make. I asked him whether Gouverneur Morris and Pinckney might not change places. He said that would be a sort of remedy, but not a radical one. That if the French ministry conceived Gouverneur Morris to be hostile to them; if they would be jealous merely on his proposing to visit London, they would never be satisfied with us at placing him at London permanently. He then observed, that though I had unfixed the day on which I had intended to resign, yet I appeared fixed in doing it at no great distance of time; that in this case, he could not but wish that I would go to Paris;

that the moment was important: I possessed the confidence of both sides, and might do great good; that he wished I could do it, were it only to stay there a year or two. I told him that my mind was so bent on retirement that I could not think of launching forth again in a new business; that I could never again cross the Atlantic; and that as to the opportunity of doing good, this was likely to be the scene of action, as Genet was bringing powers to do the business here; but that I could not think of going abroad. He replied that I had pressed him to continue in the public service, and refused to do the same myself. I said the case was very different; he united the confidence of all America, and was the only person who did so: his services therefore were of the last importance; but for myself, my going out would not be noted or known. A thousand others could supply my place to equal advantage, therefore I felt myself free; and that as to the mission to France, I thought perfectly proper. He desired me then to consider maturely what arrangement should be made.

Smith, in speaking of Morris, said, that at his own table, in presence of his company and servants, he cursed the French ministers, as a set of damned rascals; said the king would still be replaced upon his throne. He said he knew they had written to have him recalled, and expected to be recalled. He consulted Smith to know whether he would bring his furniture here duty free. Smith has mentioned the situation of Gouverneur Morris freely to others here. Smith said also that the ministers told him they meant to begin their attack at the mouth of the Mississippi, and to sweep along the Bay of Mexico southwardly, and that they would have no objection to our incorporating into our government the two Floridas.

❧ February the 25th, 1793. The President desires the opinions of the heads of the three departments, and of the Attorney General, on the following question, to wit.: Mr. Ternant having applied for money equivalent to three millions of livres, to be furnished on account of our debt to France at the request of the executive of that country, which sum is to be laid out in provisions within the United States, to be sent to France. Shall the money be furnished?

The Secretary of the Treasury stated it as his opinion, that making a liberal allowance for the depreciation of assignats (no rule of liquidation having been yet fixed), a sum of about three hundred and eighteen thousand dollars may not exceed the arrearages equitably due to France to the end of 1792, and that the whole sum asked for may be furnished within periods capable of answering the purpose of Mr. Ternant's application, without a derangement of the Treasury.

Whereupon the Secretaries of State and War, and the Attorney General, are of opinion that the whole sum asked for by Mr. Ternant ought to be furnished: the Secretary of the Treasury is of opinion that the supply ought not exceed the above-mentioned sum of three hundred and eighteen thousand dollars.

The President having required the attendance of the heads of the three departments, and of the Attorney General, at his house, on Monday the 25th of February, 1793, the following questions were proposed, and answers given:

1. The Governor of Canada having refused to let us obtain provisions from that province, or to pass them along the water communication to the place of treaty with the Indians; and the Indians having refused to let them pass peaceably along what they call the bloody path, the Governor of Canada at the same time proposing to furnish the whole provisions necessary, ought the treaty to proceed? Answer unanimously, it ought to proceed.

2. Have the Executive, or the Executive and Senate together, authority to relinquish to the Indians the right of soil of any part of the land north of the Ohio, which has been validly obtained by former treaties?

The Secretary of the Treasury, the Secretary at War, and Attorney General, are of opinion that the Executive and Senate have such authority, provided that no grants to individuals, nor reservations to States, be thereby infringed. The Secretary of State is of opinion they have no such authority to relinquish.

3. Will it be expedient to make any such relinquishments to the Indians, if essential to peace?

The Secretaries of the Treasury and War, and the Attorney General, are of opinion it will be expedient to make such relinquishments if essential to peace, provided it do not include any lands sold or received for special purposes (the reservations for trading places excepted). The Secretary of State is of opinion that the Executive and Senate have authority to stipulate with the Indians, and that if essential to peace, it will be expedient to stipulate that we will not settle any lands between those already sold, or reserved for special purposes, and the lines heretofore validly established with the Indians.

Whether the Senate shall be previously consulted on this point. The opinion unanimously is, that it will be better not to consult them previously.

⋙ February the 26th, 1793. Notes on the proceedings of yesterday. [See the formal opinions given to the President in writing, and signed.]

First question. We are all of opinion that the treaty should proceed merely to gratify the public opinion, and not from an expectation of success. I expressed myself strongly, that the event was so unpromising, that I thought the preparations for a campaign should go on without the least relaxation, and that a day should be fixed with the commissioners for the treaty, beyond which they should not permit the treaty to be protracted, by which day orders should be given for our forces to enter into action. The President took up the thing instantly, after I had said this, and declared that he was so much in the opinion that the treaty would end in nothing, that he then, in the presence of us all, gave orders to General Knox, not to slacken the preparations for the campaign in the least, but to exert every nerve in preparing for it. Knox said something about the ultimate day for continuing the negotiations. I acknowledged myself not a judge on what day the campaign should begin, but that whatever it was, that day should terminate the treaty. Knox said he thought a winter campaign was always the most efficacious against the Indians. I was of opinion, since Great Britain insisted on furnishing provisions, that we should offer to repay. Hamilton thought we should not.

Second question. I considered our right of pre-emption of the Indian lands, not as amounting to any dominion, or jurisdiction, or paramountship whatever, but merely in the nature of a remainder after the extinguishment of a present right, which gave us no present right whatever, but of preventing other nations from taking possession, and so defeating our expectancy; that the Indians had the full, undivided and independent sovereignty as long as they choose to keep it, and that this might be forever; that as fast as we extend our rights by purchase from them, so fast we extend the limits of our society, and as soon as a new portion became encircled within our line, it became a fixed limit of our society; that the executive, with either or both branches of the legislature, could not alien any part of our territory; that by the law of nations it was settled, that the unity and indivisibility of the society was so fundamental, that it could not be dismembered by the constituted authorities, except, 1, where *all power* was delegated to them (as in the case of despotic governments), or, 2, where it was expressly delegated; that neither of these delegations had been made to our General Government, and therefore, that it had no right to dismember or alienate any portion of territory once ultimately consolidated with us; and that we could no more cede to the Indians than to the English or Spaniards, as it might, according to acknowledged principles, remain as irrevocably and eternally with the one as the other. But I thought, that as we had a right to sell and settle lands once comprehended within our lines, so we might forbear to exercise that right, retaining the property till circumstances should be more favorable to the settlement, and this I agreed to do in the present instance, if necessary for peace.

Hamilton agreed to the doctrine of the law of nations, as laid down in Europe, but that it was founded on the universality of settlement there; consequently, that no lopping off of territory could be made without a lopping off of citizens, which required their consent; but that the law of nations for us must be adapted to the circumstance of our unsettled country, which he conceived the President and Senate may cede; that the power of treaty was given to them by the Constitution, without restraining it to particular objects; consequently, that it was given in as plenipotentiary a form as held by any sovereign in any other society. Randolph was of opinion there was a difference between a cession to Indians and to any others, because it only restored the ceded part to the condition in which it was before we bought it, and consequently, that we might buy it again hereafter; therefore, he thought the Executive and Senate could cede it. Knox joined in the main opinion. The President discovered no opinion, but he made some efforts to get us to join in some terms which could unite us all, and he seemed to direct those efforts more towards me; but the thing could not be done.

Third question. We agreed in idea as to the line to be drawn, to wit, so as to retain all lands appropriated, or granted, or reserved.

Fourth question. We all thought if the Senate should be consulted, and consequently apprized of our line, it would become known to Hammond, and we should lose all chance of saving anything more at the treaty than our ultimatum.

The President, at this meeting, mentioned the declaration of some person, in a paper of Fenno,* that he would commence an attack on the character of Dr. Franklin. He said the theme was to him excessively disagreeable on other considerations, but most particularly so, as the party seemed to do it as a means of defending him (the President) against the late attacks on him; that such a mode of defence would be peculiarly painful to him, and he wished it could be stopped. Hamilton and Randolph undertook to speak to Fenno to suppress it, without mentioning it as the President's wish. Both observed that they had heard this declaration mentioned in many companies, and that it had excited universal horror and detestation.

* John Fenno, published *Gazette of the United States*, a federalist organ under favor of Alexander Hamilton.

The paper in Fenno must lie between two persons, *viz.*, Adams and Izard, because they are the only persons who could know such facts as are there promised to be unfolded. Adams is an enemy to both characters, and might choose this ground as an effectual position to injure both. Izard hated Franklin with unparalleled bitterness, but humbly adores the President, because he is in *loco regis*. If the paper proceeds, we shall easily discover which of these two gentlemen is the champion. In the meantime, the first paper leads our suspicions more towards Izard than Adams, from the circumstance of style, and because he is quite booby enough not to see the injury he would do to the President by such a mode of defence.

➤➤ February the 28th. Knox, E. Randolph and myself met at Knox's, where Hamilton was also to have met, to consider the time, manner and place of the President's swearing in. Hamilton had been there before, and had left his opinion with Knox, to wit, that the President should ask a judge to attend him in his own house to administer the oath, in the presence of the Heads of departments, which oath should be deposited in the Secretary of State's office. I concurred in this opinion. Randolph was for the President's going to the Senate's chamber to take the oath, attended by the marshal of the United States, who should then make proclamation, &c. Knox was for this, and for adding the House of Representatives to the presence, as they would not yet be departed. Our individual opinions were written, to be communicated to the President, out of which he might form one. In the course of our conversation, Knox, stickling for parade, got into great warmth, and swore that our government must either be entirely new modeled, or it would be knocked to pieces in less than ten years; and that as it is at present, he would not give a copper for it; that it is the President's character, and not the written constitution, which keeps it together.

Same day. Conversation with Lear. He expressed the strongest confidence that republicanism was the universal creed of America, except of a very few; that a republican administration must of necessity immediately overbear the contrary faction; said that he had seen with extreme regret that a number of gentlemen had for a long time been endeavoring to instil into the President, that the noise against the administration of the government was that of a little faction, which would soon be silent, and which was detested by the people, who were contented and prosperous; that this very party, however, began to see their error, and that the sense of America was bursting forth to their conviction.

⋙ March the 2d, 1793. See in the papers of this date, Mr. Giles's resolutions. He and one or two others were sanguine enough to believe that the palpableness of these resolutions rendered it impossible the House could reject them. Those who knew the composition of the House, 1, of bank directors; 2, holders of bank stock; 3, stock jobbers; 4, blind devotees; 5, ignorant persons, who did not comprehend them; 6, lazy and good-humored persons, who comprehended and acknowledged them, yet were too lazy to examine, or unwilling to pronounce censure; the persons who knew these characters, foresaw that the three first descriptions making one-third of the House, the three latter would make one-half of the residue; and, of course, that they would be rejected by a majority of two to one. But they thought that even this rejection would do good, by showing the public the desperate and abandoned dispositions with which their affairs were conducted. The resolutions were proposed, and nothing spared to present them in the fulness of demonstration. There were not more than three or four who voted otherwise than had been expected.

⋙ March the 30th, 1793. At our meeting at the President's, February the 25th, in discussing the question, whether we should furnish to France the three millions of livres desired, Hamilton, in speaking on the subject, used this expression, "When Mr. Genet arrives, whether we shall receive him or not, will then be a question for discussion," which expression I did not recollect till E. Randolph reminded me of it a few days after. Therefore, on the 20th instant, as the President was shortly to set out for Mount Vernon, I observed to him, that as Genet might arrive in his absence, I wished to know beforehand how I should treat him, whether as a person who would or would not be received? He said he could see no ground of doubt but that he ought to be received. On the 24th he asked E. Randolph's opinion on the subject, saying he had consulted Colonel Hamilton thereon, who went into lengthy considerations of doubt and difficulty, and viewing it as a very unfortunate thing that the President should have the decision of so critical a point forced on him; but, in conclusion, said, since he was brought into that situation, he did not see but that he must receive Mr. Genet. Randolph told the President he was clear he should be received, and the President said he had never had any doubt on the subject in his mind. Afterwards, on the same day, he spoke to me again on it, and said Mr. Genet should unquestionably be received; but he thought not with too much warmth or cordiality, so only as to be satisfactory to him. I wondered at first at this restriction; but when Randolph afterwards communicated to me his conversation of the 24th, I became satisfied it was a small sacrifice to the opinion of Hamilton.

≫ March the 31st. Mr. Beckley tells me, that the merchants' bonds for duties on six months' credit became due the 1st instant to a very great amount, that Hamilton went to the bank on that day, and directed the bank to discount for those merchants all their bonds at thirty days, and that he would have the collectors credited for the money at the treasury. Hence, the treasury lumping its receipts by the month in its printed accounts, these sums will be considered by the public as only received on the last day; consequently, the bank makes the month's interest out of it. Beckley had this from a merchant who had a bond discounted, and supposes a million of dollars were discounted at the bank here. Mr. Brown got the same information from another merchant, who supposed only six hundred thousand dollars discounted here. But they suppose the same orders went to all the branch banks to a great amount.

Eodem die. Mr. Brown tells me he has it from a merchant, that during the last winter the directors of the bank ordered the freest discounts. Every man could obtain it. Money being so flush, the six per cents run up to twenty-one and twenty-two shillings. Then the directors sold out their private stocks. When the discounted notes were becoming due, they stopped discounts, and not a dollar was to be had. This reduced six per cents to eighteen shillings and three pence; then the same directors bought in again.

⋙ April the 7th, 1793. Mr. Lear called on me, and introduced of himself a conversation on the affairs of the United States. He laughed at the cry of prosperity, and the deriving it from the establishment of the treasury: he said, that so far from giving into this opinion, and that we were paying off our national debt, he was clear the debt was growing on us; that he had lately expressed this opinion to the President, who appeared much astonished at it. I told him I had given the same hint to the President last summer, and lately again had suggested, that we were even depending for the daily subsistence of government on borrowed money. He said, that was certain, and was the only way of accounting for what was become of the money drawn over from Holland to this country. He regretted that the President was not in the way of hearing full information, declared he communicated to him everything he could learn himself; that the men who vaunted the present government so much on some occasions, were the very men who at other times declared it was a poor thing, and such a one as could not stand, and he was sensible they only esteemed it as a stepping stone to something else, and had availed themselves of the first moments of the enthusiasm in favor of it, to pervert its principles and make of it what they wanted; and that though they raised the cry of anti-federalism against those who censured the mode of administration, yet he was satisfied, whenever it should come to be tried, that the very men whom they called anti-federalists, were the men who would save the government, and he looked to the next Congress for much rectification.

⋙ April the 18th. The President sends a set of questions to be considered, and calls a meeting. Though those sent me were in his own hand writing, yet it was palpable from the style, their ingenious tissue and suite, that they were not the President's, that they were raised upon a prepared chain of argument, in short, that the language was Hamilton's, and the doubts his alone. They led to a declaration of the executive, that our treaty with France is void. E. Randolph, the next day, told me that the day before the date of these questions, Hamilton went with him through the whole chain of reasoning of which these questions are the skeleton, and that he recognized them the moment he saw them.

We met. The first question, whether we should receive the French minister, Genet, was proposed, and we agreed unanimously that he should be received; Hamilton, at the same time, expressing his great regret that any incident had happened, which should oblige us to recognize the government. The next question was, whether he should be received absolutely, or with qualifications. Here Hamilton took up the whole subject, and went through it in the order in which the questions sketch it. See the chain of his reasoning in my opinions of April the 28th. Knox subscribed at once to Hamilton's opinion that we ought to declare the treaty void, acknowledging, at the same time, like a fool as he is, that he knew nothing about it. I was clear it remained valid. Randolph declared himself of the same opinion, but on Hamilton's undertaking to present to him the authority in Vattel (which we had not present) and to prove to him, that if the authority was admitted, the treaty might be declared void, Randolph agreed to take further time to consider. It was adjourned. We determined, unanimously, the last question, that Congress should not be called. There having been an intimation by Randolph, that in so great a question he should choose to give a written opinion, and this being approved by the President, I gave in mine April the 28th. Hamilton gave in his. I believe Knox's was never thought worth offering or asking for. Randolph gave his May the 6th, concurring with mine. The President told me, the same day, he had never had a doubt about the validity of the treaty; but that since a question had been suggested, he thought it ought to be considered; that this being done, I might now issue passports to sea vessels in the form prescribed by the French treaty. I had for a week past only issued the Dutch form; to have issued the French, would have been presupposing the treaty to be in existence. The President suggested, that he thought it would be as well that nothing should be said of such a question having been under consideration.   *Written May the 6th.*

⇶ May the 6th, 1793. When the question was, whether the proclamation of April the 22d should be issued, Randolph observed, that there should be a letter written by me to the ministers of the belligerent powers, to declare that it should not be taken as conclusive evidence against our citizens in foreign courts of admiralty, for contraband goods. Knox suddenly adopted the opinion, before Hamilton delivered his. Hamilton opposed it pretty strongly. I thought it an indifferent thing, but rather approved Randolph's opinion. The President was against it; but observed that *as there were three for it, it should go.* This was the first instance I had seen of an opportunity to decide by a mere majority, including his own vote.

⇶ May the 12th. Lear called on me today. Speaking of the lowness of stocks, (sixteen shillings), I observed it was a pity we had not money to buy on public account. He said, yes, and that it was the more provoking, as two millions had been borrowed for that purpose, and drawn over here, and yet were not here. That he had no doubt those would take notice of the circumstance whose duty it was to do so. I suppose he must mean the President.

⇶ May the 23d. I had sent to the President yesterday, draughts of a letter from him to the Provisory Executive Council of France, and of one from myself to Mr. Ternant, both on the occasion of his recall. I called on him today. He said there was an expression in one of them, which he had never before seen in any of our public communications, to wit, "our republic." The letter prepared for him to the Council, began thus: "The Citizen Ternant has delivered to me the letter wherein you inform me, that yielding, &c., you had determined to recall him from his mission, as your Minister Plenipotentiary to *our republic.*" He had underscored the words, *our republic.* He said that certainly ours was a republican government, but yet we had not used that style in this way; that if any body wanted to change its form into a monarchy, he was sure it was only a few individuals, and that no man in the United States would set his face against it more than himself; but that this was not what he was afraid of; his fears were from another quarter; that there was more danger of anarchy being introduced. He averted to a piece in Freneau's paper of yesterday; he said he despised all their attacks on him personally, but that there never had been an act of the government, not meaning in the executive line only, but in any line, which that paper had not abused. He has also marked the word republic thus √, where it was applied to the French republic. (See the original paper.) He was evidently sore and warm, and I took his intention to be, that I should interpose in some way with Freneau, perhaps withdraw his appointment of translating clerk to my office. But I will not do it. His paper has saved our constitution, which was galloping fast into monarchy, and has been checked by no one means so powerfully as by that paper. It is well and universally known, that it has been that paper which has checked the career of the monocrats; and the President, not sensible of the designs of the party, has not with his usual good sense and *sang froid*, looked on the efforts and effects of this free press, and seen that, though some bad things have passed through it to the public, yet the good have preponderated immensely.

⋙ June the 7th, 1793. Mr. Beckley, who has returned from New York within a few days, tells me that while he was there, Sir John Temple, Consul General of the northern States for Great Britain, showed him a letter from Sir Gregory Page Turner, a member of Parliament for a borough in Yorkshire, who, he said, had been a member for twenty-five years, and always confidential for the ministers, in which he permitted him to read particular passages of the following purport: "that the government was well apprized of the predominancy of the British interest in the United States; that they considered Colonel Hamilton, Mr. King, and Mr. W. Smith of South Carolina, as the main supports of that interest; that particularly, they considered Colonel Hamilton, and not Mr. Hammond, as their effective minister here; that if the anti-federal interest (that was his term), at the head of which they considered Mr. Jefferson to be, should prevail, these gentlemen *had secured* an asylum to themselves in England." Beckley could not understand whether they had secured it *themselves*,* or whether they were only

* Jefferson wrote in the margin: "Impossible as to Hamilton; he was far above that."

notified that it was secured to them. So that they understand that they may go on boldly in their machinations to change the government, and if they should be overset and choose to withdraw, they will be secure of a pension in England, as Arnold, Deane, &c., had. Sir John read passages of a letter (which he did not put into Beckley's hand, as he did the other) from Lord Grenville, saying nearly the same things. This letter mentions to Sir John, that though they had divided the Consul General-ship, and given the southern department to Bond, yet he, Sir John, was to retain his whole salary. [By this it would seem, as if, wanting to use Bond, they had covered his employment with this cloak.] Mr. Beckley says that Sir John Temple is a strong republican. I had a proof of his intimacy with Sir John in this circumstance. Sir John received his new commission of Consul for the northern department, and instead of sending it through Mr. Hammond, got Beckley to enclose it to me for his exequatur. I wrote to Sir John that it must come through Mr. Hammond, enclosing it back to him. He accordingly then sent it to Mr. Hammond.

In conversation with the President today, and speaking about General Greene, he said that he and General Greene had always differed in opinion about the manner of using militia. Greene always placed them in his front: himself was of opinion, they should always be used as a reserve to improve any advantage, for which purpose they were the *finest fellows* in the world. He said he was on the ground of the battle of Guilford, with a person who was in the action, and who explained the whole of it to him. That General Greene's front was behind a fence at the edge of a large field, through which the enemy were obliged to pass to get at them; and that in their passage through this, they must have been torn all to pieces, if troops had been posted there who would have stood their ground; and that the retreat from that position was through a thicket, perfectly secure. Instead of this, he posted the North Carolina militia there, who only gave one fire and fell back, so that the whole benefit of their position was lost. He thinks that the regulars, with their field pieces, would have hardly let a single man get through that field.

Eodem die (June the 7th). Beckley tells me that he has the following fact from Governor Clinton. That before the proposition for the present General Government, *i.e.*, a little before Hamilton conceived a plan for establishing a monarchial government in the United States, he wrote a draught of a circular letter, which was to be sent to about —— persons, to bring it about. One of these letters, in Hamilton's handwriting, is now in possession of an old militia General up the North River, who, at that time, was thought *orthodox* enough to be entrusted in the execution. This General has given notice to Governor Clinton that he has this paper, and that he will deliver it into his hands, and no one's else. Clinton intends, the first interval of leisure, to go for it, and he will bring it to Philadelphia. Beckley is a man of perfect truth as to what he affirms of his own knowledge, but too credulous as to what he hears from others.

≫ June the 10th, 1793. Mr. Brown gives me the following specimen of the phrenzy which prevailed at New York on the opening of the new government. The first public ball which took place after the President's arrival there, Colonel Humphreys, Colonel W. S. Smith and Mrs. Knox were to arrange the ceremonials. These arrangements were as follows: a sofa at the head of the room, raised on several steps, whereon the President and Mrs. Washington were to be seated. The gentlemen were to dance in swords. Each one, when going to dance, was to lead his partner to the foot of the sofa, make a low obeisance to the President and his lady, then go and dance, and when done, bring his partner again to the foot of the sofa for new obeisances, and then to retire to their chairs. It was to be understood, too, that gentlemen should be dressed in bags. Mrs. Knox contrived to come with the President, and to follow him and Mrs. Washington to their destination, and she had the design of forcing an invitation from the President to a seat on the sofa. She mounted up the steps after them unbidden, but unfortunately the wicked sofa was so short, that when the President and Mrs. Washington were seated, there was not room for a third person; and she was obliged, therefore, to descend in the face of the company, and to sit where she could. In other respects the ceremony was conducted rigorously according to the arrangements, and the President made to pass an evening which his good sense rendered a very miserable one to him.

≫ June the 12th. Beckley tells me that Klingham has been with him today, and relates to him the following fact: A certificate of the old Congress had been offered at the treasury and refused payment, and so indorsed in red ink as usual. This certificate came to the hands of Francis (the quondam clerk of the treasury, who, on account of his being dipped in the infamous case of the Baron Glaubec, Hamilton had been

obliged to dismiss, to save appearances, but with an assurance of all future service, and he accordingly got him established in New York). Francis wrote to Hamilton that such a ticket was offered him, but he could not buy it unless he would inform him and give him his certificate that it was good. Hamilton wrote him a most friendly letter, and sent him the certificate. He bought the paper, and came on here and got it recognized, whereby he made twenty-five hundred dollars. Klingham saw both the letter and certificate.

Irving, a clerk in the treasury, an Irishman, is the author of the pieces now coming out under the signature of Veritas, and attacking the President. I have long suspected this detestable game was playing by the fiscal party, to place the President on their side.

❧ June the 17th, 1793. At a meeting of the Heads of department at the President's this day, on summons from him, a letter from Mr. Genet of the 15th inst. (addressed to the Secretary of State on the subject of the seizure of a vessel by the Governor of New York, as having been armed, equipped and manned in that port, with a design to cruise on the enemies of France), was read, as also the draught of an answer prepared by the Secretary of State, which was approved.

Read, also, a letter of June 14th from Mr. Hammond to the Secretary of State, desiring to know whether the French privateers, the Citizen Genet, and Sans Culottes, are to be allowed to return or send their prizes into the ports of the United States. It is the opinion that he be informed that they were required to depart to the dominions of their own sovereign, and nothing expressed as to their ulterior proceedings; and that in answer to that part which states that the Sans Culottes had increased its force in the port of Baltimore, and remained there in the avowed intention of watching the motions of a valuable ship now lying there, it be answered that we expect the speedy departure of those privateers will obviate the inconveniences apprehended, and that it will be considered whether any practical arrangements can be adopted to prevent the augmentations of the force of armed vessels.

Thomas Jefferson, Alexander Hamilton, Henry Knox.

❧ June the 20th, 1793. At a meeting this day of the Heads of department at the President's, on summons from him, a letter from Messrs. Viar and Jaudines, dated June 18th, and addressed to the Secretary of State, was read; whereupon it is the opinion that a full detail of the proceedings of the United States with respect to the southern Indians and the Spaniards be prepared, and a justification as to the particular matters charged in the said letter; that this be sent, with all the necessary documents, to our commissioners at the court of Madrid, leaving to them a discretion to change expressions in it which to them may appear likely to give offence in the circumstances under which they may be at the time of receiving it; and that a copy be sent to Mr. Pinckney for his information, and to make such use of the matter it contains as to him should seem expedient; that an answer be written to Messrs. Viar and Jaudines informing them that we shall convey our sentiments on the subject to their court through our commissioners at Madrid, and letting them see that we are not insensible to the style and manner of their communications.

A draught of a letter from the Secretary of State to Mr. Hammond, asking when an answer to his letter of May 29th, 1792, might be expected, was read and approved.

Thomas Jefferson, Alexander Hamilton, Henry Knox.

⋙ July the 5th, 1793. A meeting desired by Alexander Hamilton at my office. Himself, Knox, and myself met accordingly. He said that according to what had been agreed on in presence of the President, in consequence of Mr. Genet's declining to pay the $45,000 at his command in the treasury, to the holders of the St. Domingo bills, we had agreed to pay the holders out of other moneys to that amount; that he found, however, that these bills would amount to $90,000, and the question was whether he should assume $90,000 to be paid out of the September instalment. This, he said, would enable holders to get discounts at the banks, would therefore be equal to ready money, and save them from bankruptcy. Unanimously agreed to. We also agreed to a letter written by General Knox to Governor Mifflin, to have a particular inquiry made whether the Little Sarah is arming, &c., or not. I read also Governor Lee's letter about the Governor of South Carolina's proclamation respecting pestilential disease in West Indies. We are all of opinion the evidence is too slight for interference, and doubt the power to interfere. Therefore let it lie.

Mr. Genet called on me, and read to me very rapidly instructions he had prepared for Michaud, who is going to Kentucky; an address to the inhabitants of Louisiana, and another to those of Canada. In these papers it appears that, besides encouraging those inhabitants to insurrection, he speaks of two generals in Kentucky who have proposed to him to go and take New Orleans, if he will furnish the expense, about £3,000 sterling. He declines advancing it, but promises that sum ultimately for their expenses; proposes that officers shall be commissioned by himself in Kentucky and Louisiana; that they shall rendezvous *out of the territories of the United States,*—suppose in Louisiana, and there making up a battalion to be called the —— of inhabitants of Louisiana and Kentucky, and getting what Indians they could, to undertake the expedition against New Orleans, and then Louisiana to be established into an independent State, connected in commerce with France and the United States; that two frigates shall go into the river Mississippi, and co-operate against New Orleans. The address to Canada was to encourage them to shake off English yoke, to call Indians to their assistance, and to assure them of the friendly dispositions of their neighbors of the United States.

He said he communicated these things to me, not as Secretary of State, but as Mr. Jefferson. I told him that his enticing officers and soldiers from Kentucky to go against Spain, was really putting a halter about their necks; for that they would assuredly be hung if they commenced hostilities against a nation at peace with the United States. That leaving out that article I did not care what insurrections should be excited in Louisiana. He had about a fortnight ago sent me a communication for Michaud as consul of France at Kentucky, and desired an Exequatur. I told him this could not be given, that it was only in the *ports* of the United States they were entitled to consuls, and that if France should have a consul at Kentucky, England and Spain would soon demand the same, and we should have all our interior country filled with foreign agents. He acquiesced, and asked me to return the commission and his note, which I did; but he desired I would give Michaud a letter of introduction for Governor Shelby. I sent him one a day or two after. He now observes to me that in that letter I speak of him only as a person of botanical and natural pursuits, but that he wished the Governor to view him as something more; as a French citizen possessing his confidence. I took back the letter and wrote another.

The Anas

≫ *Memorandum of a Meeting at the State House, Philadelphia, relative to the case of the Little Sarah:* July the 8th, 1793. At a meeting at the State House of the City of Philadelphia, Present: the Secretary of State, the Secretary of the Treasury, the Secretary of War.

It appears that a brigantine, called the Little Sarah, has been fitted out at the port of Philadelphia, with fourteen cannon and all other equipment, indicating that she is intended to cruise under the authority of France, and that she is now lying in the river Delaware, at some place between this city and Mud Island; that a conversation has been had between the Secretary of State and the Minister Plenipotentiary of France, in which conversation the Minister refused to give any explicit assurance that the brigantine would continue until the arrival of the President, and his decision in the case, but made declarations respecting her not being ready to sail within the time of the expected return of the President, from which the Secretary of State infers with confidence, that she will not sail till the President will have an opportunity of considering and determining the case; that in the course of the conversation, the Minister declared that the additional guns which had been taken in by the Little Sarah were French property, but the Governor of Pennsylvania declared that he has good ground to believe that two of her cannon were purchased here of citizens of Philadelphia.

The Governor of Pennsylvania asks advice what steps, under the circumstances, he shall pursue?

The Secretary of the Treasury and the Secretary of War are of opinion, that it is expedient that immediate measures should be taken provisionally for establishing a battery on Mud Island, under cover of a party of militia, with direction that if the brig Sarah should attempt to depart before the pleasure of the President shall be known concerning her, military coercion be employed to arrest and prevent her progress.

The Secretary of State dissents from this opinion.

Reasons for his Dissent: I am against the preceding opinion of the Secretaries of the Treasury and War, for ordering a battery to be erected on Mud Island, and firing on the Little Sarah, an armed vessel of the Republic of France:

Because I am satisfied, from what passed between Mr. Genet and myself at our personal interview yesterday, that the vessel will not be ordered to sail till the return of the President, which, by a letter of this day's post, we may certainly expect within eight and forty hours from this time.

Because the erecting a battery and mounting guns to prevent her passage might cause a departure not now intended, and produce the fact it is meant to prevent.

Because were such battery and guns now in readiness and to fire on her, in the present ardent state of her crew just in the moment of leaving port, it is morally certain that bloody consequences would follow. No one could say how many lives would be lost on both sides, and all experience has shown, that blood once seriously spilled between nation and nation, the contest is continued by subordinate agents, and the door of peace is shut. At this moment, too, we expect in the river twenty of their ships of war, with a fleet of from one hundred to one hundred and fifty of their private vessels, which will arrive at the scene of blood in time to continue it, if not to partake in it.

Because the actual commencement of hostilities against a nation, for such this act may be, is an act of too serious consequence to our countrymen to be brought on their heads by subordinate officers, not chosen by them nor clothed with their confidence; and too presumptuous on the part of those officers, when the chief magistrate, into whose hands the citizens have committed their safety, is within eight and forty hours of his arrival here, and may have an opportunity of judging for himself and them, whether the buying and carrying away two cannon (for according to information, the rest are the nation's own property), is sufficient cause of war between Americans and Frenchmen.

Because, should the vessel, contrary to expectation, depart before the President's arrival, the adverse powers may be told the truth of the case: that she went off contrary to what we had a right to expect; that we shall be justifiable in future cases to measure our confidence accordingly; that for the present we shall demand satisfaction from France, which, with the proof of good faith we have already given, ought to satisfy them. Above all, Great Britain ought not to complain: for, since the date of the order forbidding that any of the belligerent powers should equip themselves in our ports with our arms, these two cannon are all that have escaped the vigilance of our officers on the part of their enemies, while their vessels have carried off more than ten times the number, without any impediment; and if the suggestion be true (and as yet it is but suggestion) that there are fifteen or twenty Americans on board the Little Sarah, who have gone with their own consent, it is equally true that more than ten times that number of Americans are at this moment on board English ships of war, who have been taken forcibly from our merchant vessels at sea or in port, wherever met with, and compelled to bear arms against the friends of their country. And is it less a breach of our neutrality towards France to suffer England to strengthen herself with our force, than towards England to suffer France to do so? And are we equally ready and disposed to sink the British vessels in our ports by way of reprisal for this notorious and avowed practice?

Because it is inconsistent for a nation which has been patiently bearing for ten years the grossest insults and injuries from their late enemies, to rise at a feather against their friends and benefactors; and that, too, in a moment when circumstances have kindled the most ardent affections of the two people towards each other; when the little subjects of displeasure which have arisen are the acts of a particular individual, not yet important enough to have been carried to his government as causes of complaint; are such as nations of moderation and justice settle by negotiation, not making war their first step; are such as that government would correct at a word, if we may judge from the late unequivocal demonstrations of their friendship towards us; and are very slight shades of the acts committed against us by England, which we have been endeavoring to rectify by negotiation, and on which they have never condescended to give any answer to our minister.

Because I would not gratify the combination of kings with the spectacle of the two only republics on earth destroying each other for two cannon; nor would I, for infinitely greater cause, add this country to that combination, turn the scale of contest, and let it be from our hands that the hopes of man received their last stab.

It has been observed that a general order has been already given to stop by force vessels arming contrary to rule in our ports, in which I concurred. I did so because it was highly presumable that the destination of such a vessel would be discovered in some early stage, when there would be few persons on board, these not yet disposed nor prepared to resist, and a small party of militia put aboard would stop the procedure without a marked infraction of the peace. But it is a much more serious thing when a vessel has her full complement of men (here said to be one hundred and twenty), with every preparation and probably with disposition to go through with their enterprise. A serious engagement is then a certain consequence. Besides, an act of force, committed by an officer in a distant port, under general orders, given long ago, to take effect on all cases, and with less latitude of discretion in him, would be a much more negotiable case than a recent order, given by the general government itself (for that is the character we are to assume) on the spot, in the very moment, pointed at this special case, professing full discretion and not using it. This would be a stubborn transaction, not admitting those justifications and explanations which might avert a war, or admitting such only as would be entirely humiliating to the officers giving the order, and to the government itself.

On the whole, respect to the chief magistrate, respect to our countrymen, their lives, interests, and affection, respect to a most friendly nation, who, if we give them the opportunity, will answer our wrongs by correcting and not by repeating them; respect to the most sacred cause that ever man was engaged in, poising maturely the evils which may flow from the commitment of an act which it would be in the power and probably in the temper of subordinate agents to make an act of continued war, and those which may flow from an eight and forty hours suspension of the act, are motives with me for suspending it eight and forty hours, even should we thereby lose the opportunity of committing it altogether.

❧ *Copy of a minute given to the President:* July the 12th, 1793. At a meeting of the Heads of the departments at the President's, on summons from him, and on consideration of various representations from the Minister Plenipotentiary of France and Great Britain, on the subject of vessels arming and arriving in our ports, and of prizes;—it is their opinion that letters be written to the said ministers, informing them that the executive of the United States is desirous of having done what shall be strictly conformable to the treaties of the United States and the laws respecting the said cases; has determined to refer the questions arising therein to persons learned in the laws; that as this reference will occasion some delay, it is expected that, in the meantime, the Little Sarah, or Little Democrat, the ship Jane, and the ship William, in the Delaware, the Citoyen Genet and her prizes, the brigs Lovely-Lass and Prince William Henry, and the brig in the Chesapeake, do not depart till the further order of the President.

That letters be addressed to the judges of the Supreme Court of the United States, requesting their attendance at this place on Thursday the 18th instant, to give their advice on certain matters of public concern, which will be referred to them by the President.

That the Governor be desired to have the ship Jane attended to with vigilance, and if she be found augmenting her force and about to depart, that he cause her to be stopped.

Thomas Jefferson, Alexander Hamilton, Henry Knox.

⋙ *A recapitulation of questions whereon we have given opinions:* Does the treaty with France leave us free to prohibit her from arming vessels in our ports? Thomas Jefferson, Hamilton, Knox, and Randolph—unanimous—it does. As the treaty obliges us to prohibit the enemies of France from arming in our ports, and leaves us free to prohibit France, do not the laws of neutrality oblige us to prohibit her? Same persons answer they do.

How far may a prohibition now declared be retrospective to the vessels armed in Charleston before the prohibition, to wit, the Citoyen Genet and Sans Culottes, and what is to be done with these prizes? Thomas Jefferson,—It cannot be retrospective at all; they may sell their prizes, and continue to act freely as other armed vessels of France. Hamilton and Knox,—The prizes ought to be given up to the English, and the privateers suppressed. Randolph,—They are free to sell their prizes, and the privateers should be ordered away, not to return here till they shall have been to the dominions of their own sovereign, and thereby purged the illegality of their origin. This last opinion was adopted by the President.

Our citizens who have joined in these hostilities against nations at peace with the United States, are they punishable? E. Randolph gave an official opinion—they were. Thomas Jefferson, Hamilton and Knox joined in the opinion. All thought it our duty to have prosecutions instituted against them, that the laws might pronounce on their case. In the first instance, two only were prosecuted merely to try the question, and to satisfy the complaint of the British men; and because it was thought they might have offended unwittingly. But a subsequent armament of a vessel at New York taking place with full knowledge of this prosecution, all the persons engaged in it, citizens and foreigners, were ordered to be prosecuted.

May the prohibition extend to the means of the party arming, or are they only prohibited from using our means for the annoyance of their enemies? Thomas Jefferson of opinion they are free to use their own means, *i.e.*, to mount their own guns, &c. Hamilton and Knox of opinion they are not to put even their own implements or means into a posture of annoyance. The President has as yet not decided this.

May an armed vessel arriving here be prohibited to employ their own citizens found here as seamen or mariners? Thomas Jefferson,— They cannot be prohibited to recruit their own citizens. Hamilton and Knox,—They may and ought to be prohibited. No decision yet by the President.

It appears to me the President wished the Little Sarah had been stopped by military coercion, that is, by firing on her; yet I do not believe he would have ordered it himself had he been here, though he would be glad if we had ordered it. The United States being a ship-building nation, may they sell ships, prepared for war, to both parties? Thomas Jefferson,—They may sell such ships in their ports to both parties, or carry them for sale to the dominions of both parties. E. Randolph of opinion they could not sell them here; and that if they attempted to carry them to the dominions of the parties for sale, they might be seized by the way as *contraband*. Hamilton of same opinion, except that he did not consider them as seizable for contraband, but as the property of a power, making itself a party in the *war* by an aid of such a nature, and consequently that it would be a breach of neutrality.

Hamilton moves that the government of France be desired to recall Mr. Genet. Knox adds that he be in the meantime suspended from his functions. Thomas Jefferson proposes that his correspondence be communicated to his government, with friendly observations. President silent.

≫ July the 15th. Thomas Jefferson, Hamilton and Knox met at the President's. Governor Mifflin had applied to Knox for the loan of four cannon to mount at Mud Island. He informed him he should station a guard of thirty-five militia there, and asked what arrangement for rations the general government had taken. Knox told him nothing could be done as to rations, and he would ask the President for the cannon. In the meantime, he promised him to put the cannon on board a boat, ready to send off as soon as permission was obtained. The President declared his own opinion *first* and fully, that when the orders were given to the government to stop vessels arming, &c., in our ports, even by military force, he took for granted the government would use such diligence as to stop those projects in embryo, and stop them when no force was requisite, or a very small party of militia would suffice; that here was a demand from the government of Pennsylvania to land four cannon under pretext of executing orders of the general government; that if this was granted, we should be immediately applied to by every other governor, and that not for one place only, but for several, and our cannon would be dispersed all over the United States; that for this reason we would refuse the same request to the governors of South Carolina, Virginia, and Rhode Island; that if they erected batteries, they must establish men for them, and would come on us for this too. He did not think the executive had a power to establish permanent guards: he had never looked to anything permanent when the orders were given to the governors, but only an occasional call on small parties of militia in the moments requiring it. These sentiments were so entirely my own, that I did little more than combat on the same grounds the opinions of Hamilton and Knox. The latter said he would be ready to lend an equal number to every government to carry into effect orders of such importance; and Hamilton, that he would be willing to lend them in cases where they happened to be as near the place where they were to be mounted.

Hamilton submitted the purchase of a large quantity of saltpetre, which would outrun the funds destined to objects of that class by Congress. We were unanimous we ought to venture on it, and to the procuring supplies of military stores in the present circumstances, and take on us the responsibility to Congress, before whom it should be laid.

The President was fully of the same opinion.

In the above case of the cannon, the President gave no final order while I remained; but I saw that he was so impressed with the disagreeableness of taking them out of the boat again, that he would yield. He spoke sharply to Knox for having put them in that position without consulting him, and declared that, but for that circumstance, he would not have hesitated one moment to refuse them.

July the 18th, 1793. Lear calls on me. I told him that Irving, an Irishman, and a writer in the treasury, who, on a former occasion, had given the most decisive proofs of his devotion to his principal, was the author of the pieces signed Veritas; and I wished he could get at some of Irving's acquaintances and inform himself of the fact, as the person who told me of it would not permit the name of his informer to be mentioned; [*Note.*—Beckley told me of it, and he had it from Swaine, the printer to whom the pieces were delivered]; that I had long before suspected this excessive foul play in that party, of writing themselves in the character of the most exaggerated democrats, and incorporating with it a great deal of abuse on the President, to make him believe it was that party who were his enemies, and so throw him entirely into the scale of the monocrats. Lear said he no longer ago than yesterday expressed to the President his suspicions of the artifices of that party to work on him. He mentioned the following fact as a proof of their writing in the character of their adversaries; to wit, the day after the little incident of Richet's toasting "the man of the people" (see the gazettes), Mrs. Washington was at Mrs. Powel's who mentioned to her that when the toast was given, there was a good deal of disapprobation appeared in the audience, and that many put on their hats and went out; on inquiry, he had not found the fact true, and yet it was put into ———'s paper, and written under the character of a republican, though he is satisfied it is altogether a slander of the monocrats. He mentioned this to the President, but he did not mention to him the following fact, which he knows; that in New York, the last summer, when the parties of Jay and Clinton were running so high, it was an agreed point with the former, that if any circumstances should ever bring it to a question, whether to drop Hamilton or the President, they had decided to drop the President. He said that lately one of the loudest pretended friends to the government, damned it, and said it was good for nothing, that it could not support itself, and it was time to put it down and set up a better; and yet the same person, in speaking to the President, puffed off that party as the only friends to the government. He said he really feared, that by their artifices and industry, they would aggravate the President so much against the republicans, as to separate him from the body of the people. I told him what the same cabals had decided to do, if the President had refused his assent to the bank bill; also what Brockhurst Livingston said to ———, that Hamilton's life was much more precious to the community than the President's.

≫ July the 29th, 1793. At a meeting at the President's on account of the British letter-of-marque, ship Jane, said to have put up waste boards, to have pierced two port holes, and mounted two cannon (which she brought in) on new carriages which she did not bring in, and consequently having sixteen, instead of fourteen, guns mounted, it was agreed that a letter-of-marque, or vessel armé en guerre, and en marchandise, is not a privateer, and therefore not to be ordered out of our ports. It was agreed by Hamilton, Knox, and myself, that the case of such a vessel does not depend on the treaties, but on the law of nations. Edmund Randolph thought, as she had a mixed character of merchant vessel and privateer, she might be considered under the treaty; but this being overruled, the following paper was written:

Rules proposed by Attorney General: 1st. That all equipments purely for the accommodation of vessels, as merchantmen, be admitted. [Agreed.] 2d. That all equipments, doubtful in their nature, and applicable equally to commerce or war, be admitted, as producing too many minutia. [Agreed.] 3d. That all equipments, solely adapted to military objects, be prohibited. [Agreed.]

Rules proposed by the Secretary of the Treasury: 1st. That the original arming and equipping of vessels for military service, offensive or defensive, in the ports of the United States, be considered as prohibited to all. [Agreed.] 2d. That vessels which were armed before their coming into our ports, shall not be permitted to augment these equipments in the ports of the United States, but may repair or replace any military equipments which they had when they began their voyage for the United States; that this, however, shall be with the exception of privateers of the parties opposed to France, who shall not refit or repair. [Negatived—the Secretary of the Treasury only holding the opinion.] 3d. That for convenience, vessels armed and commissioned before they come into our ports, may engage their own citizens, not being inhabitants of the United States. [Agreed.]

I subjoined the following:

I concur in the rules proposed by the Attorney General, as far as respects materials or means of annoyance furnished by us; and I should be for an additional rule, that as to means or materials brought into this country, and belonging to themselves, they are free to use them.

≫ August the 1st. Met at the President's, to consider what was to be done with Mr. Genet. All his correspondence with me was read over. The following propositions were made: 1. That a full statement of Mr. Genet's conduct be made in a letter to G. Morris, and be sent with his correspondence, to be communicated to the Executive Council of France; the letter to be so prepared, as to serve for the form of communication to the Council. Agreed unanimously. 2. That in that letter his recall be required. Agreed by all, though I expressed a preference of expressing that desire with great delicacy; the others were for peremptory terms. 3. To send him off. This was proposed by Knox; but rejected by every other. 4. To write a letter to Mr. Genet, the same in substance with that written to G. Morris, and let him know we had applied for his recall. I was against this, because I thought it would render him extremely active in his plans, and endanger confusion. But I was overruled by the other three gentlemen and the President. 5. That a publication of the whole correspondence, and statement of the proceedings, should be made by way of appeal to the people. Hamilton made a jury speech of three-quarters of an hour, as inflammatory and declamatory as if he had been speaking to a jury. E. Randolph opposed it. I chose to leave the contest between them. Adjourned to next day.

>>> August the 2d. Met again. Hamilton spoke again three-quarters of an hour. I answered on these topics. *Object* of the appeal.—The democratic society; this the great circumstance of alarm; afraid it would extend its connections over the continent; chiefly meant for the local object of the ensuing election of Governor. If left alone, would die away after that is over. If opposed, if proscribed, would give it importance and vigor; would give it a new object, and multitudes would join it merely to assert the right of voluntary associations. That the measure was calculated to make the President assume the station of the head of a party, instead of the head of the nation. *Plan* of the appeal.—To consist of *facts* and the *decisions* of the President. As to facts we are agreed; but as to the decisions, there have been great differences of opinion among us. Sometimes as many opinions as persons. This proves there will be ground to attack the decisions. Genet will appeal also; it will become a contest between the President and Genet—anonymous writers—will be same difference of opinion in *public*, as in our cabinet—will be same difference in *Congress*, for it must be laid before them—would, therefore, work very unpleasantly *at home*. How would it work *abroad?* France—unkind—after such proofs of her friendship, should rely on that friendship, and her justice. Why appeal to the world? Friendly nations always negotiate little differences in private. Never appeal

to the world, but when they appeal to the sword. Confederacy of Pill-nitz was to overthrow the government of France. The interference of France to disturb other governments and excite insurrections, was a measure of reprisal. Yet these Princes have been able to make it be-lieved to be the system of France. Colonel Hamilton supposes Mr. Genet's proceedings here are in pursuance of that system; and we are so to declare it to the world, and to add our testimony to this base calumny of the Princes. What a triumph to them to be backed by our testimony. What a fatal stroke at the cause of liberty; *et tu Brute.* We indispose the French government, and they will retract their offer of the treaty of commerce. The President manifestly inclined to the appeal to the people.* Knox, in a foolish incoherent sort of a speech, introduced the pasquinade lately printed, called the funeral of George W—n, and James W—n, King and Judge, &c., where the President was placed on a guillotine. The President was much inflamed; got into one of those passions when he cannot command himself; ran on much on the per-sonal abuse which had been bestowed on him; defied any man on earth to produce one single act of his since he had been in the government, which was not done on the purest motives; that he had never repented but once the having slipped the moment of resigning his office, and that

* He said that Mr. Morris, taking a family dinner with him the other day, went largely, and of his own accord, into this subject; advised this appeal, and promised, if the President adopted it, that he would support it himself, and engage for all his connections. The President repeated this twice, and with an air of importance. Now, Mr. Morris has no family connections: he engaged them for his political friends. This shows that the President has not confidence enough in the virtue and good sense of mankind, to confide in a government bottomed on them, and thinks other props necessary.
—T.J.

was every moment since; that *by God* he had rather be in his grave than in his present situation; that he had rather be on his farm than to be made *Emperor of the world*; and yet that they were charging him with wanting to be a King. That that *rascal Freneau* sent him three of his papers every day, as if he thought he would become the distributor of his papers; that he could see in this, nothing but an impudent design to insult him: he ended in this high tone. There was a pause. Some difficulty in resuming our question; it was, however, after a little while, presented again, and he said there seemed to be no necessity for deciding it now; the propositions before agreed on might be put into a train of execution, and perhaps events would show whether the appeal would be necessary or not. He desired we would meet at my office the next day, to consider what should be done with the vessels armed in our ports by Mr. Genet, and their prizes.

August the 3d. We met. The President wrote to take our opinions, whether Congress should be called. Knox pronounced at once against it. Randolph was against it. Hamilton said his judgment was against it, but that if any two were for it, or against it, he would join them to make a majority. I was for it. We agreed to give separate opinions to the President. Knox said we should have had fine work, if Congress had been sitting these last two months. The fool thus let out the secret. Hamilton endeavored to patch up the indiscretion of this blabber, by saying "he did not know; he rather thought they would have strengthened the executive arm." It is evident they do not wish to lengthen the session of the *next Congress*, and probably they particularly wish it should not meet till Genet is gone. At this meeting I received a letter from Mr. Remson at New York, informing me of the event of the combat between the Ambuscade and the Boston. Knox broke out into the most unqualified abuse of Captain Courtany. Hamilton, with less fury, but with the deepest vexation, loaded him with censures. Both showed the most unequivocal mortification at the event.

August the 6th, 1793. The President calls on me at my house in the country, and introduces my letter of July the 31st, announcing that

I should resign at the close of the next month. He again expressed his repentance at not having resigned himself, and how much it was increased by seeing that he was to be deserted by those on whose aid he had counted; that he did not know where he should look to find characters to fill up the offices; that mere talents did not suffice for the department of State, but it required a person conversant in foreign affairs, perhaps acquainted with foreign courts; that without this, the best talents would be awkward and at a loss. He told me that Colonel Hamilton had three or four weeks ago written to him, informing him that private as well as public reasons had brought him to the determination to retire, and that he should do it towards the close of the next session. He said he had often before intimated dispositions to resign, but never as decisively before; that he supposed he had fixed on the latter part of next session, to give an opportunity to Congress to examine into his conduct; that our going out at times so different, increased his difficulty; for if he had both places to fill at once, he might consult both the particular talents and geographical situation of our successors. He expressed great apprehensions at the fermentation which seemed to be working in the mind of the public; that many descriptions of persons, actuated by different causes, appeared to be uniting; what it would end in he knew not; a new Congress was to assemble, more numerous, perhaps of a different spirit; the first expressions of their sentiments would be important; if I would only stay to the end of that, it would relieve him considerably.

I expressed to him my excessive repugnance to public life, the particular uneasiness of my situation in this place, where the laws of society oblige me always to move exactly in the circle which I know to bear me peculiar hatred; that is to say, the wealthy aristocrats, the merchants connected closely with England, the new created paper fortunes; that thus surrounded, my words were caught, multiplied, misconstrued, and even fabricated and spread abroad to my injury; that he saw also, that there was such an opposition of views between myself and another part of the administration, as to render it peculiarly unpleasing, and to destroy the necessary harmony. Without knowing the views of what is called the republican party here, or having any com-

munication with them, I could undertake to assure him, from my intimacy with that party in the late Congress, that there was not a view in
the republican party as spread over the United States, which went to
the frame of the government; that I believed the next Congress would
attempt nothing material, but to render their own body independent;
that that party were firm in their dispositions to support the government; that the manœuvres of Mr. Genet might produce some little
embarrassment, but that he would be abandoned by the republicans the
moment they knew the nature of his conduct; and on the whole, no
crisis existed which threatened anything.

He said he believed the views of the republican party were perfectly
pure, but when men put a machine into motion, it is impossible for them
to stop it exactly where they would choose, or to say where it will stop.
That the constitution we have is an excellent one, if we can keep it
where it is; that it was, indeed, supposed there was a party disposed to
change it into a monarchical form, but that he could conscientiously
declare there was not a man in the United States who would set his
face more decidedly against it than himself. Here I interrupted him, by
saying, "No rational man in the United States suspects you of any other
disposition; but there does not pass a week, in which we cannot prove
declarations dropping from the monarchical party that our government
is good for nothing, is a milk and water thing which cannot support
itself, we must knock it down, and set up something of more energy."
He said if that was the case, he thought it a proof of their insanity, for
that the republican spirit of the Union was so manifest and so solid,
that it was astonishing how anyone could expect to move it.

He returned to the difficulty of naming my successor; he said Mr.
Madison would be his first choice, but that he had always expressed to
him such a decision against public office, that he could not expect he
would undertake it. Mr. Jay would prefer his present office. He said
that Mr. Jay had a great opinion of the talents of Mr. King; that there
was also Mr. Smith of South Carolina, and E. Rutledge; but he observed, that name whom he would, some objections would be made,
some would be called speculators, some one thing, some another; and
he asked me to mention any characters occurring to me. I asked him if

Governor Johnson of Maryland had occurred to him? He said he had; that he was a man of great good sense, an honest man, and he believed, clear of speculations; but this, says he, is an instance of what I was observing; with all these qualifications, Governor Johnson, from a want of familiarity with foreign affairs, would be in them like a fish out of water; everything would be new to him, and he awkward in everything. I confessed to him that I had considered Johnson rather as fit for the Treasury Department. Yes, says he, for that he would be the fittest appointment that could be made; he is a man acquainted with figures, and having as good a knowledge of the resources of this country as any man. I asked him if Chancellor Livingston had occurred to him? He said yes; but he was from New York, and to appoint him while Hamilton was in, and before it should be known he was going out, would excite a newspaper conflagration, as the ultimate arrangement would not be known. He said McLurg had occurred to him as a man of first-rate abilities, but it is said that he is a speculator. He asked me what sort of a man Wolcott was. I told him I knew nothing of him myself; I had heard him characterized as a cunning man. I asked him whether some person could not take my office *per interim*, till he should make an appointment, as Mr. Randolph, for instance. Yes, says he, but there you would raise the expectation of keeping it, and I do not know that he is fit for it, nor what is thought of Mr. Randolph. I avoided noticing the last observation, and he put the question to me directly. I then told him, I went into society so little as to be unable to answer it: I knew that the embarrassments in his private affairs had obliged him to use expedients, which had injured him with the merchants and shop-keepers, and affected his character of independence; that these embarrassments were serious, and not likely to cease soon. He said if I would only stay in till the end of another quarter (the last of December) it would get us through the difficulties of this year, and he was satisfied that the affairs of Europe would be settled with this campaign; for that either France would be overwhelmed by it, or the confederacy would give up the contest. By that time, too, Congress will have manifested its character and view. I told him that I had set my private affairs in motion in a line which had powerfully called for my presence the last spring, and that they had suffered immensely from my not going home; that I had now calculated them to my return in the fall, and to fail in going then, would be the loss of another year, and prejudicial beyond measure. I asked him whether he could not name Governor Johnson to my office, under an express arrangement that at the close of the session he should take that of the Treasury. He said that men never chose to descend; that being once in a higher department, he would not like to go into a lower one. He asked me whether I could not arrange my affairs by going home. I told him I did not think the public business would admit of it; that there never was a day now in which the absence of the Secretary of State would not be inconvenient to the public. And he concluded by desiring that I would take two or three days to consider whether I could not stay in till the end of another quarter, for that like a man going to the gallows, he was willing to put it off as long as he could; but if I persisted, he must then look about him and make up his mind to do the best he could; and so he took leave.

⟫ August the 20th. We met at the President's to examine by paragraphs the draught of a letter I had prepared to Gouverneur Morris on the conduct of Mr. Genet. There was no difference of opinion on any part of it, except on this expression, "An attempt to embroil both, to add still another nation to the enemies of his country, and to draw on both a reproach which it is hoped will never stain the history of either, that of *liberty warring on herself.*" Hamilton moved to strike out these words, "that of liberty warring on herself." He urged generally that it would give offence to the combined powers; that it amounted to a declaration that they were warring on liberty; that we were not called on to declare that the cause of France was that of liberty; that he had at first been with them with all his heart, but that he had long since left them, and was not for encouraging the idea here, that the cause of France was the cause of liberty in general, or could have either connection or influence in our affairs. Knox, according to custom, jumped plump into all his opinions. The President, with a good deal of positiveness, declared in favor of the expression; that he considered the pursuit of France to be that of liberty, however they might sometimes fail of the best means of obtaining it; that he had never at any time entertained a doubt of their ultimate success, if they hung well together; and that as to their dissensions, there were such contradictory accounts given, that no one could tell what to believe. I observed that it had been supposed among us all along that the present letter might become public; that we had therefore three parties to attend to,—1st, France; 2d, her enemies; 3d, the people of the United States; that as to the enemies of France, it ought not to offend them because the passage objected to, only spoke of an attempt to make the United States, a *free nation*, war on France, a *free nation*, which would be liberty warring against liberty; that as to France, we were taking so harsh a measure (desiring her to recall her minister) that a precedent for it could scarcely be found; that we knew that minister would represent to his government that our executive was hostile to liberty, leaning to monarchy, and would endeavor to parry the charges on himself, by rendering suspicious the source from which they flowed; that, therefore, it was essential to satisfy France, not only of our friendship to her, but our attachment to the general cause of liberty, and to hers in particular; that as to the people of the United States, we knew there were suspicions abroad that the executive, in some of its parts, was tainted with a hankering after monarchy, an indisposition towards liberty, and towards the French cause; and that it was important, by an explicit declaration, to remove these suspicions, and restore the confidence of the people in their government. Randolph opposed the passage on nearly the same ground with Hamilton. He added, that he thought it had been agreed that this correspondence should contain no expressions which could give offence to either party. I replied that it had been my opinion in the beginning of the correspondence, that while we were censuring the conduct of the French minister, we should make the most cordial declarations of friendship to them; that in the first letter or two of the correspondence, I had inserted expressions of that kind, but that himself and the other two gentlemen had struck them out; that I thereupon conformed to their opinions in my subsequent letters, and had carefully avoided the insertion of a single term of friendship to the French nation, and the letters were as dry and husky as if written between the generals of two enemy nations; that on the present occasion, however, it had been agreed that such expressions ought to be inserted in the letter now under consideration, and I had accordingly charged it pretty well with them; that I had further thought it essential to satisfy the French and our own citizens of the light in which we viewed their cause, and of our fellow feeling for the general cause of liberty, and had ventured only four words on the subject; that there was not from beginning to end of the letter one other expression or word in favor of liberty, and I should think it singular, at least, if the single passage of that character should be struck out.

The President again spoke. He came into the idea that attention was due to the two parties who had been mentioned, France and the United States; that as to the former, thinking it certain their affairs would issue in a government of some sort—of considerable freedom—it was the only nation with whom our relations could be counted on; that as to the United States, there could be no doubt of their universal attachment to the cause of France, and of the solidity of their republicanism. He declared his strong attachment to the expression, but finally left it to us to accommodate. It was struck out, of course, and the expressions of affection in the context were a good deal taken down.

≫ August the 23d, 1793. In consequence of my note of yesterday to the President, a meeting was called this day at his house to determine what should be done with the proposition of France to treat. The importance of the matter was admitted; and being of so old a date as May 22d, we might be accused of neglecting the interests of the United States, to have left it so long unanswered, and it could not be doubted Mr. Genet would avail himself of this inattention. The President declared it had not been inattention, that it had been the subject of conversation often at our meetings, and the delay had proceeded from the difficulty of the thing.

If the struggles of France should end in the old despotism, the formation of such a treaty with the present government would be a matter of offence; if it should end in any kind of free government, he should be very unwilling, by inattention to their advances, to give offence, and lose the opportunity of procuring terms so advantageous to our country. He was, therefore, for writing to Mr. Morris to get the powers of Mr. Genet renewed to his successor. [As he had expressed this opinion to me the afternoon before, I had prepared the draught of a letter accordingly.] But how to explain the delay? The Secretary of the Treasury observed on the letter of the National Convention, that as it did not seem to require an answer, and the matters it contained would occasion embarrassment if answered, he should be against answering it; that he should be for writing to Mr. Morris, mentioning our readiness to treat with them, and suggesting a renewal of Mr. Genet's powers to his successor, but not in as strong terms as I had done in my draught of the letter—not as a thing anxiously wished for by us, lest it should suggest to them the asking a price; and he was for my writing to Mr. Genet *now*, an answer to his letter of May 22d, referring to the meeting of the Senate the entering on the treaty. Knox concurred with him, the Attorney General also,—except that he was against suggesting the renewal of Mr. Genet's powers, because that would amount to a declaration that we would treat with that government, would commit us to lay the subject before the Senate, and his principle had ever been to do no act, not unavoidably necessary, which, in the event of a counter revolution, might offend the future governing powers of that country. I stated to them that having observed from our conversations that the propositions to treat might not be acceded to immediately, I had endeavored to prepare Mr. Genet for it, by taking occasion in conversations to apprize him of the control over treaties which our constitution had given to the Senate; that though this was indirectly done (because not having been authorized to say anything official on the subject, I did not venture to commit myself directly), yet, on some subsequent conversation, I found it had struck him exactly as I had wished; for, speaking on some other matter, he mentioned incidentally his propositions to treat, and said, however, as I know now that you cannot take up that subject till the meeting of the Senate, I shall say no more about it now, and so proceeded with his other subject, which I do not now recollect. I said I thought it possible by recalling the substance of these conversations to Mr. Genet, in a letter to be written now, I might add that the Executive had at length come to a conclusion, that on account of the importance of the matter, they would await the meeting of the Senate; but I pressed strongly the urging Mr. Morris to procure a renewal of Genet's powers, that we might not lose the chance of obtaining so advantageous a treaty. Edmund Randolph had argued against our acceding to it, because it was too advantageous; so much so that they would certainly break it, and it might become the cause of war. I answered that it would be easy, in the course of the negotiation, to cure it of its inequality by giving some compensation; but I had no fear of their revoking it, that the islanders themselves were too much interested in the concessions ever to suffer them to be revoked; that the best thinkers in France had long been of opinion that it would be for the interest of the mother country to let the colonies obtain subsistence wherever they could cheapest; that I was confident the present struggles in France would end in a free government of some sort, and that such a government would consider itself as growing out of the present one, and respect its treaties. The President recurred to the awkwardness of writing a letter now to Mr. Genet, in answer to his of May 22d; that it would certainly be construed as merely done with a design of exculpation of ourselves, and he would thence inculpate us. The more we reflected on this, the more the justice of the observation struck us. Hamilton and myself came into it—Knox still for the letter—Randolph half for it, half against it, according to custom.

It was at length agreed I should state the substance of my verbal observations to Mr. Genet, in a letter to Mr. Morris, and let them be considered as the answer intended; for being from the Secretary of State, they might be considered as official, though not in writing.

It is evident that taking this ground for their future justification to France and to the United States, they were sensible they had censurably neglected these overtures of treaty; for not only what I had said to Mr. Genet was without authority from them, but was never communicated to them till this day. To rest the justification of delay on answers given, it is true in time; but of which they had no knowledge till now, is an ostensible justification only.

⇶ September the 4th, 1793. At a meeting held some days ago, some letters from the Governor of Georgia were read, in which a consultation of officers, and a considerable expedition against the Creeks was proposed. We were all of opinion no such expedition should be undertaken. My reasons were that such a war might bring on a Spanish, and even an English war; that for this reason the aggressions of the Creeks

had been laid before the last Congress, and they had not chosen to declare war, therefore the Executive should not take on itself to do it; and that according to the opinions of Pickens and Blount, it was too late in the season.

I thought, however, that a temperate and conciliatory letter should be written to the Governor, in order that we might retain the disposition of the people of the State to assist in an expedition when undertaken. The other gentlemen thought a strong letter of disapprobation should be written. Such a one was this day produced, strong and reprehendatory enough, in which I thought were visible the personal enmities of Knox and Hamilton, against Telfair, Gun, and Jackson—the two last having been of the council of officers. The letter passed without objection, being of the complexion before determined.

Wayne's letter was read, proposing that six hundred militia should set out from Fort Pitt to attack certain Miami towns, while he marched against the principal towns. The President disapproved it, because of the difficulty of concerted movements at six hundred miles distance; because these six hundred men might, and probably would have the whole force of the Indians to contend with; and because the object was not worth the risking such a number of men. We all concurred. It appeared to me, further, that to begin an expedition from Fort Pitt, the very first order for which is to be given now, when we have reason to believe Wayne advanced as far as Fort Jefferson, would be either too late for his movements, or would retard them very injuriously. [*Note.* —The letters from the Commissioners were now read, announcing the refusal of the Indians to treat, unless the Ohio were made the boundary; and that they were on their return.]

A letter from Governor Clinton read, informing of his issuing a warrant to arrest Governor Galbaud, at the request of the French Consul, and that he was led to interfere because the judge of the district lived at Albany. It was proposed to write to the judge of the district, that the place of his residence was not adapted to his duties; and to Clinton, that Galbaud was not liable to arrest. Hamilton said, that by the laws of New York, the Governor has the powers of a justice of peace, and had issued the warrant as such.

I was against writing letters to judiciary officers. I thought them independent of the Executive, not subject to its coercion, and, therefore, not obliged to attend to its admonitions.

The other three were for writing the letters. They thought it the duty of the President to see that the laws were executed; and if he found a failure in so important an officer, to communicate it to the legislature for impeachment.

Edmund Randolph undertook to write the letters, and I am to sign them as if mine. The President brought forward the subject of the ports, and thought a new demand of answers should be made to Mr. Hammond. As we had not Mr. Hammond's last answer (of June 20th) on that subject, agreed to let it lie over to Monday.

Hammond proposed, that on Monday we should take into consideration the fortification of the rivers and ports of the United States, and that though the Executive could not undertake to do it, preparatory surveys should be made to be laid before Congress, to be considered on Monday.

The letters to Genet covering a copy of mine to Gouv. Morris—

of —— to the French consuls, threatening the revocation of their Exequaturs—to Mr. Pinckney on the additional instructions of Great Britain to their navy for shipping our corn, flour, &c., and to Gouv. Morris on the similar order of the French National Assembly, are to be ready on Monday.

My letter to Mr. Hammond, in answer to his of August 30th, was read and approved. Hamilton wished not to narrow the ground of compensation so much as to cases after August 7th. Knox joined him, and by several observations showed he did not know what the question was. He could not comprehend that the letter of August 7th, which promised compensation (because we had not used all the means in our power for restricting), would not be contradicted by a refusal to compensate in cases after August 7th, where we should naturally use all the means in our power for restriction, and these means should be insufficient. The letter was agreed to on Mr. Randolph's opinion and mine; Hamilton acquiescing, Knox opposing.

➤➤ At sundry meetings of the Heads of departments and Attorney General, from the 1st to the 28th of November, 1793, at the President's, several matters were agreed upon, as stated in the following letters from the Secretary of State, to wit:

November the 8th. Circular letter to the representatives of France, Great Britain, Spain, and the United Netherlands, fixing provisionally the extent of our jurisdiction into the sea at a sea league.

10th. Circular letter to the district attorneys, notifying the same, and committing to them the taking depositions in those cases.

10th. Circular to the foreign representatives, notifying how depositions are to be taken in those cases.

The substance of the preceding letters was agreed to by all; the rough draughts were submitted to them and approved.

November the 14th. To Mr. Hammond, that the United States are not bound to restore the Rochampton. This was agreed by all. The rough draught was submitted to and approved by Colonel Hamilton and Mr. Randolph. General Knox was on a visit to Trenton.

10th. Letters to Mr. Genet and Hammond, and the 14th to Mr. Hollingsworth, for taking depositions in the cases of the Conningham and Pilgrim.

13th. Ditto, to Mr. Genet, Hammond, and Bowle, for depositions in the case of the William.

14th. Ditto, to Hollingsworth, to ascertain whether Mr. Moissonier had passed sentence on the Rochampton and Pilgrim.

These last-mentioned letters of the 10th, 13th, and 14th were, as to their substance, agreed to by all, the draughts were only communicated to Mr. Randolph, and approved by him.

November the 13th. To Mr. Hammond, inquiring when we shall have an answer on the inexecution of the treaty. The substance agreed by all. The letter was sent off without communication, none of the gentlemen being at Germantown.

22d. To Mr. Genet, returning the commissions of Pennevert and Chervi, because not addressed to the President.

22d. To Mr. Genet, inquiring whether the Lovely-Lass, Prince William Henry, and Jane, of Dublin, have been given up; and if not, requiring that they be restored to owners. These were agreed to by all, as to their matter, and the letters themselves were submitted before they were sent to the President, the Secretary of War, and the Attorney General.

22d. To Mr. Gore, for authentic evidence of Dannery's protest on the President's revocation of Duplaine's Exequatur. The substance agreed by all. The letter sent off before communication. *November 23d, 1793. Thomas Jefferson, Henry Knox, Edmund Randolph, Alexander Hamilton.*

⇒ November the 5th, 1793. E. Randolph tells me, that Hamilton, in conversation with him yesterday, said, "Sir, if all the people in America were now assembled, and to call on me to say whether I am a friend to the French revolution, I would declare that *I have it in abhorrence.*"

⇒ November the 8th, 1793. At a conference at the President's, where I read several letters of Mr. Genet; on finishing one of them, I asked what should be the answer? The President thereupon took occasion to observe, that Mr. Genet's conduct continued to be of so extraordinary a nature, that he meant to propose to our serious consideration, whether he should not have his functions discontinued, and be ordered away? He went lengthily into observations on his conduct, to raise against the executive, 1, the people; 2, the State governments; 3, the Congress. He showed he felt the venom of Genet's pen, but declared he would not choose his insolence should be regarded any further, than as might be thought to affect the honor of the country. Hamilton and Knox readily and zealously argued for dismissing Mr. Genet. Randolph opposed it with firmness, and pretty lengthily. The President replied to him lengthily, and concluded by saying he did not wish to have the thing hastily decided, but that we should consider of it, and give our opinions on his return from Reading and Lancaster.

Accordingly, November the 18th, we met at his house; read new volumes of Genet's letters, received since the President's departure; then took up the discussion of the subjects of communication to Congress. 1. The Proclamation. E. Randolph read the statement he had prepared; Hamilton did not like it; said much about his own views; that the President had a right to declare his opinion to our citizens and foreign nations; that it was not the interest of this country to join in the war, and that we were under no obligation to join in it; that though the declaration would not legally bind Congress, yet the President had a right to give his opinion of it, and he was against any explanation in the speech, which should yield that he did not intend that foreign nations should consider it as a declaration of neutrality, future as well as present; that he understood it as meant to give them that sort of assurance and satisfaction, and to say otherwise now, would be a deception on them. He was for the President's using such expressions, as should neither affirm his right to make such a declaration to foreign nations, nor yield it. Randolph and myself opposed the right of the President to declare anything future on the question, shall there or shall there not be war, and that no such thing was intended; that Hamilton's construction of the effect of the proclamation, would have been a determination of the question of the *guarantee*, which we both denied to have intended, and I had at the time declared the executive incompetent to. Randolph said he meant that foreign nations should understand it as an intimation

of the President's opinion, that neutrality would be our interest. I declared my meaning to have been, that foreign nations should understand no such thing; that on the contrary, I would have chosen them to be doubtful, and to come and bid for our neutrality. I admitted the President, having received the nation at the close of Congress in a state of peace, was bound to preserve them in that state till Congress should meet again, and might proclaim anything which went no farther. The President declared he never had an idea that he could bind Congress against declaring war, or that anything contained in his proclamation could look beyond the first day of their meeting. His main view was to keep our people in peace; he apologized for the use of the term neutrality in his answers, and justified it, by having submitted the first of them (that to the merchants, wherein it was used) to our consideration, and we had not objected to the term. He concluded in the end, that Colonel Hamilton should prepare a paragraph on this subject for the speech, and it should then be considered. We were here called to dinner.

After dinner, the *renvoi* of Genet was proposed by himself. I opposed it on these topics. France, the only nation on earth sincerely our friend. The measure so harsh a one, that no precedent is produced where it has not been followed by war. Our messenger has now been gone eighty-four days; consequently, we may hourly expect the return, and to be relieved by their revocation of him. Were it now resolved on, it would be eight or ten days before the matter on which the order should be founded, could be selected, arranged, discussed, and forwarded. This would bring us within four or five days of the meeting of Congress. Would it not be better to wait and see how the pulse of that body, new as it is, would beat? They are with us now, probably, but such a step as this may carry many over to Genet's side. Genet will not obey the order, &c., &c. The President asked me what I would do if Genet sent the accusation to us to be communicated to Congress, as he threatened in the letter to Moultrie? I said I would not send it to Congress; but either put it in the newspapers, or send it back to him to be published if he pleased. Other questions and answers were put and returned in a quicker altercation than I ever before saw the President use. Hamilton was for the *renvoi;* spoke much of the dignity of the nations; that they were now to form their character; that our conduct now would tempt or deter other foreign ministers from treating us in the same manner; touched on the President's personal feelings; did not believe France would make it a cause of war; if she did, we ought to do what was right, and meet the consequences, &c. Knox on the same side, and said he thought it very possible Mr. Genet would either declare us a department of France, or levy troops here and endeavor to reduce us to obedience. Randolph of my opinion, and argued chiefly on the resurrection of popularity to Genet, which might be produced by this measure. That at present he was dead in the public opinion, if we would but leave him so. The President lamented there was not unanimity among us; that as it was, we had left him exactly where we found him; and so it ended.

⋙ November the 21st. We met at the President's. The manner of explaining to Congress the intentions of the proclamation, was the matter of debate. Randolph produced his way of stating it. This expressed its views to have been, 1, to keep our citizens quiet; 2, to intimate to foreign nations that it was the President's opinion, that the interests and dispositions of this country were for peace. Hamilton produced his statement, in which he declared his intention to be, to say nothing which could be laid hold of for any purpose; to leave the proclamation to explain itself. He entered pretty fully into all the argumentation of Pacificus; he justified the right of the President to declare his opinion for a *future neutrality*, and that there existed no circumstances to oblige the United States to enter into the war on account of the guarantee; and that in agreeing to the proclamation, he meant it to be understood as conveying both those declarations; *viz.*, neutrality, and that the *casus fœderis** on the guarantee did not exist. He admitted the Congress might declare war, notwithstanding these declarations of the President. In like manner, they might declare war in the face of a treaty, and in direct infraction of it. Among other positions laid down by him, this was with great positiveness; that the constitution having given power to the President and Senate to make treaties, they might make a treaty of neutrality which should take from Congress the right to declare war in that particular case, and that under the form of a treaty they might exercise any powers whatever, even those exclusively given by the constitution to the House of Representatives. Randolph opposed this position, and seemed to think that where they undertook to do acts by treaty (as to settle a tariff of duties), which were exclusively given to the Legislature, that an act of the Legislature would be necessary to confirm them, as happens in England, when a treaty interferes with duties established by law. I insisted that in giving to the President and Senate a power to make treaties, the constitution meant only to authorize them to carry into effect, by way of treaty, any powers they might constitutionally exercise. I was sensible of the weak points in this position, but there were still weaker in the other hypothesis; and if it be impossible to discover a rational measure of authority to have been given by this clause, I would rather suppose that the cases which my hypothesis would leave unprovided, were not thought of by the convention, or if thought of, could not be agreed on, or were thought of and deemed unnecessary to be invested in the government. Of this last description, were treaties of neutrality, treaties offensive and defensive, &c. In every event, I would rather construe so narrowly as to oblige the nation to amend, and thus declare what powers they would agree to yield, than too broadly, and indeed, so broadly as to enable the executive and Senate to do things which the constitution forbids. On the question, which form of explaining the principles of the proclamation should be adopted, I declared for Randolph's, though it gave to that instrument more objects than I had contemplated. Knox declared for Hamilton's. The President said he had had but one object, the keep-

* I.e., a case within its provisions.

ing our people quiet till Congress should meet; that nevertheless, to declare he did not mean a declaration of neutrality, in the technical sense of the phrase, might perhaps be crying *peccavi* before he was charged. However, he did not decide between the two draughts.

⮆ November the 23d. At the President's. Present, Knox, Randolph, and Th: Jefferson. Subject, the heads of the speech. One was, a proposition to Congress to fortify the principal harbors. I opposed the expediency of the General Government's undertaking it, and the expediency of the President's proposing it. It was amended, by substituting a proposition to adopt means for enforcing respect to the jurisdiction of the United States within its waters. It was proposed to recommend the establishment of a military academy. I objected that none of the specified powers given by the constitution to Congress, would authorize this. It was, therefore, referred for further consideration and inquiry. Knox was for both propositions. Randolph against the former, but said nothing as to the latter. The President acknowledged he had doubted of the expediency of undertaking the former; and as to the latter, though it would be a good thing, he did not wish to bring on anything which might generate hate and ill humor. It was agreed that Randolph should draw the speech and the messages.

⮆ November the 28th. Met at the President's. I read over a list of the papers copying, to be communicated to Congress on the subject of Mr. Genet. It was agreed that Genet's letter of August the 13th to the President, mine of August the 16th, and Genet's of November to myself and the Attorney General, desiring a prosecution of Jay and King should not be sent to the legislature: on a general opinion, that the discussion of the fact certified by Jay and King had better be left to the channel of the newspapers, and in the private hands in which it now is, than for the President to meddle in it, or give room to a discussion of it in Congress.

Randolph had prepared a draught of the speech. The clause recommending fortifications was left out; but that for a military academy was inserted. I opposed it, as unauthorized by the constitution. Hamilton and Knox approved it without discussion. Randolph was for it, saying that the words of the constitution authorizing Congress to lay taxes, &c., *for the common defence*, might comprehend it. The President said he would not choose to recommend anything against the constitution, but if it was *doubtful*, he was so impressed with the necessity of this measure, that he would refer it to Congress, and let them decide for themselves whether the constitution authorized it or not. It was, therefore, left in. I was happy to see that Randolph had, by accident, used the expression "our republic," in the speech. The President, however, made no objection to it, and so, as much as it had disconcerted him on a former occasion with me, it was now put into his own mouth to be pronounced to the two Houses of legislature.

No material alterations were proposed or made in any part of the draught.

After dinner, I produced the draught of messages on the subject of France and England, proposing that that relative to Spain should be subsequent and secret.

Hamilton objected to the draught *in toto*; said that the contrast drawn between the conduct of France and England amounted to a declaration of war; he denied that France had ever done us favors; that it was mean for a nation to acknowledge favors; that the dispositions of the people of this country towards France, he considered as a serious calamity; that the executive ought not, by an echo of this language, to nourish that disposition in the people; that the offers in commerce made us by France, were the offspring of the moment, of circumstances which would not last, and it was wrong to receive as permanent, things merely temporary; that he could demonstrate that Great Britain showed us more favors than France. In complaisance to him I whittled down the expressions without opposition; struck out that of "favors ancient and recent" from France; softened some terms, and omitted some sentiments respecting Great Britain. He still was against the whole, but insisted that, at any rate, it should be a secret communication, because the matters it stated were still depending. These were, 1, the inexecution of the treaty; 2, the restraining our commerce to their own ports and those of their friends. Knox joined Hamilton in everything. Randolph was for the communications; that the documents respecting the first should be given in as public; but that those respecting the second should not be given to the legislature at all, but kept secret. I began to tremble now for the whole, lest all should be kept secret. I urged, especially, the duty now incumbent on the President, to lay before the legislature and the public what had passed on the inexecution of the treaty, since Mr. Hammond's answer of this month might be considered as the last we should ever have; that, therefore, it could no longer be considered as a negotiation pending. I urged that the documents respecting the stopping our corn ought also to go, but insisted that if it should be thought better to withhold them, the restrictions should not go to those respecting the treaty; that neither of these subjects was more in a state of *pendency* than the recall of Mr. Genet, on which, nevertheless, no scruples had been expressed. The President took up the subject with more vehemence than I have seen him show, and decided without reserve, that not only what had passed on the inexecution of the treaty should go in as public (in which Hamilton and Knox had divided in opinion from Randolph and myself), but also that those respecting the stopping our corn should go in as public (wherein, Hamilton, Knox, and Randolph had been against me). This was the first instance I had seen of his deciding on the opinion of one against that of three others, which proved his own to have been very strong.

➤ December the 1st, 1793. Beckley tells me he had the following fact from Lear. Langdon, Cabot, and some others of the Senate, standing in a knot before the fire after the Senate had adjourned, and growling together about some measure which they had just lost; "Ah!" said Cabot, "things will never go right till you have a President for life, and an hereditary Senate." Langdon told this to Lear, who mentioned it to the President. The President seemed struck with it, and declared he had not supposed there was a man in the United States who could have entertained such an idea.

➤ March the 2d, 1797. I arrived at Philadelphia to qualify as Vice-President, and called instantly on Mr. Adams, who lodged at Francis's, in Fourth street. The next morning he returned my visit at Mr. Madison's, where I lodged. He found me alone in my room, and shutting the door himself, he said he was glad to find me alone, for that he wished a free conversation with me. He entered immediately on an explanation of the situation of our affairs with France, and the danger of rupture with that nation, a rupture which would convulse the attachments of this country; that he was impressed with the necessity of an immediate mission to the Directory; that it would have been the first wish of his heart to have got me to go there, but that he supposed it was out of the question, as it did not seem justifiable for him to send away the person destined to take his place in case of accident to himself, nor decent to remove from competition one who was a rival in the public favor. That he had, therefore, concluded to send a mission, which, by its dignity, should satisfy France, and by its selection from the three great divisions of the continent, should satisfy all parts of the United States; in short, that he had determined to join Gerry and Madison to Pinckney, and he wished me to consult Mr. Madison for him. I told him that as to myself, I concurred in the opinion of the impropriety of my leaving the post assigned me, and that my inclinations, moreover, would never permit me to cross the Atlantic again; that I would, as he desired, consult Mr. Madison, but I feared it was desperate, as he had refused that mission on my leaving it, in General Washington's time, though it was kept open a twelvemonth for him. He said that if Mr. Madison should refuse, he would still appoint him, and leave the responsibility on him. I consulted Mr. Madison, who declined as I expected. I think it was on Monday the 6th of March, Mr. Adams and myself met at dinner at General Washington's, and we happened, in the evening, to rise from table and come away together. As soon as we got into the street, I told him the event of my negotiation with Mr. Madison. He immediately said, that, on consultation, some objections to that nomination had been raised which he had not contemplated; and was going on with excuses which evidently embarrassed him, when we came to Fifth street, where our road separated, his being down Market street, mine off along Fifth, and we took leave; and he never after that said one word to me on the subject, or ever consulted me as to any measures of the government.

The opinion I formed at the time on this transaction, was, that Mr. Adams, in the first moments of the enthusiasm of the occasion (his inauguration), forgot party sentiments, and as he never acted on any system, but was always governed by the feeling of the moment, he thought, for a moment, to steer impartially between the parties; that Monday, the 6th of March, being the first time he had met his cabinet, on expressing ideas of this kind, he had been at once diverted from them, and returned to his former party views.

➤ July, 1797. Murray is rewarded for his services by an appointment to Amsterdam; W. Smith of Charleston, to Lisbon.

➤ August the 24th. About the time of the British treaty, Hamilton and Talleyrand, bishop of Autun, dined together, and Hamilton drank freely. Conversing on the treaty, Talleyrand says, *"mais vraiment, Monsieur Hamilton, ce n'est pas bien honnête,* after making the Senate ratify the treaty, to advise the President to reject it." "The treaty," says Hamilton, "is an execrable one, and Jay was an old woman for making it; but the whole credit of saving us from it must be given to the President." After circumstances had led to a conclusion that the President also must ratify it, he said to the same Talleyrand, "though the treaty is a most execrable one, yet when once we have come to a determination on it, we must carry it through thick and thin, right or wrong." Talleyrand told this to Volney, who told it to me.

There is a letter now appearing in the papers, from Pickering to Monroe, dated July the 24th, 1797, which I am satisfied is written by Hamilton. He was in Philadelphia at that date.

➤ December the 26th, 1797. Langdon tells me, that at the second election of President and Vice-President of the United States, when there was a considerable vote given to Clinton in opposition to Mr. Adams, he took occasion to remark it in conversation in the Senate chamber with Mr. Adams, who, gritting his teeth, said, "damn 'em, damn 'em, damn 'em, you see that an elective government will not do." He also tells me that Mr. Adams, in a late conversation, said, "republicanism must be disgraced, Sir." The Chevalier Yruho called on him at Braintree, and conversing on French affairs, and Yruho expressing his belief of their stability, in opposition to Mr. Adams, the latter lifting up and shaking his finger at him, said, "I'll tell you what, the French republic will not last three months." This I had from Yruho.

Harper, lately in a large company, was saying that the best thing the friends of the French could do, was to pray for the restoration of their monarch. "Then," says a bystander, "the best thing we could do, I suppose, would be to pray for the establishment of a monarch in the United States." "Our people," says Harper, "are not yet ripe for it, but it is the best thing we can come to, and we shall come to it." Something like this was said in presence of Findlay. He now denies it in the public papers, though it can be proved by several members.

⫸ December the 27th. Tenche Coxe tells me, that a little before Hamilton went out of office, or just as he was going out, taking with him his last conversation, and among other things, on the subject of their differences, "for my part," says he, "I avow myself a monarchist; I have no objection to a trial being made of this thing of a republic, but," &c.

⫸ January the 5th, 1798. I receive a very remarkable fact indeed in our history, from Baldwin and Skinner. Before the establishment of our present government, a very extensive combination had taken place in New York and the eastern States, among that description of people who were partly monarchical in principle, or frightened with Shays's rebellion and the impotence of the old Congress. Delegates in different places had actually had consultations on the subject of seizing on the powers of a government, and establishing them by force; had corresponded with one another, and had sent a deputy to General Washington to solicit his co-operation. He refused to join them. The new convention was in the meantime proposed by Virginia and appointed. These people believed it impossible the States should ever agree on a government, as this must include the impost and all the other powers which the States had, a thousand times, refused to the general authority. They therefore let the proposed convention go on, not doubting its failure, and confiding that on its failure would be a still more favorable moment for their enterprise. They therefore wished it to fail, and especially, when Hamilton, their leader, brought forward his plan of government, failed entirely in carrying it, and retired in disgust from the convention. His associates then took every method to prevent any form of government being agreed to. But the well-intentioned never ceased trying, first one thing, then another, till they could get something agreed to. The final passage and adoption of the constitution completely defeated the views of the combination, and saved us from an attempt to establish a government over us by force. This fact throws a blaze of light on the conduct of several members from New York and the eastern States in the convention of Annapolis, and the grand convention. At that of Annapolis, several eastern members most vehemently opposed Madison's proposition for a more general convention, with more general powers. They wished things to get more and more into confusion, to justify the violent measure they proposed. The idea of establishing a government by reasoning and agreement, they publicly ridiculed as an Utopian project, visionary and unexampled.

≫ February the 6th, 1798. Mr. Baldwin tells me that in a conversation yesterday with Goodhue, on the state of our affairs, Goodhue said, "I'll tell you what, I have made up my mind on the subject; I would rather the old ship should go down than not"; (meaning the Union of the States). Mr. Hillhouse coming up, "well," says Mr. Baldwin, "I'll tell my old friend Hillhouse what you say"; and he told him. "Well," says Goodhue, "I repeat that I would rather the old ship should go down, if we are to be always kept pumping so." "Mr. Hillhouse," says Baldwin, "you remember when we were learning logic together at school, there was the case *categorical* and the case *hypothetical*. Mr. Goodhue stated it to me first as the case categorical. I am glad to see that he now changes it to the case hypothetical, by adding, 'if we are always to be kept pumping so.' " Baldwin went on then to remind Goodhue what an advocate he had been for our tonnage duty, wanting to make it one dollar instead of fifty cents; and how impatiently he bore the delays of Congress in proceeding to retaliate on Great Britain before

Mr. Madison's propositions came on. Goodhue acknowledged that his opinions had changed since that.

⇒⇒ February the 15th, 1798. I dined this day with Mr. Adams (the President). The company was large. After dinner I was sitting next to him, and our conversation was first on the enormous price of labor,* house rent, and other things. We both concurred in ascribing it chiefly to the floods of bank paper now afloat, and in condemning those institutions. We then got on the constitution; and in the course of our conversation he said, that no republic could ever last which had not a Senate, and a Senate deeply and strongly rooted, strong enough to bear up against all popular storms and passions; that he thought our Senate as well constituted as it could have been, being chosen by the legislatures; for if these could not support them, he did not know what could do it; that perhaps it might have been as well for them to be chosen by the State at large, as that would insure a choice of distinguished men, since none but such could be known to a whole people; that the only fault in our Senate was, that it was not durable enough; that hitherto, it had behaved very well; however, he was afraid they would give way in the end. That as to trusting to a popular assembly for the preservation of our liberties, it was the merest chimera imaginable; they never had any rule of decision but their own will; that he would as lieve be again in the hands of our old committees of safety, who made the law and executed it at the same time; that it had been observed by some writer (I forget whom he named), that anarchy did more mischief in one night, than tyranny in an age; and that in modern times we might say with truth, that in France, anarchy had done more harm in one night, than all the despotism of their Kings had ever done in twenty or thirty years. The point in which he views our Senate, as the colossus of the constitution, serves as a key to the politics of the Senate, who are two-thirds of them in his sentiments, and accounts for the bold line of conduct they pursue.

* He observed, that eight or ten years ago, he gave only fifty dollars to a common laborer for his farm, finding him food and lodging. Now he gives one hundred and fifty dollars, and even two hundred dollars to one.—T.J.

➤ March the 1st. Mr. Tazewell tells me, that when the appropriations for the British treaty were on the carpet, and very uncertain in the lower House, there being at that time a number of bills in the hands of committees of the Senate, none reported, and the Senate idle for want of them, he, in his place, called on the committees to report, and particularly on Mr. King, who was on most of them. King said that it was true the committees kept back their reports, waiting the event of the question about appropriation; that if that was not carried, they considered legislation as at an end; that they might as well break up and consider the Union as dissolved. Tazewell expressed his astonishment at these ideas, and called on King to know if he had misapprehended him. King rose again and repeated the same words. The next day, Cabot took an occasion in debate, and so awkward a one as to show it was a thing agreed to be done, to repeat the same sentiments in stronger terms, and carried further, by declaring a determination on their side to break up and dissolve the government.

➤ March the 11th. In conversation with Baldwin, and Brown of Kentucky, Brown says that in a private company once, consisting of Hamilton, King, Madison, himself, and someone else making a fifth, speaking of the *"federal government"*: "Oh!" says Hamilton, "say the *federal monarchy*, let us call things by their right names, for a monarchy it is."

Baldwin mentions at table the following fact: When the bank bill was under discussion in the House of Representatives, Judge Wilson came in, and was standing by Baldwin. Baldwin reminded him of the following fact which passed in the grand convention: Among the enumerated powers given to Congress, was one to erect corporations. It was, on debate, struck out. Several particular powers were then proposed. Among others, Robert Morris proposed to give Congress a power to establish a national bank. Gouverneur Morris opposed it, observing that it was extremely doubtful whether the constitution they were framing could ever be passed at all by the people of America; that to give it its best chance, however, they should make it as palatable as possible, and put nothing into it not very essential, which might raise up enemies; that his colleague (Robert Morris) well knew that "a bank" was, in their State (Pennsylvania), the very watch-word of party; that *a bank* had been the great bone of contention between the two parties of the State from the establishment of their constitution, having been erected, put down, and erected again, as either party preponderated; that therefore, to insert this power, would instantly enlist against the whole instrument, the whole of the anti-bank party in Pennsylvania. Whereupon it was rejected, as was every other special power, except that of giving copyrights to authors, and patents to inventors; the general power of incorporating being whittled down to this shred. Wilson agreed to the fact.

Mr. Hunter, of South Carolina, who lodges with Rutledge, tells me that Rutledge was explaining to him the plan they proposed to pursue as to war measures when Otis came in. Rutledge addressed Otis. Now, sir, says he, you must come forward with something liberal for the southern States, fortify their harbors, and build gallies, in order to obtain their concurrence. Otis said, we insist on convoys for our European trade, and *guarda costas*, on which conditions alone we will give them gallies and fortifications. Rutledge observed, that in the event of war, McHenry and Pickering must go out; Wolcott, he thought, might remain, but the others were incapable of conducting a war. Otis said the eastern people would never abandon Pickering, he must be retained; McHenry might go. They considered together whether General Pinckney would accept the office of Secretary of War. They apprehended he would not. It was agreed in this conversation that Sewall had more the ear of the President than any other person.

» March the 12th. When the bill for appropriations was before the Senate, Anderson moved to strike out a clause recognizing (by way of appropriation) the appointment of a committee by the House of Representatives to sit during their recess to collect evidence on Blount's case, denying they had power, but by a law, to authorize a committee to sit during recess. Tracy advocated the motion, and said, "We may as well speak out. The committee was appointed by the House of Representatives to take care of the British minister, to take care of the Spanish minister, to take care of the Secretary of State, in short, to take care of the President of the United States. They were afraid the President and Secretary of State would not perform the office of collecting evidence faithfully; that there would be collusion, &c. Therefore, the House appointed a committee of their own. We shall have them next sending a committee to Europe to make a treaty, &c. Suppose that the House of Representatives should resolve, that after the adjournment of Congress, they should continue to sit as a committee of the whole House during the whole recess." This shows how the appointment of that committee has been viewed by the President's friends.

⇒ April the 5th. Doctor Rush tells me he had it from Mrs. Adams, that not a scrip of a pen has passed between the late and present President since he came into office.

⇒ April the 13th. New instructions of the British government to their armed ships now appear, which clearly infringe their treaty with us, by authorizing them to take our vessels carrying produce of the French colonies from those colonies to Europe, and to take vessels bound to a blockaded port. See them in Brown's paper, of April the 18th, in due form.

The President has sent a government brig to France, probably to carry despatches. He has chosen as the bearer of these one Humphreys, the son of a ship carpenter, ignorant, under age, not speaking a word of French, most abusive of that nation, whose only merit is, the having mobbed and beaten Bache on board the frigate built here, for which he was indicted and punished by fine.

⇒ April the 25th. At a dinner given by the bar to the federal judges, Chase and Peters, present about twenty-four lawyers, and William Tilghman in the chair, this toast was given, "Our *King* in old England." Observe the double *entendre* on the word King. Du Ponceau, who was one of the bar present, told this to Tenche Coxe, who told me in presence of H. Tazewell. Dallas was at the dinner; so was Colonel Charles Sims, of Alexandria, who is here on a lawsuit *vs*. General Irving.

≫ May the 3d. The President some time ago appointed Steele, of Virginia, a commissioner to the Indians, and recently Secretary of the Mississippi Territory. Steele was a Counsellor of Virginia, and was voted out by the Assembly because he turned tory. He then offered for Congress, and was rejected by the people. Then offered for the Senate of Virginia, and was rejected. The President has also appointed Joseph Hopkinson commissioner to make a treaty with the Oneida Indians. He is a youth of about twenty-two or twenty-three, and has no other claims to such an appointment than extreme toryism, and the having made a poor song to the tune of the President's March.

≫ October the 13th, 1798. Littlepage, who has been on one or two missions from Poland to Spain, said that when Gardoqui returned from America, he settled with his court an account of secret service money of six hundred thousand dollars. *Ex-relatione** Colonel Monroe.

≫ January, 1799. In a conversation between Dr. Ewen and the President, the former said one of his sons was an aristocrat, the other a democrat. The President asked if it was not the youngest who was the democrat. "Yes," said Ewen. "Well," said the President, "a boy of fifteen who is not a democrat is good for nothing, and he is no better who is a democrat at twenty." Ewen told Hurt, and Hurt told me.

≫ January the 14th. Logan tells me that in his conversation with Pickering on his arrival, the latter abused Gerry very much; said he was a traitor to his country, and had deserted the post to which he was appointed; that the French temporized at first with Pinckney, but found him too much of a man for their purpose. Logan observing, that notwithstanding the pacific declarations of France, it might still be well to keep up the military ardor of our citizens, and to have the militia in good order; "the militia," said Pickering, "the militia never did any good to this country, except in the single affair of Bunker Hill; that we must have a standing army of fifty thousand men, which being stationed in different parts of the continent, might serve as rallying points for

* On the information of.

the militia, and so render them of some service." In his conversation with Mr. Adams, Logan mentioned the willingness of the French to treat with Gerry. "And do you know why?" said Mr. Adams. "Why, sir?" said Logan. "Because," said Mr. Adams, "they know him to have been an anti-federalist, against the constitution."

❧ January the 2d, 1800. Information from Tenche Coxe. Mr. Liston had sent two letters to the Governor of Canada by one Sweezy. He had sent copies of them, together with a third (original) by one Cribs. Sweezy was arrested (being an old horse thief), and his papers examined. T. Coxe had a sight of them. As soon as a rumor got out that there were letters of Mr. Liston disclosed, but no particulars yet mentioned, Mr. Liston suspecting that *Cribs* had betrayed him, thought it best to bring all his *three* letters, and lay them before Pickering, Secretary of State. Pickering thought them all very innocent. In his office they were seen by a Mr. Hodgen of New Jersey, commissary of military stores, and the intimate friend of Pickering. It happens that there is some land partnership between Pickering, Hodgen and Coxe, so that the latter is freely and intimately visited by Hodgen, who, moreover, speaks freely with him on political subjects. They were talking the news of the day, when Mr. Coxe observed that these intercepted letters of Liston were serious things; (nothing being yet out but a general rumor). Hodgen asked which he thought the most serious. Coxe said the second; (for he knew yet of no other). Hodgen said he thought little of any of them, but that the third was the most exceptionable. This struck Coxe, who, not betraying his ignorance of a third letter, asked generally what part of that he alluded to. Hodgen said to that wherein he *assured the Governor of Canada, that if the French invaded Canada, an army would be marched from these States to his assistance.* After this it became known that it was Sweezy who was arrested, and not Cribs; so that Mr. Liston had made an unnecessary disclosure of his third letter to Mr. Pickering, who, however, keeps his secret for him. In the beginning of the conversation between Hodgen and Coxe, Coxe happened to name Sweezy as the bearer of the letters. "That's not his name," says Hodgen (for he did not know that two of the letters had been sent by Sweezy also), "his name is Cribs." This put Coxe on his guard, and sent him fishing for the new matter.

⊗ January the 10th. Doctor Rush tells me that he had it from Samuel Lyman, that during the X. Y. Z. Congress, the federal members held the largest caucus they have ever had, at which he was present, and the question was proposed and debated, whether they should declare war against France, and determined in the negative. Lyman was against it.

He tells me, that Mr. Adams told him, that when he came on in the fall to Trenton, he was there surrounded constantly by the opponents of the late mission to France. That Hamilton pressing him to delay it, said, "Why, sir, by Christmas, Louis the XVIII will be seated on his throne." Mr. A. "By whom?" H. "By the coalition." Mr. A. "Ah! then farewell to the independence of Europe. If a coalition moved by the finger of England, is to give a government to France, there is an end to the independence of every country."

⊗ January the 12th. General Samuel Smith says that Pickering, Wolcott, and McHenry, wrote a joint letter from Trenton to the President, then at Braintree, dissuading him from the mission to France. Stoddard refused to join in it. Stoddard says the instructions are such, that if the Directory have any disposition to reconciliation, a treaty will be made. He observed to him, also, that Ellsworth looks beyond this mission to the Presidential chair. That with this view, he will endeavor to make a treaty, and a good one. That Davie has the same vanity and views. All this communicated by Stoddard to S. Smith.

⊗ January the 13th. Baer and Harrison G. Otis told J. Nicholas, that in the caucus mentioned ante 10th, there wanted but five votes to produce a declaration of war. Baer was against it.

⊗ January the 19th. W. C. Nicholas tells me, that in a conversation with Dexter three or four days ago, he asked Dexter whether it would not be practicable for the States to agree on some uniform mode of choosing electors of President. Dexter said, "I suppose you would prefer an election by districts." "Yes," said Nicholas, "I think it would be best; but would nevertheless agree to any other consistent with the constitution." Dexter said he did not know what might be the opinion of his State, but his own was, that no mode of *election* would answer any good purpose; that he should prefer one *for life*. "On that reasoning," said Nicholas, "you should prefer an hereditary one." "No," he said, "we are not ripe for that yet. I suppose," added he, "this doctrine is not very popular with you." "No," said Nicholas, "it would effectually damn any man in my State." "So it would in mine," said Dexter; "but I am under no inducement to belie my sentiment, I have nothing to ask from anybody; I had rather be at home than here, therefore I speak my sentiments freely." Mr. Nicholas, a little before or after this, made the same proposition of a uniform election to Ross, who replied that he saw no good in any kind of election. "Perhaps," said he, "the present one may last awhile." On the whole, Mr. Nicholas thinks he perceives in that party, a willingness and a wish to let everything go from bad to worse, to amend nothing, in hopes it may bring on confusion, and open a door to the kind of government they wish. In a conversation with Gunn, who goes with them, but thinks in some degree with us, Gunn told him that the very game which the minority of Pennsylvania is now playing with McKean (see substitute of minority in lower House, and address of Senate in upper), was meditated by the same party in the federal government, in case of the election of a republican President; and that the eastern States would in that case throw things into confusion, and break the Union. That they have in a great degree got rid of their paper, so as no longer to be creditors, and the moment they cease to enjoy the plunder of the immense appropriations now exclusively theirs, they would aim at some other order of things.

≫ January the 24th. Mr. Smith, a merchant of Hamburg, gives me the following information: The St. Andrew's Club of New York (all of Scotch tories), gave a public dinner lately. Among other guests, Alexander Hamilton was one. After dinner, the first toast was, "The President of the United States." It was drank without any particular approbation. The next was, "George the Third." Hamilton started up on his feet, and insisted on a bumper and three cheers. The whole company accordingly rose and gave the cheers. One of them, though a federalist, was so disgusted at the partiality shown by Hamilton to a foreign sovereign over his own President, that he mentioned it to a Mr. Schwarthouse, an American merchant of New York, who mentioned it to Smith.

Mr. Smith also tells me, that calling one evening on Mr. Evans, then Speaker of the House of Representatives of Pennsylvania, and ask-

ing the news, Evans said, Harper had just been there, and speaking of the President's setting out to Braintree, said, "he prayed to God that his horses might run away with him, or some other accident happen to break his neck before he reached Braintree." This was indignation at his having named Murray, &c., to negotiate with France. Evans approved of the wish.

⟫ February the 1st. Doctor Rush tells me that he had it from Asa Green, that when the clergy addressed General Washington on his departure from the government, it was observed in their consultation, that he had never, on any occasion, said a word to the public which showed a belief in the Christian religion, and they thought they should so pen their address, as to force him at length to declare publicly whether he was a Christian or not. They did so. However, he observed, the old fox was too cunning for them. He answered every article of their address particularly except that, which he passed over without notice. Rush observes, he never did say a word on the subject in any of his public papers, except in his valedictory letter to the Governors of the States, when he resigned his commission in the army, wherein he speaks of "the benign influence of the Christian religion."

I know that Gouverneur Morris, who pretended to be in his secrets and believed himself to be so, has often told me that General Washington believed no more of that system than he himself did.

≫ March, 1800. Heretical doctrines maintained in Senate, on the motion against the Aurora. That there is in every legal body of men a right of self-preservation, authorizing them to do whatever is necessary for that purpose: by Tracy, Read, and Lawrence. That the common law authorizes the proceeding proposed against the Aurora, and is in force here: by Read. That the privileges of Congress are and ought to be indefinite: by Read.

Tracy says, he would not say exactly that the common law of England in all its extent is in force here; but common sense, reason and morality, which are the foundations of the common law, are in force here, and establish a common law. He held himself so nearly half way between the common law of England and what everybody else has called natural law, and not common law, that he could hold to either the one or the other, as he should find expedient.

Dexter maintained that the common law, as to crimes, is in force in the United States.

Chipman says, that the principles of common right are common law.

≫ March the 11th. Conversing with Mrs. Adams on the subject of the writers in the newspapers, I took occasion to mention that I never in my life had, directly or indirectly, written one sentence for a newspaper; which is an absolute truth. She said that Mr. Adams, she believed, had pretty well ceased to meddle in the newspapers, since he closed the pieces on Davila. This is the first direct avowal of that work to be his, though long and universally understood to be so.

≫ March the 14th. Freneau, in Charleston, had the printing of the laws in his paper. He printed a pamphlet of Pinckney's letters on Robbins' case. Pickering has given the printing of the laws to the tory paper of that place, though not of half the circulation. The printing amounted to about one hundred dollars a year.

≫ March the 24th. Mr. Perez Morton of Massachusetts tells me that Thatcher, on his return from the war Congress, declared to him he had been for a declaration of war against France, and many others also; but that on counting noses they found they could not carry it, and therefore did not attempt it.

≫ March the 27th. Judge Breckenridge gives me the following information: He and Mr. Ross were originally very intimate; indeed, he says, he found him keeping a little Latin school, and advised and aided him in the study of law, and brought him forward. After Ross became a Senator, and particularly at the time of the western insurrection, they still were in concert. After the British treaty, Ross, on his return, informed him there was a party in the United States who wanted to overturn the government, who were in league with France; that France, by a secret article of treaty with Spain, was to have Louisiana; and that Great Britain was likely to be our best friend and dependence. On this information, he, Breckenridge, was induced to become an advocate for the British treaty. During this intimacy with Ross, he says, that General Collot, in his journey to the western country, called on him, and he frequently led Breckenridge into conversations on their grievances under the government, and particularly the western expedition; that he spoke to him of the advantages that country would have in joining France when she should hold Louisiana; showed him a map he had drawn of that part of the country; pointed out the passes in the mountain, and the facility with which they might hold them against the United States, and with which France could support them from New Orleans. He says, that in these conversations, Collot let himself out with common prudence. He says, Michaud (to whom I, at the request of Genet, had given a letter of introduction to the Governor of Kentucky as a botanist, which was his real profession), called on him; that Michaud had a commissary's commission for the expedition, which Genet had planned from that quarter against the Spaniards; that ———, the late Spanish commandant of St. Genevieve, with one Powers, an Englishman, called on him. That from all these circumstances, together with Ross's stories, he did believe that there was a conspiracy to deliver our country, or some part of it at least, to the French; that he made notes of what passed between himself and Collot and the others, and lent them to Mr. Ross, who gave them to the President, by whom they were deposited in the office of the Board of War; that when he complained to Ross of this breach of confidence, he endeavored to get off by compliments on the utility and importance of his notes. They now cooled towards each other; and his opposition to Ross's election as Governor has separated them in truth, though not entirely to appearance.

Doctor Rush tells me, that within a few days he has heard a member of Congress lament our separation from Great Britain, and express his sincere wishes that we were again dependent on her.

»» December the 25th, 1800. Colonel Hitchburn tells me what Col. Monroe had before told me of, as coming from Hitchburn. He was giving me the characters of persons in Massachusetts. Speaking of Lowell, he said he was, in the beginning of the Revolution, a timid whig, but as soon as he found we were likely to prevail, he became a great office hunter. And in the very breath of speaking of Lowell, he stopped: says he, I will give you a piece of information which I do not venture to speak of to others. There was a Mr. Hale in Massachusetts, a reputable, worthy man, who becoming a little embarrassed in his affairs, I aided him, which made him very friendly to me. He went to Canada on some business. The Governor there took great notice of him. On his return, he took occasion to mention to me that he was authorized by the Governor of Canada to give from three to five thousand guineas each to himself and some others, to induce them, not to do anything to the injury of their country, but to befriend a good connection between England and it. Hitchburn said he would think of it, and asked Hale to come and dine with him tomorrow. After dinner he drew Hale fully out. He told him he had his doubts, but particularly, that he should not like to be alone in such a business. On that, Hale named to him four others who were to be engaged, two of whom, said Hitchburn, are now dead, and two living. Hitchburn, when he had got all he wanted out of Hale, declined in a friendly way. But he observed those four men, from that moment, to espouse the interests of England in every point and on every occasion. Though he did not name the men to me, yet as the speaking of Lowell was what brought into his head to tell me this anecdote, I concluded he was one. From other circumstances respecting Stephen Higginson, of whom he spoke, I conjectured him to be the other living one.

December the 26th. In another conversation, I mentioned to Colonel Hitchburn, that though he had not named names, I had strongly suspected Higginson to be one of Hale's men. He smiled and said, if I had strongly suspected any man wrongfully from his information, he would undeceive me; that there were no persons he thought more strongly to be suspected himself, than Higginson and Lowell. I considered this as saying they were the men. Higginson is employed in an important business about our navy.

✤ February the 12th, 1801. Edward Livingston tells me, that Bayard applied today or last night to General Samuel Smith, and represented to him the expediency of his coming over to the States who vote for Burr,* that there was nothing in the way of appointment which he might not command, and particularly mentioned the Secretaryship of the Navy.

---

* Because of the tie with Aaron Burr in the popular vote of 1800, Jefferson was elected President in February, 1801, by the House of Representatives. Burr thus became Vice-President. Jefferson served two terms (1801–1809).

Smith asked him if he was authorized to make the offer. He said he was authorized. Smith told this to Livingston, and to W. C. Nicholas who confirms it to me. Bayard in like manner tempted Livingston, not by offering any particular office, but by representing to him his, Livingston's, intimacy and connection with Burr; that from him he had everything to expect, if he would come over to him. To Doctor Linn of New Jersey, they have offered the government of New Jersey. See a paragraph in Martin's Baltimore paper of February the 10th, signed, "A LOOKER ON," stating an intimacy of views between Harper and Burr.

✤ February the 14th. General Armstrong tells me, that Gouverneur Morris, in conversation with him today on the scene which is passing, expressed himself thus. "How comes it," says he, "that Burr who is four hundred miles off (at Albany), has agents here at work with great activity, while Mr. Jefferson, who is on the spot, does nothing?" This explains the ambiguous conduct of himself and his nephew, Lewis Morris, and that they were holding themselves free for a prize; *i.e.*, some office, either to the uncle or nephew.

✤ February the 16th. See in the Wilmington Mirror of February the 14th, Mr. Bayard's elaborate argument to prove that the common law, as modified by the laws of the respective States at the epoch of the ratification of the constitution, attached to the courts of the United States.

✤ June the 23d, 1801. Andrew Ellicot tells me, that in a conversation last summer with Major William Jackson of Philadelphia, on the subject of our intercourse with Spain, Jackson said we had managed our affairs badly; that he himself was the author of the papers against the Spanish ministers signed Americanus; that his object was irritation; that he was anxious, if it could have been brought about, to have plunged us in a war with Spain, that the people might have been occupied with that, and not with the conduct of the administration, and other things they had no business to meddle with.

✤ December the 13th, 1803. The Reverend Mr. Coffin of New England, who is now here soliciting donations for a college in Greene county, in Tennessee, tells me that when he first determined to engage in this enterprise, he wrote a paper recommendatory of the enterprise, which he meant to get signed by clergymen, and a similar one for persons in a civil character, at the head of which he wished Mr. Adams to put his name, he being then President, and the application going only for his name, and not for a donation. Mr. Adams, after reading the paper and considering, said, "he saw no possibility of continuing the union of the States; that their dissolution must necessarily take place; that he therefore saw no propriety in recommending to New England men to promote a literary institution in the south; that it was in fact giving strength to those who were to be their enemies; and, therefore, he would have nothing to do with it."

≫ December the 31st. After dinner today, the pamphlet on the conduct of Colonel Burr being the subject of conversation, Matthew Lyon noticed the insinuations against the republicans at Washington, pending the Presidential election, and expressed his wish that everything was spoken out which was known; that it would then appear on which side there was a bidding for votes, and he declared that John Brown of Rhode Island, urging him to vote for Colonel Burr, used these words: "What is it you want, Colonel Lyon? Is it office, is it money? Only say what you want, and you shall have it."

≫ January the 2d, 1804. Colonel Hitchburn of Massachusetts, reminding me of a letter he had written me from Philadelphia, pending the Presidential election, says he did not therein give the details. That he was in company at Philadelphia with Colonel Burr and . . . that in the course of the conversation on the election, Colonel Burr said, "we must have a President, and a constitutional one, in some way." "How is it to be done," says Hitchburn; "Mr. Jefferson's friends will not quit him, and his enemies are not strong enough to carry another." "Why," says Burr, "our friends must join the federalists, and give the President." The next morning at breakfast, Colonel Burr repeated nearly the same, saying, "we cannot be without a President, our friends must join the federal vote." "But," says Hitchburn, "we shall then be without a Vice-President; who is to be our Vice-President?" Colonel Burr answered, "Mr. Jefferson."

⁂ January the 26th. Colonel Burr, the Vice-President, calls on me in the evening, having previously asked an opportunity of conversing with me. He began by recapitulating summarily, that he had come to New York a stranger, some years ago; that he found the country in possession of two rich families (the Livingstons and Clintons); that his pursuits were not political, and he meddled not. When the crisis, however, of 1800 came on, they found their influence worn out, and solicited his aid with the people. He lent it without any views of promotion. That his being named as a candidate for Vice-President was unexpected by him. He acceded to it with a view to promote my fame and advancement, and from a desire to be with me, whose company and conversation had always been fascinating to him. That since, those great families had become hostile to him, and had excited the calumnies which I had seen published. That in this Hamilton had joined, and had even written some of the pieces against him. That his attachment to me had been sincere, and was still unchanged, although many little stories had been carried to him, and he supposed to me also, which he despised; but that attachments must be reciprocal or cease to exist, and therefore he asked if any change had taken place in mine towards him; that he had chosen to have this conversation with myself directly, and not through any intermediate agent. He reminded me of a letter written to him about the time of counting the votes (say February, 1801), mentioning that his election had left a chasm in my arrangements; that I had lost him from my list in the administration, &c. He observed, he believed it would be for the interest of the republican cause for him to retire; that a disadvantageous schism would otherwise take place; but that were he to retire, it would be said he shrunk from the public sentence, which he never would do; that his enemies were using my name to destroy him, and something was necessary from me to prevent and deprive them of that weapon, some mark of favor from me which would declare to the world that he retired with my confidence.

I answered by recapitulating to him what had been my conduct previous to the election of 1800. That I had never interfered directly or indirectly with my friends or any others, to influence the election either for him or myself; that I considered it as my duty to be merely passive, except that in Virginia, I had taken some measures to procure for him the unanimous vote of that State, because I thought any failure there might be imputed to me. That in the election now coming on, I was observing the same conduct, held no councils with anybody respecting it, nor suffered anyone to speak to me on the subject, believing it my duty to leave myself to the free discussion of the public; that I do not at this moment know, nor have ever heard, who were to be proposed as candidates for the public choice, except so far as could be gathered from the newspapers. That as to the attack excited against him in the newspapers, I had noticed it but as the passing wind; that I had seen complaints that Cheetham, employed in publishing the laws, should be permitted to eat the public bread and abuse its second officer; that as to this, the publishers of the laws were appointed by the Secretary of the State, without any reference to me; that to make the notice general, it was often given to one republican and one federal printer of the same place; that these federal printers did not in the least intermit their abuse of me, though receiving emoluments from the governments and that I have never thought it proper to interfere for myself, and consequently not in the case of the Vice-President. That as to the letter he referred to, I remembered it, and believed he had only mistaken the date at which it was written; that I thought it must have been on the first notice of the event of the election of South Carolina; and that I had taken that occasion to mention to him, that I had intended to have proposed to him one of the great offices, if he had not been elected; but that his election in giving him a higher station had deprived me of his aid in the administration. The letter alluded to was, in fact, mine to him of December the 15th, 1800. I now went on to explain to him verbally, what I meant by saying I had lost him from my list. That in General Washington's time, it had been signified to him that Mr. Adams, the Vice-President, would be glad of a foreign embassy; that General Washington mentioned it to me, expressed his doubts whether Mr. Adams was a fit character for such an office, and his still greater doubts, indeed his conviction, that it would not be justifiable to send away the person who, in case of his death, was provided by the constitution to take his place; that it would moreover appear indecent for him to be disposing of the public trusts, in apparently buying off a competitor for the public favor. I concurred with him in the opinion, and, if I recollect rightly,

Hamilton, Knox, and Randolph were consulted and gave the same opinions. That when Mr. Adams came to the administration, in his first interview with me, he mentioned the necessity of a mission to France, and how desirable it would have been to him if he could have got me to undertake it; but that he conceived it would be wrong in him to send me away, and assigned the same reasons General Washington had done; and therefore, he should appoint Mr. Madison, &c. That I had myself contemplated his (Colonel Burr's) appointment to one of the great offices, in case he was not elected Vice-President; but that as soon as that election was known, I saw it could not be done, for the good reasons which had led General Washington and Mr. Adams to the same conclusion; and therefore, in my first letter to Colonel Burr, after the issue was known, I had mentioned to him that a chasm in my arrangements had been produced by this event. I was thus particular in rectifying the date of this letter, because it gave me an opportunity of explaining the grounds on which it was written, which were, indirectly, an answer to his present hints. He left the matter with me for consideration, and the conversation was turned to indifferent subjects. I should here notice, that Colonel Burr must have thought that I could swallow strong things in my own favor, when he founded his acquiescence in the nomination as Vice-President, to his desire of promoting my honor, the being with me, whose company and conversation had always been fascinating with him, &c. I had never seen Colonel Burr till he came as a member of Senate. His conduct very soon inspired me with distrust. I habitually cautioned Mr. Madison against trusting him too much. I saw afterwards, that under General Washington's and Mr. Adams' administrations, whenever a great military appointment or a diplomatic one was to be made, he came post to Philadelphia to show himself, and in fact that he was always at market, if they had wanted him. He was indeed told by Dayton in 1800, he might be Secretary at War; but this bid was too late. His election as Vice-President was then foreseen. With these impressions of Colonel Burr, there never had been an intimacy between us, and but little association. When I destined him for a high appointment, it was out of respect for the favor he had obtained with the republican party, by his extraordinary exertions and successes in the New York election in 1800.

⋙ April the 15th, 1806. About a month ago, Colonel Burr called on me, and entered into a conversation, in which he mentioned, that a little before my coming into office, I had written to him a letter intimating that I had destined him for a high employ, had he not been placed by the people in a different one; that he had signified his willingness to resign as Vice-President, to give aid to the administration in any other place, that he had never asked an office, however; he asked aid of nobody, but could walk on his own legs and take care of himself; that I had always used him with politeness, but nothing more; that he aided in bringing on the present order of things; that he had supported the administration; and that he could do me much harm; he wished, however, to be on different ground; he was now disengaged from all particular business—willing to engage in something—should be in town some days, if I should have anything to propose to him. I observed to him, that I had always been sensible that he possessed talents which might be employed greatly to the advantage of the public, and that as to myself, I had a confidence that if he were employed, he would use his talents for the public good; but that he must be sensible the public had withdrawn their confidence from him, and that in a government like ours it was necessary to embrace in its administration as great a mass of public confidence as possible, by employing those who had a character with the public, of their own, and not merely a secondary one through the executive. He observed, that if we believed a few newspapers, it might be supposed he had lost the public confidence, but that I knew how easy it was to engage newspapers in anything. I observed, that I did not refer to that kind of evidence of his having lost the public confidence, but to the late Presidential election, when, though in possession of the office of Vice-President, there was not a single voice heard for his retaining it. That as to any harm he could do me, I knew no cause why he should desire it, but, at the same time, I feared no injury which any man could do me; that I never had done a single act, or been concerned in any transaction, which I feared to have fully laid open, or which could do me any hurt, if truly stated; that I had never done a single thing with a view to my personal interest, or that of any friend, or with any other view than that of the greatest public good; that, therefore, no threat or fear on that head would ever be a motive of action with me. He has continued in town to this time; dined with me this day week, and called on me to take leave two or three days ago.

I did not commit these things to writing at the time, but I do it now, because in a suit between him and Cheetham, he has had a deposition of Mr. Bayard taken, which seems to have no relation to the suit, nor to any other object than to calumniate me. Bayard pretends to have addressed to me, during the pending of the Presidential election in February, 1801, through General Samuel Smith, certain conditions on which my election might be obtained, and that General Smith, after conversing with me, gave answers from me. This is absolutely false. No proposition of any kind was ever made to me on that occasion by General Smith, nor any answer authorized by me. And this fact General Smith affirms at this moment.

For some matters connected with this, see my notes of February the 12th and 14th, 1801, made at the moment. But the following transactions took place about the same time, that is to say, while the Presidential election was in suspense in Congress, which, though I did not enter at the time, they made such an impression on my mind, that they are now as fresh, as to their principal circumstances, as if they had happened yesterday. Coming out of the Senate chamber one day, I found Gouverneur Morris on the steps. He stopped me, and began a conversation on the strange and portentous state of things then existing, and went on to observe, that the reasons why the minority of States was so opposed to my being elected, were, that they apprehended that, 1, I would turn all federalists out of office; 2, put down the navy; 3, wipe off the public debt. That I need only to declare, or authorize my friends to declare, that I would not take these steps, and instantly the event of the election would be fixed. I told him, that I should leave the world to judge of the course I meant to pursue by that which I had pursued hitherto, believing it to be my duty to be passive and silent during the present scene; that I should certainly make no terms; should never go into the office of President by capitulation, nor with my hands tied by any conditions which should hinder me from pursuing the measures which I should deem for the public good. It was understood that Gouverneur Morris had entirely the direction of the vote of Lewis Morris of Vermont, who, by coming over to Matthew Lyon, would have added another vote, and decided the election. About the same time, I called on Mr. Adams. We conversed on the state of things. I observed to him, that a very dangerous experiment was then in contemplation, to defeat the Presidential election by an act of Congress declaring the right of the Senate to name a President of the Senate, to devolve on him the government during any interregnum; that such a measure would probably produce resistance by force, and incalculable consequences, which it would be in his power to prevent by negativing such an act. He seemed to think such an act justifiable, and observed, it was in my power to fix the election by a word in an instant, by declaring I would not turn out the federal officers, nor put down the navy, nor spunge the national debt. Finding his mind made up as to the usurpation of the government by the President of the Senate, I urged it no further, observed the world must judge as to myself of the future by the past, and turned the conversation to something else. About the same time, Dwight Foster of Massachusetts called on me in my room one night, and went into a very long conversation on the state of affairs, the drift of which was to let me understand, that the fears above mentioned were the only obstacle to my election, to all of which I avoided giving any answer the one way or the other. From this moment he became most bitterly and personally opposed to me, and so has ever continued. I do not recollect that I ever had any particular conversation with General Samuel Smith on this subject. Very possibly I had, however, as the general subject and all its parts were the constant themes of conversation in the private *tête à têtes* with our friends. But certain I am that neither he, nor any other republican ever uttered the most distant hint to me about submitting to any conditions or giving any assurances to anybody; and still more certainly was neither he nor any other person ever authorized by me to say what I would or would not do. See a very exact statement of Bayard's conduct on that occasion in a piece among my notes of 1801, which was published by G. Granger with some alterations in the papers of the day under the signature of —— [blank].

Jefferson's Services to His Country

c. 1800

I HAVE sometimes asked myself, whether my country is the better for my having lived at all? I do not know that it is. I have been the instrument of doing the following things; but they would have been done by others; some of them, perhaps, a little better.

The Rivanna had never been used for navigation; scarcely an empty canoe had ever passed down it. Soon after I came of age, I examined its obstructions, set on foot a subscription for removing them, got an Act of Assembly passed, and the thing effected, so as to be used completely and fully for carrying down all our produce.

The Declaration of Independence.

I proposed the demolition of the church establishment, and the freedom of religion. It could only be done by degrees; to wit, the Act of 1776, c. 2, exempted dissenters from contributions to the Church, and left the Church clergy to be supported by voluntary contributions of their own sect; was continued from year to year, and made perpetual 1779, c. 36. I prepared the act for religious freedom in 1777, as part of the revisal, which was not reported to the Assembly till 1779, and that particular law not passed till 1785, and then by the efforts of Mr. Madison.

The act putting an end to entails.

The act prohibiting the importation of slaves.

The act concerning citizens, and establishing the natural right of man to expatriate himself, at will.

The act changing the course of descents, and giving the inheritance to all the children, &c., equally, I drew as part of the revisal.

The act for apportioning crimes and punishments, part of the same work, I drew. When proposed to the legislature, by Mr. Madison, in 1785, it failed by a single vote. G. K. Taylor afterwards, in 1796, proposed the same subject; avoiding the adoption of any part of the diction of mine, the text of which had been studiously drawn in the technical terms of the law, so as to give no occasion for new questions by new expressions. When I drew mine, public labor was thought the best punishment to be substituted for death. But, while I was in France, I heard of a society in England, who had successfully introduced solitary confinement, and saw the drawing of a prison at Lyons, in France, formed on the idea of solitary confinement. And, being applied to by the Governor of Virginia for the plan of a Capitol and Prison, I sent him the Lyons plan, accompanying it with a drawing on a smaller scale, better adapted to our use. This was in June, 1786. Mr. Taylor very judiciously adopted this idea (which had now been acted on in Philadelphia, probably from the English model), and substituted labor in confinement, to the public labor proposed by the Committee of revisal; which themselves would have done, had they been to act on the subject again. The public mind was ripe for this in 1796, when Mr. Taylor proposed it, and ripened chiefly by the experiment in Philadelphia; whereas, in 1785, when it had been proposed to our Assembly, they were not quite ripe for it.

In 1789 and 1790, I had a great number of olive plants, of the best kind, sent from Marseilles to Charleston, for South Carolina and Georgia. They were planted, and are flourishing; and, though not yet multiplied, they will be the germ of that cultivation in those States.

In 1790, I got a cask of heavy upland rice, from the river Denbigh, in Africa, about lat. 9° 30′ North, which I sent to Charleston, in hopes it might supersede the culture of the wet rice, which renders South Carolina and Georgia so pestilential through the summer. It was divided, and a part sent to Georgia. I know not whether it has been attended to in South Carolina; but it has spread in the upper parts of Georgia, so as to have become almost general, and is highly prized. Perhaps it may answer in Tennessee and Kentucky. The greatest service which can be rendered any country is, to add an useful plant to its culture; especially, a bread grain; next in value to bread is oil.

Whether the act for the more general diffusion of knowledge will ever be carried into complete effect, I know not. It was received by the legislature with great enthusiasm at first; and a small effort was made in 1796, by the act to establish public schools, to carry a part of it into effect, *viz.*, that for the establishment of free English schools; but the option given to the courts has defeated the intention of the act.

Testament

I, THOMAS JEFFERSON, of Monticello, in Albemarle, being of sound mind and in my ordinary state of health, make my last will and testament in manner and form as follows:

I give to my grandson Francis Eppes, son of my dear deceased daughter Mary Eppes, in fee simple, all that part of my lands at Poplar Forest lying west of the following lines, to wit: beginning at Radford's upper corner, near the double branches of Bear Creek and the public road, and running thence in a straight line to the fork of my private road, near the barn; thence along that private road (as it was changed in 1817), to its crossing of the main branch of North Tomahawk Creek; and from that crossing, in a direct line over the main ridge which divides the North and South Tomahawk, to the South Tomahawk, at the confluence of two branches where the old road to the Waterlick crossed it, and from that confluence up the northernmost branch (which separate M'Daniels' and Perry's fields), to its source; and thence by the shortest line to my western boundary. And having, in a former correspondence with my deceased son-in-law John W. Eppes, contemplated laying off for him, with remainder to my grandson Francis, a certain portion in the southern part of my lands in Bedford and Campbell, which I afterwards found to be generally more indifferent than I had supposed, and therefore determined to change its location for the better; now to remove all doubt, if any could arise on a purpose merely voluntary and unexecuted, I hereby declare that what I have herein given to my said grandson Francis, is instead of, and not additional to, what I had formerly contemplated. I subject all my other property to the payment of my debts in the first place. Considering the insolvent state of the affairs of my friend and son-in-law Thomas Mann Randolph, and that what will remain of my property will be the only resource against the want in which his family would otherwise be left, it must be his wish, as it is my duty, to guard that resource against all liability for his debts, engagements or purposes whatsoever, and to preclude the rights, powers, and authorities over it, which might result to him by operation of law, and which might, independently of his will, bring it within the power of his creditors, I do hereby devise and bequeath all the residue of my property, real and personal, in possession or in action, whether held in my own right, or in that of my dear deceased wife, according to the powers vested in me by deed of settlement for that purpose, to my grandson Thomas J. Randolph, and my friends Nicholas P. Trist and Alexander Garrett, and their heirs, during the life of my said son-in-law Thomas M. Randolph, to be held and administered by them, in trust, for the sole and separate use and behoof of my dear daughter Martha Randolph, and her heirs; and aware of the nice and difficult distinction of the law in these cases, I will further explain by saying, that I understand and intend the effect of these limitations to be, that the legal estate and actual occupation shall be vested in my said trustees, and held by them in base fee, determinable on the death of my said son-in-law, and the remainder during the same time be vested in my said daughter and her heirs, and of course disposable by her last will, and that at the death of my said son-in-law, the particular estate of the trustees shall be determined, and the remainder, in legal estate, possession, and use, become vested in my said daughter and her heirs, in absolute property forever. In consequence of the variety and indescribableness of the articles of property within the house at Monticello, and the difficulty of inventorying and appraising them separately and specifically, and its inutility, I dispense with having them inventoried and appraised; and it is my will that my executors be not held to give any security for the administration of my estate. I appoint my grandson Thomas Jefferson Randolph, my sole executor during his life, and after his death, I constitute executors my friends Nicholas P. Trist and Alexander Garrett, joining to them my daughter Martha Randolph, after the death of my said son-in-law Thomas M. Randolph. Lastly, I revoke all former wills by me heretofore made; and in witness that this is my will, I have written the whole with my own hand on two pages, and have subscribed my name to each of them this sixteenth day of March, one thousand eight hundred and twenty-six.

I, Thomas Jefferson, of Monticello, in Albemarle, make and add the following codicil to my will, controlling the same so far as its provisions go:

I recommend to my daughter Martha Randolph, the maintenance and care of my well beloved sister Anne Scott, and trust confidently that from affection to her, as well as for my sake, she will never let her want a comfort. I have made no specific provision for the comfortable maintenance of my son-in-law Thomas M. Randolph, because of the difficulty and uncertainty of devising terms which shall vest any beneficial interest in him, which the law will not transfer to the benefit of his creditors, to the destitution of my daughter and her family, and disablement of her to supply him: whereas, property placed under the exclusive control of my daughter and her independent will, as if she were a feme sole, considering the relation in which she stands both to him and his children, will be a certain resource against want for all.

I give to my friend James Madison, of Montpellier, my gold-mounted walking staff of animal horn, as a token of the cordial and affectionate friendship which for nearly now an half century, has united us in the same principles and pursuits of what we have deemed for the greatest good of our country.

I give to the University of Virginia my library, except such particular books only, and of the same edition, as it may already possess, when this legacy shall take effect; the rest of my said library, remaining after those given to the University shall have been taken out, I give to my two grandsons-in-law Nicholas P. Trist and Joseph Coolidge. To my grandson Thomas Jefferson Randolph, I give my silver watch in preference of the golden one, because of its superior excellence. My papers of business going of course to him, as my executor, all others of a literary or other character I give to him as of his own property.

I give a gold watch to each of my grandchildren, who shall not have already received one from me, to be purchased and delivered by my executor to my grandsons, at the age of twenty-one, and granddaughters at that of sixteen.

I give to my good, affectionate, and faithful servant Burwell, his freedom, and the sum of three hundred dollars, to buy necessaries to commence his trade of glazier, or to use otherwise, as he pleases.

I give also to my good servants John Hemings and Joe Fosset, their freedom at the end of one year after my death; and to each of them respectively, all the tools of their respective shops or callings; and it is my will that a comfortable log-house be built for each of the three servants so emancipated, on some part of my lands convenient to them with respect to the residence of their wives, and to Charlottesville and the University, where they will be mostly employed, and reasonably convenient also to the interests of the proprietor of the lands, of which houses I give the use of one, with a curtilage of an acre to each, during his life or personal occupation thereof.

I give also to John Hemings the service of his two apprentices Madison and Eston Hemings, until their respective ages of twenty-one years, at which period respectively, I give them their freedom; and I humbly and earnestly request of the legislature of Virginia a confirmation of the bequest of freedom to these servants, with permission to remain in this State, where their families and connections are, as an additional instance of the favor, of which I have received so many other manifestations in the course of my life, and for which I now give them my last, solemn, and dutiful thanks.

In testimony that this is a codicil to my will of yesterday's date, and that it is to modify so far the provisions of that will, I have written it all with my own hand in two pages, to each of which I subscribe my name, this seventeenth day of March, one thousand eight hundred and twenty-six. *March 16 and 17, 1826.*

PART TWO

——

Affairs of State, Education, Religion, and Slavery

PREFACE

THIS section contains a sampling of Jefferson's political and social papers, both official and private. They were selected as being particularly fine examples of his thought and style. Some of them—notably the *Declaration of Independence* and the two *Inaugural Addresses*—are, of course, American classics.

These documents are also characteristic of Jefferson's mind and concerns. They represent subjects that were close to his heart, as can be judged from what he expressly stated to be his claim to remembrance by posterity. Before his death, which took place around noon of July 4, 1826, he wrote out instructions as to what should be inscribed on his tombstone:

Here was buried
Thomas Jefferson
Author of the Declaration of American Independence
of the Statute of Virginia for religious freedom
& Father of the University of Virginia.

This was all ("& not a word more") for which, he wrote, "I wish to be remembered." The inscription is not only a form of self-evaluation; it is also a guide to what Jefferson deemed most important, namely, American self-government, freedom, and education. The papers given in the following pages are facets of all of these subjects.

A Summary View of the Rights of British America, written by Jefferson in 1774 and originally entitled "Instructions," is his first important political paper. It marked, so to speak, his historic debut. Published in Williamsburg and later in several editions in London, the pamphlet was designed to serve as a political-juridical brief for the American case against Great Britain. It is a sparkling essay, and may be considered as a reasoned forerunner of the *Declaration of Independence. A Summary*

View made Jefferson's reputation. In England, where it was read by men like Edmund Burke, the pamphlet (Jefferson tells in his *Autobiography*) "procured me the honor of having my name inserted in a long list of proscriptions" by the British Parliament.

Jefferson's two *Inaugural Addresses* are of intrinsic value to American liberty. Jefferson used them, not as customary political rhetoric, but as vehicles for the propagation of his democratic creed. In the *First Inaugural* he spelled out the meaning of republican government and the tenets on which it rests. This *Inaugural* is studded with memorable phrases: "Every difference of opinion is not a difference of principle." "Error of opinion may be tolerated where reason is left free to combat it." "Honest friendship with all nations, entangling alliances with none."

The *Second Inaugural*, a logical continuation of the First, was an exposition of how he had carried out the principles he had formulated in the First. One, he said, was *promise*; the other, *performance*. A noteworthy topic in the *Second Inaugural* is a pointed reference to American Indians, whose brutal treatment by whites moved Jefferson to mention his commiseration for their lot. In introducing this subject, he explained in a private note, he hoped "to promote the work of humanizing our citizens towards these people."

The *Bill for Establishing Religious Freedom*, as well as the essay on religion, contain the quintessence of Jefferson's ideas in this field, which he considered crucial. The Bill was introduced into the Virginia Assembly on June 13, 1779; it stirred up so much opposition that its passage was delayed until 1786. Jefferson regarded it as one of the major achievements of his life. The *Bill for the More General Diffusion of Knowledge* constituted a pioneering step in the establishment of American public schools. Both Bills are part of Virginia's codified laws, *Report of the Revisors* (Chapters LXXXII and LXXIX), of which Jefferson was the leading draftsman. The other two pieces, on religion and on slavery, are from Jefferson's only published book, *Notes on the State of Virginia*, written in 1781 and revised in 1782. Jefferson issued an anonymous edition of two hundred copies in Paris in 1785. Many editions, including a Philadelphia one in 1788, have appeared in subsequent years.

S. K. P.

A Summary View of the Rights of British America

August, 1774

THE Legislature of Virginia happened to be in session, in Williamsburg, when news was received of the passage, by the British Parliament, of the Boston Port Bill, which was to take effect on the first day of June then ensuing. The House of Burgesses, thereupon, passed a resolution, recommending to their fellow citizens, that that day should be set apart for fasting and prayer to the Supreme Being, imploring him to avert the calamities then threatening us, and to give us one heart and one mind to oppose every invasion of our liberties. The next day, May the 20th, 1774, the Governor dissolved us. We immediately repaired to a room in the Raleigh tavern, about one hundred paces distant from the Capitol, formed ourselves into a meeting, Peyton Randolph in the chair, and came to resolutions, declaring, that an attack on one colony, to enforce arbitrary acts, ought to be considered as an attack on all, and to be opposed by the united wisdom of all. We, therefore, appointed a Committee of correspondence, to address letters to the Speakers of the several Houses of Representatives of the colonies, proposing the appointment of deputies from each, to meet annually in a General Congress, to deliberate on their common interests, and on the measures to be pursued in common. The members then separated to their several homes, except those of the Committee, who met the next day, prepared letters according to instructions, and despatched them by messengers express, to their several destinations. It had been agreed, also, by the meeting, that the Burgesses, who should be elected under the writs then issuing, should be requested to meet in Convention, on a certain day in August, to learn the results of these letters, and to appoint delegates to a Congress, should that measure be approved by the other colonies. At the election, the people re-elected every man of the former Assembly, as a proof of their approbation of what they had done.

Before I left home, to attend the Convention, I prepared what I thought might be given, in instruction, to the Delegates who should be appointed to attend the General Congress proposed. They were drawn in haste, with a number of blanks, with some uncertainties and inaccuracies of historical facts, which I neglected at the moment, knowing they could be readily corrected at the meeting. I set out on my journey, but was taken sick on the road, and was unable to proceed. I therefore sent on, by express, two copies, one under cover to Patrick Henry, the other to Peyton Randolph, who I knew would be in the chair of the Convention. Of the former, no more was ever heard or known. Mr. Henry probably thought it too bold, as a first measure, as the majority of the members did. On the other copy being laid on the table of the Convention, by Peyton Randolph, as the proposition of a member, who was prevented from attendance by sickness on the road, tamer sentiments were preferred, and, I believe, wisely preferred; the leap I proposed being too long, as yet, for the mass of our citizens. The distance between these, and the instructions actually adopted, is of some curiosity, however, as it shews the inequality of pace with which we moved, and the prudence required to keep front and rear together. My creed had been formed on unsheathing the sword at Lexington. They printed the paper, however, and gave it the title of "A Summary View of the Rights of British America." In this form it got to London, where the opposition took it up, shaped it to opposition views, and, in that form, it ran rapidly through several editions:*

❧❧ Resolved, That it be an instruction to the said deputies, when assembled in General Congress, with the deputies from the other states of British America, to propose to the said Congress, that an humble and dutiful address be presented to his Majesty, begging leave to lay before him, as Chief Magistrate of the British empire, the united complaints of his Majesty's subjects in America; complaints which are excited by many unwarrantable encroachments and usurpations, attempted to be

* See Jefferson's *Autobiography*, Part I, page 12.

made by the legislature of one part of the empire, upon the rights which God, and the laws, have given equally and independently to all. To represent to his Majesty that these, his States, have often individually made humble application to his imperial Throne, to obtain, through its intervention, some redress of their injured rights; to none of which, was ever even an answer condescended. Humbly to hope that this, their joint address, penned in the language of truth, and divested of those expressions of servility, which would persuade his Majesty that we are asking favors, and not rights, shall obtain from his Majesty a more respectful acceptance; and this his Majesty will think we have reason to expect, when he reflects that he is no more than the chief officer of the people, appointed by the laws, and circumscribed with definite powers, to assist in working the great machine of government, erected for their use, and, consequently, subject to their superintendence; and, in order that these, our rights, as well as the invasions of them, may be laid more fully before his Majesty, to take a view of them, from the origin and first settlement of these countries.

To remind him that our ancestors, before their emigration to America, were the free inhabitants of the British dominions in Europe, and possessed a right, which nature has given to all men, of departing from the country in which chance, not choice, has placed them, of going in quest of new habitations, and of there establishing new societies, under such laws and regulations as, to them, shall seem most likely to promote public happiness. That their Saxon ancestors had, under this universal law, in like manner, left their native wilds and woods in the North of Europe, had possessed themselves of the Island of Britain, then less charged with inhabitants, and had established there that system of laws which has so long been the glory and protection of that country. Nor was ever any claim of superiority or dependence asserted over them, by that mother country from which they had migrated: and were such a claim made, it is believed his Majesty's subjects in Great Britain have too firm a feeling of the rights derived to them from their ancestors, to bow down the sovereignty of their state before such visionary pretensions. And it is thought that no circumstance has occurred to distinguish, materially, the British from the Saxon emigration. America was

·[245]·

conquered, and her settlements made and firmly established, at the expense of individuals, and not of the British public. Their own blood was spilt in acquiring lands for their settlement, their own fortunes expended in making that settlement effectual. For themselves they fought, for themselves they conquered, and for themselves alone they have right to hold. No shilling was ever issued from the public treasures of his Majesty, or his ancestors, for their assistance, till of very late times, after the colonies had become established on a firm and permanent footing. That then, indeed, having become valuable to Great Britain for her commercial purposes, his Parliament was pleased to lend them assistance against an enemy who would fain have drawn to herself the benefits of their commerce, to the great aggrandisement of herself, and danger of Great Britain. Such assistance, and in such circumstances, they had often before given to Portugal and other allied states, with whom they carry on a commercial intercourse. Yet these states never supposed, that by calling in her aid, they thereby submitted themselves to her sovereignty. Had such terms been proposed, they would have rejected them with disdain, and trusted for better, to the moderation of their enemies, or to a vigorous exertion of their own force. We do not, however, mean to underrate those aids, which, to us, were doubtless valuable, on whatever principles granted: but we would shew that they cannot give a title to that authority which the British Parliament would arrogate over us; and that may amply be repaid by our giving to the inhabitants of Great Britain such exclusive privileges in trade as may be advantageous to them, and, at the same time, not too restrictive to ourselves. That settlement having been thus effected in the wilds of America, the emigrants thought proper to adopt that system of laws, under which they had hitherto lived in the mother country, and to continue their union with her, by submitting themselves to the same common sovereign, who was thereby made the central link, connecting the several parts of the empire thus newly multiplied.

But that not long were they permitted, however far they thought themselves removed from the hand of oppression, to hold undisturbed the rights thus acquired at the hazard of their lives and loss of their fortunes. A family of Princes was then on the British throne, whose treasonable crimes against their people, brought on them, afterwards, the exertion of those sacred and sovereign rights of punishment, reserved in the hands of the people for cases of extreme necessity, and judged by the constitution unsafe to be delegated to any other judicature. While every day brought forth some new and unjustifiable exertion of power over their subjects on that side of the water, it was not to be expected that those here, much less able at that time to oppose the designs of despotism, should be exempted from injury. Accordingly, this country which had been acquired by the lives, the labors, and fortunes of individual adventurers, was by these Princes, several times, parted out and distributed among the favorites and followers of their fortunes; and, by an assumed right of the Crown alone, were erected into distinct and independent governments; a measure, which it is believed, his Majesty's prudence and understanding would prevent him from imitating at this day; as no exercise of such power, of dividing and dismembering a country, has ever occurred in his Majesty's realm of England, though now of very ancient standing; nor could it be justified or acquiesced under there, or in any part of his Majesty's empire.

That the exercise of a free trade with all parts of the world, possessed by the American colonists, as of natural right, and which no law of their own had taken away or abridged, was next the object of unjust encroachment. Some of the colonies having thought proper to continue the administration of their government in the name and under the authority of his Majesty, King Charles the first, whom, notwithstanding his late deposition by the Commonwealth of England, they continued in the sovereignty of their State, the Parliament, for the Commonwealth, took the same in high offence, and assumed upon themselves the power of prohibiting their trade with all other parts of the world, except the Island of Great Britain. This arbitrary act, however, they soon recalled, and by solemn treaty entered into on the 12th day of March, 1651, between the said Commonwealth, by their Commissioners, and the colony of Virginia by their House of Burgesses, it was expressly stipulated by the eighth article of the said treaty, that they should have "free trade as the people of England do enjoy to all places and with all nations, according to the laws of that Commonwealth."

But that, upon the restoration of his Majesty, King Charles the second, their rights of free commerce fell once more a victim to arbitrary power; and by several acts of his reign, as well as some of his successors, the trade of the colonies was laid under such restrictions, as show what hopes they might form from the justice of a British Parliament, were its uncontrolled power admitted over these States. History has informed us, that bodies of men as well as of individuals, are susceptible of the spirit of tyranny. A view of these acts of Parliament for regulation, as it has been affectedly called, of the American trade, if all other evidences were removed out of the case, would undeniably evince the truth of this observation. Besides the duties they impose on our articles of export and import, they prohibit our going to any markets Northward of Cape Finisterra, in the kingdom of Spain, for the sale of commodities which Great Britain will not take from us, and for the purchase of others, with which she cannot supply us; and that, for no other than the arbitrary purpose of purchasing for themselves, by a sacrifice of our rights and interests, certain privileges in their commerce with an allied state, who, in confidence, that their exclusive trade with America will be continued, while the principles and power of the British Parliament be the same, have indulged themselves in every exorbitance which their avarice could dictate or our necessity extort: have raised their commodities called for in America, to the double and treble of what they sold for, before such exclusive privileges were given them, and of what better commodities of the same kind would cost us elsewhere; and, at the same time, give us much less for what we carry thither, than might be had at more convenient ports. That these acts prohibit us from carrying, in quest of other purchasers, the surplus of our tobaccos, remaining after the consumption of Great Britain is supplied: so that we must leave them with the British merchant, for whatever he will please to allow us, to be by him re-shipped to foreign markets, where he will reap the benefits of making sale of them for full value. That, to heighten still the idea of Parliamentary justice, and to show with what moderation they are like to exercise power, where themselves are to feel no part of its weight, we take leave to mention to his Majesty, certain other acts of the British Parliament, by which they would prohibit us from manufacturing, for our own use, the articles we raise on our own lands, with our own labor. By an act passed in the fifth year of the reign of his late Majesty, King George the second, an American subject is forbidden to make a hat for himself, of the fur which he has taken, perhaps, on his own soil; an instance of despotism, to which no parallel can be produced in the most arbitrary ages of British history. By one other act, passed in the twenty-third year of the same reign, the iron which we make, we are forbidden to manufacture; and, heavy as that article is, and necessary in every branch of husbandry, besides commission and insurance, we are to pay freight for it to Great Britain, and freight for it back again, for the purpose of supporting, not men, but machines, in the island of Great Britain. In the same spirit of equal and impartial legislation, is to be viewed the act of Parliament, passed in the fifth year of the same reign, by which American lands are made subject to the demands of British creditors, while their own lands were still continued unanswerable for their debts; from which, one of these conclusions must necessarily follow, either that justice is not the same thing in America as in Britain, or else, that the British Parliament pay less regard to it here than there. But, that we do not point out to his Majesty the injustice of these acts, with intent to rest on that principle the cause of their nullity; but to show that experience confirms the propriety of those political principles, which exempt us from the jurisdiction of the British Parliament. The true ground on which we declare these acts void, is, that the British Parliament has no right to exercise authority over us.

That these exercises of usurped power have not been confined to instances alone, in which themselves were interested; but they have also intermeddled with the regulation of the internal affairs of the colonies. The act of the 9th of Anne for establishing a post office in America, seems to have had little connection with British convenience, except that of accommodating his Majesty's ministers and favorites with the sale of a lucrative and easy office.

That thus have we hastened through the reigns which preceded his Majesty's, during which the violation of our rights were less alarming, because repeated at more distant intervals, than that rapid and bold succession of injuries, which is likely to distinguish the present from all other periods of American story. Scarcely have our minds been able to emerge from the astonishment into which one stroke of Parliamentary thunder has involved us, before another more heavy and more alarming is fallen on us. Single acts of tyranny may be ascribed to the accidental opinion of a day; but a series of oppressions, begun at a distinguished period, and pursued unalterably through every change of ministers, too plainly prove a deliberate, systematical plan of reducing us to slavery.

That the act passed in the fourth year of his Majesty's reign, entitled "an act [for granting certain duties],"

One other act passed in the fifth year of his reign, entitled "an act . . ." [Stamp act],

One other act passed in the sixth year of his reign, entitled "an act [declaring the right of Parliament over the colonies],"

And one other act passed in the seventh year of his reign, entitled "an act [for granting duties on paper, tea, &c.],"

. . . form that connected chain of Parliamentary usurpation, which has already been the subject of frequent applications to his Majesty, and the Houses of Lords and Commons of Great Britain; and, no answers having yet been condescended to any of these, we shall not trouble his Majesty with a repetition of the matters they contained.

But that one other act passed in the same seventh year of his reign, having been a peculiar attempt, must ever require peculiar mention. It is entitled "an act [suspending legislature of New York]."

One free and independent legislature, hereby takes upon itself to suspend the powers of another, free and independent as itself. Thus exhibiting a phenomenon in nature, the creator, the creature of its own power. Not only the principles of common sense, but the common feelings of human nature must be surrendered up, before his Majesty's subjects here, can be persuaded to believe, that they hold their political existence at the will of a British Parliament. Shall these governments be dissolved, their property annihilated, and their people reduced to a state of nature, at the imperious breath of a body of men whom they never saw, in whom they never confided, and over whom they have no powers of punishment or removal, let their crimes against the American public be ever so great? Can any one reason be assigned, why one hundred and sixty thousand electors in the island of Great Britain, should give law to four millions in the States of America, every individual of whom is equal to every individual of them in virtue, in understanding, and in bodily strength? Were this to be admitted, instead of being a free people, as we have hitherto supposed, and mean to continue ourselves, we should suddenly be found the slaves, not of one, but of one hundred and sixty thousand tyrants; distinguished, too, from all others, by this singular circumstance, that they are removed from the reach of fear, the only restraining motive which may hold the hand of a tyrant.

That, by "an act to discontinue in such manner, and for such time as are therein mentioned, the landing and discharging, lading or shipping of goods, wares and merchandize, at the town and within the harbor of Boston, in the province of Massachusetts bay, in North America," which was passed at the last session of the British Parliament, a large and populous town, whose trade was their sole subsistence, was deprived of that trade, and involved in utter ruin. Let us for a while, suppose the question of right suspended, in order to examine this act on principles of justice. An act of Parliament had been passed, imposing duties on teas, to be paid in America, against which act the Americans had protested, as inauthoritative. The East India Company, who till that time, had never sent a pound of tea to America on their own account, step forth on that occasion, the asserters of Parliamentary right, and send hither many ship loads of that obnoxious commodity. The masters of their several vessels, however, on their arrival in America, wisely attended to admonition, and returned with their cargoes. In the province of New-England alone, the remonstrances of the people were disregarded, and a compliance, after being many days waited for, was flatly refused. Whether in this, the master of the vessel was governed by his obstinacy, or his instructions, let those who know, say. There are extraordinary situations which require extraordinary interposition. An exasperated people, who feel that they possess power, are not easily restrained within limits strictly regular. A number of them assembled in the town of Boston, threw the tea into the ocean, and dispersed without doing any other act of violence. If in this they did wrong, they were known, and were amenable to the laws of the land; against which, it could not be objected, that they had ever, in any instance, been obstructed or diverted from the regular course, in favor of popular offenders. They should, therefore, not have been distrusted on this occasion. But that ill-fated colony had formerly been bold in their enmities against the House of Stuart, and were now devoted to ruin, by that unseen hand which governs the momentous affairs of this great empire. On the partial representations of a few worthless ministerial dependants, whose constant office it has been to keep that government embroiled, and who, by their treacheries, hope to obtain the dignity of British knighthood, without calling for a party accused, without asking a proof, without attempting a distinction between the guilty and the innocent, the whole of that ancient and wealthy town, is in a moment reduced from opulence to beggary. Men who had spent their lives in extending the British commerce, who had invested, in that place, the wealth their honest endeavors had merited, found themselves and their families, thrown at once on the world, for subsistence by its charities. Not the hundredth part of the inhabitants of that town, had been concerned in the act complained of; many of them were in Great Britain, and in other parts beyond sea; yet all were involved in one indiscriminate ruin, by a new executive power, unheard of till then, that of a British Parliament. A property of the value of many millions of money, was sacrificed to revenge, not repay, the loss of a few thousands. This is administering justice with a heavy hand indeed! And when is this tempest to be arrested in its course? Two wharves are to be opened again when his Majesty shall think proper: the residue, which lined the extensive shores of the bay of Boston, are forever interdicted the exercise of commerce. This little exception seems to have been thrown in for no other purpose, than that of setting a precedent for investing his Majesty with legislative powers. If the pulse of his people shall beat calmly under this experiment, another and another will be tried, till the measure of despotism be filled up. It would be an insult on common sense, to pretend that this exception was made, in order to restore its commerce to that great town. The trade, which cannot be received at two wharves alone, must of necessity be transferred to some other place; to which it will soon be followed by that of the two wharves. Considered in this light, it would be an insolent and cruel mockery at the annihilation of the town of Boston. By the act for the suppression of riots and tumults in the town of Boston, passed also in the last session of Parliament, a murder committed there, is, if the Governor pleases, to be tried in the court of King's bench, in the island of Great Britain, by a jury of Middlesex. The witnesses, too, on receipt of such a sum as the Governor shall think it reasonable for them to expend, are to enter into recognizance to appear at the trial. This is, in other words, taxing them to the amount of their recognizance; and that amount may be whatever a Governor pleases. For who does his Majesty think can be prevailed on to cross the Atlantic for the sole purpose of bearing evidence to a fact? His expenses are to be borne, indeed, as they shall be estimated by a Governor; but who are to feed the wife and children whom he leaves behind, and who have had no other subsistence but his daily labor? Those epidemical disorders, too, so terrible in a foreign climate, is the cure of them to be estimated among the articles of expense, and their danger to be warded off by the Almighty power of a Parliament? And the wretched criminal, if he happen to have offended on the American side, stripped of his privilege of trial by peers of his vicinage, removed from the place where alone full evidence could be obtained, without money, without counsel, without friends, without exculpatory proof, is tried before Judges predetermined to condemn. The cowards who would suffer a countryman to be torn from the bowels of their society, in order to be thus offered a sacrifice to Parliamentary tyranny, would merit that everlasting infamy now fixed on the authors of the act! A clause, for a similar purpose, had been introduced into an act passed in the twelfth year of his Majesty's reign, entitled, "an act for the better securing and preserving his Majesty's Dock-yards, Magazines, Ships, Ammunition and Stores"; against which, as meriting the same censures, the several colonies have already protested.

That these are the acts of power, assumed by a body of men foreign to our constitutions, and unacknowledged by our laws; against which we do, on behalf of the inhabitants of British America, enter this, our solemn and determined protest. And we do earnestly intreat his Majesty, as yet the only mediatory power between the several States of the British empire, to recommend to his Parliament of Great Britain, the total revocation of these acts, which, however nugatory they may be, may yet prove the cause of further discontents and jealousies among us.

That we next proceed to consider the conduct of his Majesty, as holding the Executive powers of the laws of these States, and mark out his deviations from the line of duty. By the Constitution of Great Britain, as well as of the several American States, his Majesty possesses the power of refusing to pass into a law, any bill which has already passed the other two branches of the legislature. His Majesty, however, and his ancestors, conscious of the impropriety of opposing their single opinion to the united wisdom of two Houses of Parliament, while their proceedings were unbiassed by interested principles, for several ages past, have modestly declined the exercise of this power, in that part of his empire called Great Britain. But, by change of circumstances, other principles than those of justice simply, have obtained an influence on their determinations. The addition of new States to the British empire has produced an addition of new, and, sometimes, opposite interests. It is now, therefore, the great office of his Majesty to resume the exercise of his negative power, and to prevent the passage of laws by any one legislature of the empire, which might bear injuriously on the rights and interests of another. Yet this will not excuse the wanton exercise of this power, which we have seen his Majesty practice on the laws of the American legislature. For the most trifling reasons, and, sometimes for no conceivable reason at all, his Majesty has rejected laws of the most salutary tendency. The abolition of domestic slavery is the great object of desire in those colonies, where it was, unhappily, introduced in their infant state. But previous to the enfranchisement of the slaves we have, it is necessary to exclude all further importations from Africa. Yet our repeated attempts to effect this, by prohibitions, and by imposing duties which might amount to a prohibition, having been hitherto defeated by his Majesty's negative: thus preferring the immediate advantages of a few British corsairs, to the lasting interests of the American States, and to the rights of human nature, deeply wounded by this infamous practice. Nay, the single inter-position of an interested individual against a law was scarcely ever known to fail of success, though, in the opposite scale, were placed the interests of a whole country. That this is so shameful an abuse of a power, trusted with his Majesty for other purposes, as if, not reformed, would call for some legal restrictions.

With equal inattention to the necessities of his people here has his Majesty permitted our laws to lie neglected, in England, for years, nei-ther confirming them by his assent, nor annulling them by his negative: so, that such of them as have no suspending clause, we hold on the most precarious of all tenures, his Majesty's will; and such of them as sus-pend themselves till his Majesty's assent be obtained, we have feared might be called into existence at some future and distant period, when time and change of circumstances shall have rendered them destructive to his people here. And, to render this grievance still more oppressive, his Majesty, by his instructions, has laid his Governors under such re-strictions, that they can pass no law, of any moment, unless it have such suspending clause: so that, however immediate may be the call for leg-islative interposition, the law cannot be executed, till it has twice crossed the Atlantic, by which time the evil may have spent its whole force.

But in what terms reconcilable to Majesty, and at the same time to truth, shall we speak of a late instruction to his Majesty's Governor of the colony of Virginia, by which he is forbidden to assent to any law for the division of a county, unless the new county will consent to have no representative in Assembly? That colony has as yet affixed no bound-ary to the Westward. Their Western counties, therefore, are of an indefinite extent. Some of them are actually seated many hundred miles from their Eastern limits. Is it possible, then, that his Majesty can have bestowed a single thought on the situation of those people, who in order to obtain justice for injuries, however great or small, must, by the laws of that colony, attend their county court at such a distance, with all their witnesses, monthly, till their litigation be determined? Or does his Majesty seriously wish, and publish it to the world, that his subjects should give up the glorious right of representation, with all the benefits derived from that, and submit themselves the absolute slaves of his sovereign will? Or is it rather meant to confine the legislative body to their present numbers, that they may be the cheaper bargain, whenever they shall become worth a purchase?

One of the articles of impeachment against Tresilian, and the other Judges of Westminster Hall, in the reign of Richard the Second, for which they suffered death, as traitors to their country, was, that they had advised the King, that they might dissolve his Parliament at any time; and succeeding kings have adopted the opinion of these unjust Judges. Since the establishment, however, of the British constitution, at the glorious Revolution, on its free and ancient principles, neither his Majesty, nor his ancestors, have exercised such a power of dissolution in the island of Great Britain;* and when his Majesty was petitioned, by the united voice of his people there, to dissolve the present Parliament, who had become obnoxious to them, his Ministers were heard to declare, in open Parliament, that his Majesty possessed no such power by the constitution. But how different their language, and his practice, here! To declare, as their duty required, the known rights of their country, to oppose the usurpation of every foreign judicature, to disregard the imperious mandates of a Minister or Governor, have been the avowed causes of dissolving Houses of Representatives in America. But if such powers be really vested in his Majesty, can he suppose they are there placed to awe the members from such purposes as these? When the representative body have lost the confidence of their constituents, when they have notoriously made sale of their most valuable rights, when they have assumed to themselves powers which the people never put into their hands, then, indeed, their continuing in office becomes dangerous to the State, and calls for an exercise of the power of dissolution. Such being the cause for which the representative body should, and should not, be dissolved, will it not appear strange,

---

* On further inquiry, I find two instances of dissolution before the Parliament would, of itself, have been at an end: *viz.*, the Parliament called to meet August 24, 1698, was dissolved by King William, December 19, 1700, and a new one called, to meet February 6, 1701, which was also dissolved, November 11, 1701, and a new one met December 30, 1701.—T.J.

to an unbiassed observer, that that of Great Britain was not dissolved, while those of the colonies have repeatedly incurred that sentence?

But your Majesty, or your Governors, have carried this power beyond every limit known or provided for by the laws. After dissolving one House of Representatives, they have refused to call another, so that, for a great length of time, the legislature provided by the laws, has been out of existence. From the nature of things, every society must, at all times, possess within itself the sovereign powers of legislation. The feelings of human nature revolt against the supposition of a State so situated, as that it may not, in any emergency, provide against dangers which, perhaps, threaten immediate ruin. While those bodies are in existence to whom the people have delegated the powers of legislation, they alone possess, and may exercise, those powers. But when they are dissolved, by the lopping off one or more of their branches, the power reverts to the people, who may use it to unlimited extent, either assembling together in person, sending deputies, or in any other way they may think proper. We forbear to trace consequences further; the dangers are conspicuous with which this practice is replete.

That we shall, at this time also, take notice of an error in the nature of our land holdings, which crept in at a very early period of our settlement. The introduction of the feudal tenures into the kingdom of England, though ancient, is well enough understood to set this matter in a proper light. In the earlier ages of the Saxon settlement, feudal holdings were certainly altogether unknown, and very few, if any, had been introduced at the time of the Norman conquest. Our Saxon ancestors held their lands, as they did their personal property, in absolute dominion, disincumbered with any superior, answering nearly to the nature of those possessions which the feudalist term Allodial. William the Norman, first introduced that system generally. The lands which had belonged to those who fell in the battle of Hastings, and in the subsequent insurrections of his reign, formed a considerable proportion of the lands of the whole kingdom. These he granted out, subject to feudal duties, as did he also those of a great number of his new subjects, who, by persuasions or threats, were induced to surrender them for that purpose. But still, much was left in the hands of his Saxon subjects,

held of no superior, and not subject to feudal conditions. These, therefore, by express laws, enacted to render uniform the system of military
defence, were made liable to the same military duties as if they had
been feuds; and the Norman lawyers soon found means to saddle them,
also, with the other feudal burthens. But still they had not been surrendered to the King, they were not derived from his grant, and therefore they were not holden of him. A general principle was introduced,
that "all lands in England were held either mediately or immediately
of the Crown"; but this was borrowed from those holdings which were
truly feudal, and only applied to others for the purposes of illustration.
Feudal holdings were, therefore, but exceptions out of the Saxon laws
of possession, under which all lands were held in absolute right. These,
therefore, still form the basis or groundwork of the Common law, to
prevail wheresoever the exceptions have not taken place. America was
not conquered by William the Norman, nor its lands surrendered to
him or any of his successors. Possessions there are, undoubtedly, of the
Allodial nature. Our ancestors, however, who migrated hither, were
laborers, not lawyers. The fictitious principle, that all lands belong
originally to the King, they were early persuaded to believe real, and
accordingly took grants of their own lands from the Crown. And while
the Crown continued to grant for small sums and on reasonable rents,
there was no inducement to arrest the error, and lay it open to public
view. But his Majesty has lately taken on him to advance the terms of
purchase and of holding, to the double of what they were; by which
means, the acquisition of lands being rendered difficult, the population
of our country is likely to be checked. It is time, therefore, for us to lay
this matter before his Majesty, and to declare, that he has no right to
grant lands of himself. From the nature and purpose of civil institutions,
all the lands within the limits, which any particular party has circumscribed around itself, are assumed by that society, and subject to their
allotment; this may be done by themselves assembled collectively, or
by their legislature, to whom they may have delegated sovereign authority; and, if they are allotted in neither of these ways, each individual of the society, may appropriate to himself such lands as he finds
vacant, and occupancy will give him title.

That, in order to enforce the arbitrary measures before complained of, his Majesty has, from time to time, sent among us large bodies of armed forces, not made up of the people here, nor raised by the authority of our laws. Did his Majesty possess such a right as this, it might swallow up all our other rights, whenever he should think proper. But his Majesty has no right to land a single armed man on our shores; and those whom he sends here are liable to our laws, for the suppression and punishment of riots, routs, and unlawful assemblies, or are hostile bodies invading us in defiance of law. When, in the course of the late war, it became expedient that a body of Hanoverian troops should be brought over for the defence of Great Britain, his Majesty's grandfather, our late sovereign, did not pretend to introduce them under any authority he possessed. Such a measure would have given just alarm to his subjects of Great Britain, whose liberties would not be safe if armed men of another country, and of another spirit, might be brought into the realm at any time, without the consent of their legislature. He, therefore, applied to Parliament, who passed an act for that purpose, limiting the number to be brought in, and the time they were to continue. In like manner is his Majesty restrained in every part of the empire. He possesses indeed the executive power of the laws in every State; but they are the laws of the particular State, which he is to administer within that State, and not those of any one within the limits of another. Every State must judge for itself, the number of armed men which they may safely trust among them, of whom they are to consist, and under what restrictions they are to be laid. To render these proceedings still more criminal against our laws, instead of subjecting the military to the civil power, his Majesty has expressly made the civil subordinate to the military. But can his Majesty thus put down all law under his feet? Can he erect a power superior to that which erected himself? He has done it indeed by force; but let him remember that force cannot give right.

That these are our grievances, which we have thus laid before his Majesty, with that freedom of language and sentiment which becomes a free people, claiming their rights as derived from the laws of nature, and not as the gift of their Chief Magistrate. Let those flatter, who fear: it is not an American art. To give praise where it is not due might be well from the venal, but would ill beseem those who are asserting the rights of human nature. They know, and will, therefore, say, that Kings are the servants, not the proprietors of the people. Open your breast, Sire, to liberal and expanded thought. Let not the name of George the third, be a blot on the page of history. You are surrounded by British counsellors, but remember that they are parties. You have no ministers for American affairs, because you have none taken from among us, nor amenable to the laws on which they are to give you advice. It behooves you, therefore, to think and to act for yourself and your people. The great principles of right and wrong are legible to every reader; to pursue them, requires not the aid of many counsellors. The whole art of government consists in the art of being honest. Only aim to do your duty, and mankind will give you credit where you fail. No longer persevere in sacrificing the rights of one part of the empire to the inordinate desires of another; but deal out to all, equal and impartial right. Let no act be passed by any one legislature, which may infringe on the rights and liberties of another. This is the important post in which fortune has placed you, holding the balance of a great, if a well-poised empire. This, Sire, is the advice of your great American council, on the observance of which may perhaps depend your felicity and future fame, and the preservation of that harmony which alone can continue, both to Great Britain and America, the reciprocal advantages of their connection. It is neither our wish nor our interest to separate from her. We are willing, on our part, to sacrifice everything which reason can ask, to the restoration of that tranquillity for which all must wish. On their part, let them be ready to establish union on a generous plan. Let them name their terms, but let them be just. Accept of every commercial preference it is in our power to give, for such things as we can raise for their use, or they make for ours. But let them not think to exclude us from going to other markets to dispose of those commodities which they cannot use, nor to supply those wants which they cannot supply. Still less, let it be proposed, that our properties, within our own territories, shall be taxed or regulated by any power on earth, but our own. The God who gave us life, gave us liberty at the same time: the hand of force may destroy, but cannot disjoin them. This, Sire, is our last, our determined resolution. And that you will be pleased to interpose, with that efficacy which your earnest endeavors may insure, to procure redress of these great grievances, to quiet the minds of your subjects in British America against any apprehensions of future encroachment, to establish fraternal love and harmony through the whole empire, and that that may continue to the latest ages of time, is the fervent prayer of all British America.

The Declaration of Independence

A Declaration by the Representatives of the United States of America, in General Congress Assembled*

July 4, 1776

WHEN, in the course of human events, it becomes necessary for one people to dissolve the political bands which have connected them with another, and to assume among the powers of the earth the separate and equal station to which the laws of nature and of nature's God entitle them, a decent respect to the opinions of mankind requires that they should declare the causes which impel them to the separation.

We hold these truths to be self-evident; that all men are created equal; that they are endowed by their creator with [*inherent and*] *certain* inalienable rights; that among these are life, liberty, and the pursuit of happiness; that to secure these rights, governments are instituted among men, deriving their just powers from the consent of the governed; that whenever any form of government becomes destructive of these ends, it is the right of the people to alter or to abolish it, and to institute new government, laying its foundation on such principles, and organizing its powers in such form, as to them shall seem most likely to effect their safety and happiness. Prudence, indeed, will dictate that governments

* This was Jefferson's original title. Congress changed it, on July 19, 1776, to "The Unanimous Declaration of the thirteen united States of America."

Since this is Jefferson's most famous paper, the text is given here as he first wrote it and as it was finally corrected. The parts stricken out by Congress are printed in italics and bracketed; the parts substituted or inserted by Congress are printed in italics without brackets. For the last section, the final text is shown at the right of Jefferson's version.

long established should not be changed for light and transient causes; and accordingly all experience hath shown that mankind are more disposed to suffer while evils are sufferable, than to right themselves by abolishing the forms to which they are accustomed. But when a long train of abuses and usurpations [*begun at a distinguished period and*] pursuing invariably the same object, evinces a design to reduce them under absolute despotism, it is their right, it is their duty to throw off such government, and to provide new guards for their future security. Such has been the patient sufferance of these Colonies; and such is now the necessity which constrains them to [*expunge*] alter their former systems of government. The history of the present King of Great Britain is a history of [*unremitting*] repeated injuries and usurpations, [*among which appears no solitary fact to contradict the uniform tenor of the rest, but all have*] all having in direct object the establishment of an absolute tyranny over these States. To prove this, let facts be submitted to a candid world [*for the truth of which we pledge a faith yet unsullied by falsehood*].

He has refused his assent to laws the most wholesome and necessary for the public good.

He has forbidden his governors to pass laws of immediate and pressing importance, unless suspended in their operation till his assent should be obtained; and, when so suspended, he has utterly neglected to attend to them.

He has refused to pass other laws for the accommodation of large districts of people, unless those people would relinquish the right of representation in the Legislature, a right inestimable to them, and formidable to tyrants only.

He has called together legislative bodies at places unusual, uncomfortable, and distant from the depository of their public records, for the sole purpose of fatiguing them into compliance with his measures.

He has dissolved representative houses repeatedly [*and continually*] for opposing with manly firmness his invasions on the rights of the people.

He has refused for a long time after such dissolutions to cause others to be elected, whereby the legislative powers, incapable of annihilation, have returned to the people at large for their exercise, the State remaining, in the meantime, exposed to all the dangers of invasion from without and convulsions within.

He has endeavored to prevent the population of these States; for that purpose obstructing the laws for naturalization of foreigners, refusing to pass others to encourage their migrations hither, and raising the conditions of new appropriations of lands.

He has [*suffered*] obstructed the administration of justice [*totally to cease in some of these States*] by refusing his assent to laws for establishing judiciary powers.

He has made [*our*] judges dependent on his will alone for the tenure of their offices, and the amount and payment of their salaries.

He has erected a multitude of new offices [*by a self-assumed power*], and sent hither swarms of new officers to harass our people and eat out their substance.

He has kept among us in times of peace standing armies [*and ships of war*] without the consent of our Legislatures.

He has affected to render the military independent of, and superior to, the civil power.

He has combined with others to subject us to a jurisdiction foreign to our constitutions and unacknowledged by our laws, giving his assent to their acts of pretended legislation for quartering large bodies of armed troops among us; for protecting them by a mock trial from punishment for any murders which they should commit on the inhabitants of these States; for cutting off our trade with all parts of the world; for imposing taxes on us without our consent; for depriving us *in many cases* of the benefits of trial by jury; for transporting us beyond seas to be tried for pretended offences; for abolishing the free system of English laws in a neighboring province, establishing therein an arbitrary government, and enlarging its boundaries, so as to render it at once an example and fit instrument for introducing the same absolute rule into these [*States*] Colonies; for taking away our charters, abolishing our most valuable laws, and altering fundamentally the forms of our governments; for suspending our own Legislatures, and declaring themselves invested with power to legislate for us in all cases whatsoever.

He has abdicated government here [*withdrawing his governors, and declaring us out of his allegiance and protection]* by declaring us out of his protection, and waging war against us.

He has plundered our seas, ravaged our coasts, burnt our towns, and destroyed the lives of our people.

He is at this time transporting large armies of foreign mercenaries to complete the works of death, desolation, and tyranny already begun with circumstances of cruelty and perfidy *scarcely paralleled in the most barbarous ages, and totally* unworthy the head of a civilized nation.

He has constrained our fellow-citizens taken captive on the high seas to bear arms against their country, to become the executioners of their friends and brethren, or to fall themselves by their hands.

He has *excited domestic insurrection among us, and has* endeavored to bring on the inhabitants of our frontiers the merciless Indian savages, whose known rule of warfare is an undistinguished destruction of all ages, sexes, and conditions *[of existence]*.

[He has incited treasonable insurrections of our fellow-citizens, with the allurements of forfeiture and confiscation of our property.

[He has waged cruel war against human nature itself, violating its most sacred rights of life and liberty in the persons of a distant people who never offended him, captivating and carrying them into slavery in another hemisphere, or to incur miserable death in their transportation thither. This piratical warfare, the opprobrium of INFIDEL *powers, is the warfare of the* CHRISTIAN *King of Great Britain. Determined to keep open a market where* MEN *should be bought and sold, he has prostituted his negative for suppressing every legislative attempt to prohibit or to restrain this execrable commerce. And that this assemblage of horrors might want no fact of distinguished die, he is now exciting those very people to rise in arms among us, and to purchase that liberty of which he has deprived them, by murdering the people on whom he also obtruded them: thus paying off former crimes committed against the* LIBERTIES *of one people with crimes which he urges them to commit against the* LIVES *of another.]*

In every stage of these oppressions we have petitioned for redress in the most humble terms: our repeated petitions have been answered only by repeated injuries.

A Prince whose character is thus marked by every act which may define a tyrant is unfit to be the ruler of a *free* people [*who mean to be free. Future ages will scarcely believe that the hardiness of one man adventured, within the short compass of twelve years only, to lay a foundation so broad and so undisguised for tyranny over a people fostered and fixed in principles of freedom*].

Nor have we been wanting in attentions to our British brethren. We have warned them from time to time of attempts by their legislature to extend [*a*] an unwarrantable jurisdiction over [*these our States*] us. We have reminded them of the circumstances of our emigration and settlement here, [*no one of which could warrant so strange a pretension: that these were effected at the expense of our own blood and treasure, unassisted by the wealth or the strength of Great Britain: that in constituting indeed our several forms of government, we had adopted one common king, thereby laying a foundation for perpetual league and amity with them: but that submission to their parliament was no part of our Constitution, nor ever in idea, if history may be credited: and,*] we *have* appealed to their native justice and magnanimity [*as well as to*] *and we have conjured them by* the ties of our common kindred to disavow these usurpations which [*were likely to*] *would inevitably* interrupt our connection and correspondence. They too have been deaf to the voice of justice and of consanguinity[, *and when occasions have been given them, by the regular course of their laws, of removing from their councils the disturbers of our harmony, they have, by their free election, re-established them in power. At this very time too, they are permitting their chief magistrate to send over not only soldiers of our common blood, but Scotch and foreign mercenaries to invade and destroy us. These facts have given the last stab to agonizing affection, and manly spirit bids us to renounce forever these unfeeling brethren. We must endeavor to forget our former love for them, and hold them as we hold the rest of mankind, enemies in war, in peace friends. We might have been a free and a great people together; but a communication of grandeur and of freedom, it seems, is below their dignity. Be it so, since they will have it. The road to happiness and to glory is open to us too. We will tread it apart from them, and*]. *We must therefore* acquiesce in the necessity which denounces our [*eternal*] separation *and hold them as we hold the rest of mankind, enemies in war, in peace friends*[*!*].

We therefore the representatives of the United States of America in General Congress assembled, do in the name, and by the authority of the good people of these [*States reject and renounce all allegiance and subjection to the kings of Great Britain and all others who may hereafter claim by, through, or under them; we utterly dissolve all political connection which may heretofore have subsisted between us and the people or parliament of Great Britain: and finally we do assert and declare these Colonies to be free and independent States,*] and that as free and independent States, they have full power to levy war, conclude peace, contract alliances, establish commerce, and to do all other acts and things which independent States may of right do.

And for the support of this declaration, we mutually pledge to each other our lives, our fortunes, and our sacred honor.

We, therefore, the representatives of the United States of America, in General Congress assembled, appealing to the Supreme Judge of the world for the rectitude of our intentions, do in the name, and by the authority of the good people of these Colonies, solemnly publish and declare, that these united Colonies are, and of right ought to be, free and independent States; that they are absolved from all allegiance to the British crown, and that all political connection between them and the state of Great Britain is, and ought to be, totally dissolved; and that as free and independent States, they have full power to levy war, conclude peace, contract alliances, establish commerce, and to do all other acts and things which independent States may of right do.

And for the support of this declaration, with a firm reliance on the protection of Divine Providence, we mutually pledge to each other our lives, our fortunes, and our sacred honor.

First Inaugural Address

March 4, 1801

FRIENDS and fellow citizens: Called upon to undertake the duties of the first executive office of our country, I avail myself of the presence of that portion of my fellow citizens which is here assembled, to express my grateful thanks for the favor with which they have been pleased to look toward me, to declare a sincere consciousness that the task is above my talents, and that I approach it with those anxious and awful presentiments which the greatness of the charge and the weakness of my powers so justly inspire. A rising nation, spread over a wide and fruitful land, traversing all the seas with the rich productions of their industry, engaged in commerce with nations who feel power and forget right, advancing rapidly to destinies beyond the reach of mortal eye—when I contemplate these transcendent objects, and see the honor, the happiness, and the hopes of this beloved country committed to the issue and the auspices of this day, I shrink from the contemplation, and humble myself before the magnitude of the undertaking. Utterly indeed, should I despair, did not the presence of many whom I here see remind me, that in the other high authorities provided by our constitution, I shall find resources of wisdom, of virtue, and of zeal, on which to rely under all difficulties. To you, then, gentlemen, who are charged with the sovereign functions of legislation, and to those associated with you, I look with encouragement for that guidance and support which may enable us to steer with safety the vessel in which we are all embarked amid the conflicting elements of a troubled world.

During the contest of opinion through which we have passed, the animation of discussion and of exertions has sometimes worn an aspect which might impose on strangers unused to think freely and to speak and to write what they think; but this being now decided by the voice of the nation, announced according to the rules of the constitution, all will, of course, arrange themselves under the will of the law, and unite in common efforts for the common good. All, too, will bear in mind this sacred principle, that though the will of the majority is in all cases to prevail, that will, to be rightful, must be reasonable; that the minority possess their equal rights, which equal laws must protect, and to violate which would be oppression. Let us, then, fellow citizens, unite with one heart and one mind. Let us restore to social intercourse that harmony and affection without which liberty and even life itself are but dreary things. And let us reflect that having banished from our land that religious intolerance under which mankind so long bled and suffered, we have yet gained little if we countenance a political intolerance as despotic, as wicked, and capable of as bitter and bloody persecutions. During the throes and convulsions of the ancient world, during the agonizing spasms of infuriated man, seeking through blood and slaughter his long-lost liberty, it was not wonderful that the agitation of the billows should reach even this distant and peaceful shore; that this should be more felt and feared by some and less by others; that this should divide opinions as to measures of safety. But every difference of opinion is not a difference of principle. We have called by different names brethren of the same principle. We are all republicans—we are federalists. If there be any among us who would wish to dissolve this Union or to change its republican form, let them stand undisturbed as monuments of the safety with which error of opinion may be tolerated where reason is left free to combat it. I know, indeed, that some honest men fear that a republican government cannot be strong; that this government is not strong enough. But would the honest patriot, in the full tide of successful experiment, abandon a government which has so far kept us free and firm, on the theoretic and visionary fear that this government, the world's best hope, may by possibility want energy to preserve itself? I trust not. I believe this, on the contrary, the strongest government on earth. I believe it is the only one where every man, at the call of the laws, would fly to the standard of the law, and would meet invasions of the public order as his own personal concern. Sometimes it is said that man cannot be trusted with the government of himself. Can he, then, be trusted with the government of others? Or have we found angels in the forms of kings to govern him? Let history answer this question.

Let us, then, with courage and confidence pursue our own federal and republican principles, our attachment to our union and representative government. Kindly separated by nature and a wide ocean from the exterminating havoc of one quarter of the globe; too high-minded to endure the degradations of the others; possessing a chosen country, with room enough for our descendants to the hundredth and thousandth generation; entertaining a due sense of our equal right to the use of our own faculties, to the acquisitions of our industry, to honor and confidence from our fellow citizens, resulting not from birth but from our actions and their sense of them; enlightened by a benign religion, professed, indeed, and practiced in various forms, yet all of them including honesty, truth, temperance, gratitude, and the love of man; acknowledging and adoring an overruling Providence, which by all its dispensations proves that it delights in the happiness of man here and his greater happiness hereafter; with all these blessings, what more is necessary to make us a happy and prosperous people? Still one thing more, fellow citizens—a wise and frugal government, which shall restrain men from injuring one another, which shall leave them otherwise free to regulate their own pursuits of industry and improvement, and shall not take from the mouth of labor the bread it has earned. This is the sum of good government, and this is necessary to close the circle of our felicities.

About to enter, fellow citizens, on the exercise of duties which comprehend everything dear and valuable to you, it is proper that you should understand what I deem the essential principles of our government, and consequently those which ought to shape its administration. I will compress them within the narrowest compass they will bear, stating the general principle, but not all its limitations. Equal and exact justice to all men, of whatever state or persuasion, religious or political; peace, commerce, and honest friendship with all nations—entangling alliances with none; the support of the State governments in all their rights, as the most competent administrations for our domestic concerns and the surest bulwarks against anti-republican tendencies; the preservation of the general government in its whole constitutional vigor, as the sheet anchor of our peace at home and safety abroad; a jealous care of the right of election by the people—a mild and safe corrective of abuses which are lopped by the sword of the revolution where peaceable remedies are unprovided; absolute acquiescence in the decisions of the majority—the vital principle of republics, from which there is no appeal but to force, the vital principle and immediate parent of despotism; a well-disciplined militia—our best reliance in peace and for the first moments of war, till regulars may relieve them; the supremacy of the civil over the military authority; economy in the public expense, that labor may be lightly burdened; the honest payment of our debts and sacred preservation of the public faith; encouragement of agriculture, and of commerce as its handmaid; the diffusion of information and the arraignment of all abuses at the bar of public reason; freedom of religion; freedom of the press; freedom of person under the protection of the *habeas corpus*; and trial by juries impartially selected—these principles form the bright constellation which has gone before us, and guided our steps through an age of revolution and reformation. The wisdom of our sages and the blood of our heroes have been devoted to their attainment. They should be the creed of our political faith—the text of civil instruction—the touchstone by which to try the services of those we trust; and should we wander from them in moments of error or alarm, let us hasten to retrace our steps and to regain the road which alone leads to peace, liberty, and safety.

I repair, then, fellow citizens, to the post you have assigned me. With experience enough in subordinate offices to have seen the difficulties of this, the greatest of all, I have learned to expect that it will rarely fall to the lot of imperfect man to retire from this station with the reputation and the favor which bring him into it. Without pretensions to that high confidence reposed in our first and great revolutionary character, whose preëminent services had entitled him to the first place in his country's love, and destined for him the fairest page in the volume of faithful history, I ask so much confidence only as may give firmness and effect to the legal administration of your affairs. I shall often go wrong through defect of judgment. When right, I shall often be thought wrong by those whose positions will not command a view of the whole ground. I ask your indulgence for my own errors, which will never be intentional; and your support against the errors of others, who may condemn what they would not if seen in all its parts. The approbation implied by your suffrage is a consolation to me for the past; and my future solicitude will be to retain the good opinion of those who have bestowed it in advance, to conciliate that of others by doing them all the good in my power, and to be instrumental to the happiness and freedom of all.

Relying, then, on the patronage of your good will, I advance with obedience to the work, ready to retire from it whenever you become sensible how much better choice it is in your power to make. And may that Infinite Power which rules the destinies of the universe, lead our councils to what is best, and give them a favorable issue for your peace and prosperity.

Second Inaugural Address

March 4, 1805

PROCEEDING, fellow citizens, to that qualification which the constitution requires, before my entrance on the charge again conferred upon me, it is my duty to express the deep sense I entertain of this new proof of confidence from my fellow citizens at large, and the zeal with which it inspires me, so to conduct myself as may best satisfy their just expectations.

On taking this station on a former occasion, I declared the principles on which I believed it my duty to administer the affairs of our commonwealth. My conscience tells me that I have, on every occasion, acted up to that declaration, according to its obvious import, and to the understanding of every candid mind.

In the transaction of your foreign affairs, we have endeavored to cultivate the friendship of all nations, and especially of those with which we have the most important relations. We have done them justice on all occasions, favored where favor was lawful, and cherished mutual interests and intercourse on fair and equal terms. We are firmly convinced, and we act on that conviction, that with nations, as with individuals, our interests soundly calculated, will ever be found inseparable from our moral duties; and history bears witness to the fact, that a just nation is taken on its word, when recourse is had to armaments and wars to bridle others.

At home, fellow citizens, you best know whether we have done well or ill. The suppression of unnecessary offices, of useless establishments and expenses, enabled us to discontinue our internal taxes. These covering our land with officers, and opening our doors to their intrusions, had already begun that process of domiciliary vexation which, once entered, is scarcely to be restrained from reaching successively every article of produce and property. If among these taxes some minor ones fell which had not been inconvenient, it was because their amount would not have paid the officers who collected them, and because, if they had any merit, the state authorities might adopt them, instead of others less approved.

The remaining revenue on the consumption of foreign articles, is paid cheerfully by those who can afford to add foreign luxuries to domestic comforts, being collected on our seaboards and frontiers only, and incorporated with the transactions of our mercantile citizens, it may be the pleasure and pride of an American to ask, what farmer, what mechanic, what laborer, ever sees a tax-gatherer of the United States? These contributions enable us to support the current expenses of the government, to fulfil contracts with foreign nations, to extinguish the native right of soil within our limits, to extend those limits, and to apply such a surplus to our public debts, as places at a short day their final redemption, and that redemption once effected, the revenue thereby liberated may, by a just repartition among the states, and a corresponding amendment of the constitution, be applied, *in time of peace*, to rivers, canals, roads, arts, manufactures, education, and other great objects within each state. *In time of war*, if injustice, by ourselves or others, must sometimes produce war, increased as the same revenue will be increased by population and consumption, and aided by other resources reserved for that crisis, it may meet within the year all the expenses of the year, without encroaching on the rights of future generations, by burdening them with the debts of the past. War will then be but a suspension of useful works, and a return to a state of peace, a return to the progress of improvement.

I have said, fellow citizens, that the income reserved had enabled us to extend our limits; but that extension may possibly pay for itself before we are called on, and in the meantime, may keep down the accruing interest; in all events, it will repay the advances we have made. I know that the acquisition of Louisiana has been disapproved by some, from a candid apprehension that the enlargement of our territory would endanger its union. But who can limit the extent to which the federative principle may operate effectively? The larger our association, the less will it be shaken by local passions; and in any view, is it not better that the opposite bank of the Mississippi should be settled by our own brethren and children, than by strangers of another family? With which shall we be most likely to live in harmony and friendly intercourse?

In matters of religion, I have considered that its free exercise is placed by the constitution independent of the powers of the general government. I have therefore undertaken, on no occasion, to prescribe the religious exercises suited to it; but have left them, as the constitution found them, under the direction and discipline of state or church authorities acknowledged by the several religious societies.

The aboriginal inhabitants of these countries I have regarded with the commiseration their history inspires. Endowed with the faculties and the rights of men, breathing an ardent love of liberty and independence, and occupying a country which left them no desire but to be undisturbed, the stream of overflowing population from other regions directed itself on these shores; without power to divert, or habits to contend against, they have been overwhelmed by the current, or driven before it; now reduced within limits too narrow for the hunter's state, humanity enjoins us to teach them agriculture and the domestic arts; to encourage them to that industry which alone can enable them to maintain their place in existence, and to prepare them in time for that state of society, which to bodily comforts adds the improvement of the mind and morals. We have therefore liberally furnished them with the implements of husbandry and household use; we have placed among them instructors in the arts of first necessity; and they are covered with the ægis of the law against aggressors from among ourselves.

But the endeavors to enlighten them on the fate which awaits their present course of life, to induce them to exercise their reason, follow its dictates, and change their pursuits with the change of circumstances, have powerful obstacles to encounter; they are combated by the habits of their bodies, prejudice of their minds, ignorance, pride, and the influence of interested and crafty individuals among them, who feel themselves something in the present order of things, and fear to become nothing in any other. These persons inculcate a sanctimonious reverence for the customs of their ancestors; that whatsoever they did, must be done through all time; that reason is a false guide, and to advance under its counsel, in their physical, moral, or political condition, is perilous innovation; that their duty is to remain as their Creator made them, ignorance being safety, and knowledge full of danger; in short, my friends, among them is seen the action and counteraction of good sense and bigotry; they, too, have their anti-philosophers, who find an interest in keeping things in their present state, who dread reformation, and exert all their faculties to maintain the ascendency of habit over the duty of improving our reason, and obeying its mandates.

In giving these outlines, I do not mean, fellow citizens, to arrogate to myself the merit of the measures; that is due, in the first place, to the reflecting character of our citizens at large, who, by the weight of public opinion, influence and strengthen the public measures; it is due to the sound discretion with which they select from among themselves those to whom they confide the legislative duties; it is due to the zeal and wisdom of the characters thus selected, who lay the foundations of public happiness in wholesome laws, the execution of which alone remains for others; and it is due to the able and faithful auxiliaries, whose patriotism has associated with me in the executive functions.

During this course of administration, and in order to disturb it, the artillery of the press has been levelled against us, charged with whatsoever its licentiousness could devise or dare. These abuses of an institution so important to freedom and science, are deeply to be regretted, inasmuch as they tend to lessen its usefulness, and to sap its safety; they might, indeed, have been corrected by the wholesome punishments reserved and provided by the laws of the several States against falsehood and defamation; but public duties more urgent press on the time of public servants, and the offenders have therefore been left to find their punishment in the public indignation.

Nor was it uninteresting to the world, that an experiment should be fairly and fully made, whether freedom of discussion, unaided by power, is not sufficient for the propagation and protection of truth—whether a government, conducting itself in the true spirit of its constitution, with zeal and purity, and doing no act which it would be unwilling the whole world should witness, can be written down by falsehood and defamation. The experiment has been tried; you have witnessed the scene; our fellow citizens have looked on, cool and collected; they saw the latent source from which these outrages proceeded; they gathered around their public functionaries, and when the constitution called them to the decision by suffrage, they pronounced their verdict, honorable to those who had served them, and consolatory to the friend of man, who believes he may be intrusted with his own affairs.

No inference is here intended, that the laws, provided by the State against false and defamatory publications, should not be enforced; he who has time, renders a service to public morals and public tranquillity, in reforming these abuses by the salutary coercions of the law; but the experiment is noted, to prove that, since truth and reason have maintained their ground against false opinions in league with false facts, the press, confined to truth, needs no other legal restraint; the public judgment will correct false reasonings and opinions, on a full hearing of all parties; and no other definite line can be drawn between the inestimable liberty of the press and its demoralizing licentiousness. If there be still improprieties which this rule would not restrain, its supplement must be sought in the censorship of public opinion.

Contemplating the union of sentiment now manifested so generally, as auguring harmony and happiness to our future course, I offer to our country sincere congratulations. With those, too, not yet rallied to the same point, the disposition to do so is gaining strength; facts are piercing through the veil drawn over them; and our doubting brethren will at length see, that the mass of their fellow citizens, with whom they cannot yet resolve to act, as to principles and measures, think as they think, and desire what they desire; that our wish, as well as theirs, is, that the public efforts may be directed honestly to the public good, that peace be cultivated, civil and religious liberty unassailed, law and order preserved, equality of rights maintained, and that state of property, equal or unequal, which results to every man from his own industry, or that of his fathers. When satisfied of these views, it is not in human nature that they should not approve and support them; in the meantime, let us cherish them with patient affection; let us do them justice, and more than justice, in all competitions of interest; and we need not doubt that truth, reason, and their own interests, will at length prevail, will gather them into the fold of their country, and will complete their entire union of opinion, which gives to a nation the blessing of harmony, and the benefit of all its strength.

I shall now enter on the duties to which my fellow citizens have again called me, and shall proceed in the spirit of those principles which they have approved. I fear not that any motives of interest may lead me astray; I am sensible of no passion which could seduce me knowingly from the path of justice; but the weakness of human nature, and the limits of my own understanding, will produce errors of judgment sometimes injurious to your interests. I shall need, therefore, all the indulgence I have heretofore experienced—the want of it will certainly not lessen with increasing years. I shall need, too, the favor of that Being in whose hands we are, who led our forefathers, as Israel of old, from their native land, and planted them in a country flowing with all the necessaries and comforts of life; who has covered our infancy with his providence, and our riper years with his wisdom and power; and to whose goodness I ask you to join with me in supplications, that he will so enlighten the minds of your servants, guide their councils, and prosper their measures, that whatsoever they do, shall result in your good, and shall secure to you the peace, friendship, and approbation of all nations.

A Bill for the More General
Diffusion of Knowledge

Report of the Revisors, Chapter 79*

1779

SECTION I. Whereas it appeareth that however certain forms of government are better calculated than others to protect the individuals in the free exercise of their natural rights, and are at the same time themselves better guarded against degeneracy, yet experience hath shewn, that even under the best forms, those entrusted with power have, in time, and by slow operations, perverted it into tyranny; and it is believed that the most effectual means of preventing this would be, to illuminate, as far as practicable, the minds of the people at large, and more especially to give them knowledge of those facts, which history exhibiteth, that, possessed thereby of the experience of other ages and countries, they may be enabled to know ambition under all its shapes, and prompt to exert their natural powers to defeat its purposes; And whereas it is generally true that that people will be happiest whose laws are best, and are best administered, and that laws will be wisely formed, and honestly administered, in proportion as those who form and administer them are wise and honest; whence it becomes expedient for promoting the public happiness that those persons, whom nature hath endowed with genius and virtue, should be rendered by liberal education worthy to receive, and able to guard the sacred deposit of the rights and liberties of their fellow citizens, and that they should be called to that charge without regard to wealth, birth or other accidental condition or circumstance; but the indigence of the greater number disabling them from so educating, at their own ex-

* See Preface to Part ii, page 242.

pence, those of their children whom nature hath fitly formed and disposed to become useful instruments for the public, it is better that such should be sought for and educated at the common expence of all, than that the happiness of all should be confined to the weak or wicked:

SECTION II. Be it therefore enacted by the General Assembly, that in every county within this commonwealth, there shall be chosen annually, by the electors qualified to vote for Delegates, three of the most honest and able men of their county, to be called the Aldermen of the county; and that the election of the said Aldermen shall be held at the same time and place, before the same persons, and notified and conducted in the same manner as by law is directed, for the annual election of Delegates for the county.

SECTION III. The person before whom such election is holden shall certify to the court of the said county the names of the Aldermen chosen, in order that the same may be entered of record, and shall give notice of their election to the said Aldermen within a fortnight after such election.

SECTION IV. The said Aldermen on the first Monday in October, if it be fair, and if not, then on the next fair day, excluding Sunday, shall meet at the court-house of their county, and proceed to divide their said county into hundreds, bounding the same by water courses, mountains, or limits, to be run and marked, if they think necessary, by the county surveyor, and at the county expence, regulating the size of the said hundreds, according to the best of their discretion, so as that they may contain a convenient number of children to make up a school, and be of such convenient size that all the children within each hundred may daily attend the school to be established therein, and distinguishing each hundred by a particular name; which division, with the names of the several hundreds, shall be returned to the court of the county and be entered of record, and shall remain unaltered until the increase or decrease of inhabitants shall render an alteration necessary, in the opinion of any succeeding Alderman, and also in the opinion of the court of the county.

SECTION V. The electors aforesaid residing within every hundred shall meet on the third Monday in October after the first election of Aldermen, at such place, within their hundred, as the said Aldermen shall direct, notice thereof being previously given to them by such person residing within the hundred as the said Aldermen shall require who is hereby enjoined to obey such requisition, on pain of being punished by amercement and imprisonment. The electors being so assembled shall choose the most convenient place within their hundred for building a school-house. If two or more places, having a greater number of votes than any others, shall yet be equal between themselves, the Aldermen, or such of them as are not of the same hundred, on information thereof, shall decide between them. The said Aldermen shall forthwith proceed to have a school-house built at the said place, and shall see that the same shall be kept in repair, and, when necessary, that it be rebuilt; but whenever they shall think necessary that it be rebuilt, they shall give notice as before directed, to the electors of the hundred to meet at the said school-house, on such a day as they shall appoint, to determine by vote, in the manner before directed, whether it shall be rebuilt at the same, or what other place in the hundred.

SECTION VI. At every of those schools shall be taught reading, writing, and common arithmetick, and the books which shall be used therein for instructing the children to read shall be such as will at the same time make them acquainted with Graecian, Roman, English, and American history. At these schools all the free children, male and female, resident within the respective hundred, shall be intitled to receive tuition gratis, for the term of three years, and as much longer, at their private expence, as their parents, guardians, or friends shall think proper.

SECTION VII. Over every ten of these schools (or such other number nearest thereto, as the number of hundreds in the county will admit, without fractional divisions) an overseer shall be appointed annually by the Aldermen at their first meeting, eminent for his learning, integrity, and fidelity to the commonwealth, whose business and duty it shall be, from time to time, to appoint a teacher to each school, who shall give assurance of fidelity to the commonwealth, and to remove him as he shall see cause; to visit every school once in every half year at the least; to examine the scholars; see that any general plan of reading and instruction recommended by the visiters of William and Mary College shall be observed; and to superintend the conduct of the teacher in everything relative to his school.

SECTION VIII. Every teacher shall receive a salary of — by the year, which, with the expences of building and repairing the school-houses, shall be provided in such manner as other county expences are by law directed to be provided and shall also have his diet, lodging, and washing found him, to be levied in like manner, save only that such levy shall be on the inhabitants of each hundred for the board of their own teacher only.

SECTION IX. And in order that grammar schools may be rendered convenient to the youth in every part of the commonwealth, be it therefore enacted, that on the first Monday in November, after the first appointment of overseers for the hundred schools, if fair, and if not, then on the next fair day, excluding Sunday, after the hour of one in the afternoon, the said overseer appointed for the schools in the counties of Princess Ann, Norfolk, Nansemond and Isle-of-Wight, shall meet at Nansemond court-house; those for the counties of Southampton, Sussex, Surry and Prince George, shall meet at Sussex court-house; those for the counties of Brunswick, Mecklenburg and Lunenburg, shall meet at Lunenburg court-house; those for the counties of Dinwiddie, Amelia and Chesterfield, shall meet at Chesterfield court-house; those for the counties of Powhatan, Cumberland, Goochland, Henrico and Hanover, shall meet at Henrico court-house; those for the counties of Prince Edward, Charlotte and Halifax, shall meet at Charlotte court-house; those for the counties of Henry, Pittsylvania and Bedford, shall meet at Pittsylvania court-house; those for the counties of Buckingham, Amherst, Albemarle and Fluvanna, shall meet at Albemarle court-house; those for the counties of Botetourt, Rockbridge, Montgomery, Washington and Kentucky, shall meet at Botetourt court-house; those for the counties of Augusta, Rockingham and Greenbriar, shall meet at Augusta court-house; those for the counties of Accomack and Northampton, shall meet at Accomack court-house; those for the counties of Elizabeth City, Warwick, York, Gloucester, James City, Charles City and New-Kent, shall meet at James City court-house; those for the counties of Middlesex, Essex, King and Queen, King William and Caroline, shall meet at King and Queen court-house; those for the counties of Lancaster, Northumberland, Richmond and Westmoreland, shall meet at Richmond court-house; those for the counties of King George, Stafford, Spotsylvania, Prince William and Fairfax, shall meet at Spotsylvania court-house; those for the counties of Loudoun and Fauquier, shall meet at Loudoun court-house; those for the counties of Culpeper, Orange and Louisa, shall meet at Orange court-house; those for the county of Shenandoah and Frederick, shall meet at Frederick court-house; those for the counties of Hampshire and Berkeley, shall meet at Berkeley court-house; and those for the counties of Yohogania, Monongalia, and Ohio, shall meet at the Monongalia court-house; and shall fix on such place in some of the counties in their district as shall be most proper for situating a grammar school-house, endeavoring that the situation be as central as may be to the inhabitants of the said counties, that it be furnished with good water, convenient to plentiful supplies of provision and fuel, and more than all things that it be healthy. And if a majority of the overseers present should not concur in their choice of any one place proposed, the method of determining shall be as follows: If two places only were proposed, and the votes be divided, they shall decide between them by fair and equal lot; if more than two places were proposed, the question shall be put on those two which on the first division had the greater number of votes; or if no two places had a greater number of votes than the others, then it shall be decided by fair and equal lot (unless it can be agreed by a majority of votes) which of the places having equal numbers shall be thrown out of the competition, so that the question shall be put on the remaining two, and if on this ultimate question the votes shall be equally divided, it shall then be decided finally by lot.

SECTION X. The said overseers having determined the place at which the grammar school for their district shall be built, shall forthwith (unless they can otherwise agree with the proprietors of the circumjacent lands as to location and price) make application to the clerk of the county in which the said house is to be situated, who shall thereupon issue a writ, in the nature of a writ of ad quod damnum, directed to the sheriff of the said county commanding him to summon and impanel twelve fit persons to meet at the place, so destined for the grammar school-house, on a certain day, to be named in the said writ, not less than five, nor more than ten, days from the date thereof; and also to give notice of the same to the proprietors and tenants of the lands to be viewed if they be found within the county, and if not, then to their agents therein if any they have. Which freeholders shall be charged by the said sheriff impartially, and to the best of their skill and judgment to view the lands round about the said place, and to locate and circumscribe, by certain meets and bounds, one hundred acres thereof, having regard therein principally to the benefit and convenience of the said school, but respecting in some measure also the convenience of the said proprietors, and to value and appraise the same in so many several and distinct parcels as shall be owned or held by several and distinct owners or tenants, and according to their respective interests and estates therein. And after such location and appraisement so made, the said sheriff shall forthwith return the same under the hands and seals of the said jurors, together with the writ, to the clerk's office of the said county and the right and property of the said proprietors and tenants in the said lands so circumscribed shall be immediately devested and be transferred to the commonwealth for the use of the said grammar school, in full and absolute dominion, any want of consent or disability to consent in the said owners or tenants notwithstanding. But it shall not be lawful for the said overseers so to situate the grammar school-house, nor to the said jurors so to locate the said lands, as to include the mansion-house of the proprietor of the lands, nor the offices, curtilage, or garden, thereunto immediately belonging.

SECTION XI. The said overseers shall forthwith proceed to have a house of brick or stone, for the said grammar school, with necessary offices, built on the said lands, which grammar school-house shall contain a room for the school, a hall to dine in, four rooms for a master and usher, and ten or twelve lodging rooms for the scholars.

SECTION XII. To each of the said grammar schools shall be allowed out of the public treasury, the sum of—pounds, out of which shall be paid by the Treasurer, on warrant from the Auditors, to the proprietors or tenants of the lands located, the value of their several interests as fixed by the jury, and the balance thereof shall be delivered to the said overseers to defray the expence of the said buildings.

SECTION XIII. In either of these grammar schools shall be taught the Latin and Greek languages, English Grammar, geography, and the higher part of numerical arithmetic, to wit, vulgar and decimal fractions, and the extrication of the square and cube roots.

SECTION XIV. A visiter from each county constituting the district shall be appointed, by the overseers, for the county, in the month of October annually, either from their own body or from their county at large, which visiters, or the greater part of them, meeting together at the said grammar school on the first Monday in November, if fair, and if not, then on the next fair day, excluding Sunday, shall have power to choose their own Rector, who shall call and preside at future meetings, to employ from time to time a master, and if necessary, an usher, for the said school, to remove them at their will, and to settle the price of tuition to be paid by the scholars. They shall also visit the school twice in every year at the least, either together or separately at their discretion, examine the scholars, and see that any general plan of instruction recommended by the visiters, of William and Mary College shall be observed. The said masters and ushers, before they enter on the execution of their office, shall give assurance of fidelity to the commonwealth.

SECTION XV. A steward shall be employed, and removed at will by the master, on such wages as the visiters shall direct; which steward shall see to the procuring provisions, fuels, servants for cooking, waiting, house cleaning, washing, mending, and gardening on the most reasonable terms; the expence of which, together with the steward's wages, shall be divided equally among all the scholars boarding either on the public or private expence. And the part of those who are on private expence, and also the price of their tuitions due to the master or usher, shall be paid quarterly by the respective scholars, their parents, or guardians, and shall be recoverable, if withheld, together with costs, on motion in any Court of Record, ten days' notice thereof being previously given to the party, and a jury impanelled to try the issue joined, or enquire of the damages. The said steward shall also, under the direction of the visiters, see that the houses be kept in repair, and necessary enclosures be made and repaired, the accounts for which, shall, from time to time, be submitted to the Auditors, and on their warrant paid by the Treasurer.

SECTION XVI. Every overseer of the hundred schools shall, in the month of September annually, after the most diligent and impartial examination and enquiry, appoint from among the boys who shall have been two years at the least at some one of the schools under his superintendence, and whose parents are too poor to give them farther education, some-one of the best and most promising genius and disposition, to proceed to the grammar school of his district; which appointment shall be made in the court-house of the county, and on the court day for that month if fair, and if not, then on the next fair day, excluding Sunday, in the presence of the Aldermen, or two of them at the least, assembled on the bench for that purpose, the said overseer being previously sworn by them to make such appointment, without favor or affection, according to the best of his skill and judgment, and being interrogated by the Aldermen, either on their own motion, or on suggestions from the parents, guardians, friends, or teachers of the children, competitors for such appointment; which teachers the parents shall attend for the information of the Aldermen. On which interrogatories the said Aldermen, if they be not satisfied with the appointment proposed, shall have right to negative it; whereupon the said visiter may proceed to make a new appointment, and the said Aldermen again to interrogate and negative, and so toties quoties until an appointment be approved.

Section xvii. Every boy so appointed shall be authorized to proceed to the grammar school of his district, there to be educated and boarded during such time as is hereafter limited; and his quota of the expences of the house together with a compensation to the master or usher for his tuition, at the rate of twenty dollars by the year, shall be paid by the Treasurer quarterly on warrant from the Auditors.

Section xviii. A visitation shall be held, for the purpose of probation, annually at the said grammar school on the last Monday in September, if fair, and if not, then on the next fair day, excluding Sunday, at which one third of the boys sent thither by appointment of the said overseers, and who shall have been there one year only, shall be discontinued as public foundationers, being those who, on the most diligent examination and enquiry, shall be thought to be the least promising in genius and disposition; and of those who shall have been there two years, all shall be discontinued save one only the best in genius and disposition, who shall be at liberty to continue there four years longer on the public foundation, and shall thence forward be deemed a senior.

Section xix. The visiters for the districts which, or any part of which, be southward and westward of James river, as known by that name, or by the names of Fluvanna and Jackson's river, in every other year, to wit, at the probation meetings held in the years, distinguished in the Christian computation by odd numbers, and the visiters for all the other districts at their said meetings to be held in those years, distinguished by even numbers, after diligent examination and enquiry as before directed, shall chuse one among the said seniors, of the best learning and most hopeful genius and disposition, who shall be authorized by them to proceed to William and Mary College; there to be educated, boarded, and clothed, three years; the expence of which annually shall be paid by the Treasurer on warrant from the Auditors.

A Bill for
Establishing Religious Freedom

Report of the Revisors, Chapter 82*

1779

SECTION I. Well aware that the opinions and belief of men depend on their own will, but follow involuntarily the evidence proposed to their minds; that Almighty God hath created the mind free, and manifested his supreme will that free it shall remain by making it altogether insusceptible of restraint; that all attempts to influence it by temporal punishments, or burthens, or by civil incapacitations, tend only to beget habits of hypocrisy and meanness, and are a departure from the plan of the holy author of our religion, who being lord both of body and mind, yet chose not to propagate it by coercions on either, as was in his Almighty power to do, but to exalt it by its influence on reason alone; that the impious presumption of legislature and ruler, civil as well as ecclesiastical, who, being themselves but fallible and uninspired men, have assumed dominion over the faith of others, setting up their own opinions and modes of thinking as the only true and infallible, and as such endeavoring to impose them on others, hath established and maintained false religions over the greatest part of the world and through all time: That to compel a man to furnish contributions of money for the propagation of opinions which he disbelieves and abhors, is sinful and tyrannical; that even the forcing him to support this or that teacher of his own religious persuasion, is depriving him of the comfortable liberty of giving his contributions to the particular pastor whose morals

* See Preface to Part II, page 242.

he would make his pattern, and whose powers he feels most persuasive to righteousness; and is withdrawing from the ministry those temporary rewards, which proceeding from an approbation of their personal conduct, are an additional incitement to earnest and unremitting labors for the instruction of mankind; that our civil rights have no dependence on our religious opinions, any more than our opinions in physics or geometry; and therefore the proscribing any citizen as unworthy the public confidence by laying upon him an incapacity of being called to offices of trust or emolument, unless he profess or renounce this or that religious opinion, is depriving him injudiciously of those privileges and advantages to which, in common with his fellow citizens, he has a natural right; that it tends also to corrupt the principles of that very religion it is meant to encourage, by bribing with a monopoly of worldly honors and emoluments, those who will externally profess and conform to it; that though indeed these are criminals who do not withstand such temptation, yet neither are those innocent who lay the bait in their way; that the opinions of men are not the object of civil government, nor under its jurisdiction; that to suffer the civil magistrate to intrude his powers into the field of opinion and to restrain the profession or propagation of principles on supposition of their ill tendency is a dangerous fallacy, which at once destroys all religious liberty, because he being of course judge of that tendency will make his opinions the rule of judgment, and approve or condemn the sentiments of others only as they shall square with or suffer from his own; that it is time enough for the rightful purposes of civil government for its officers to interfere when principles break out into overt acts against peace and good order; and finally, that truth is great and will prevail if left to herself; that she is the proper and sufficient antagonist to error, and has nothing to fear from the conflict unless by human interposition disarmed of her natural weapons, free argument and debate; errors ceasing to be dangerous when it is permitted freely to contradict them.

SECTION II. We the General Assembly of Virginia do enact that no man shall be compelled to frequent or support any religious worship, place, or ministry whatsoever, nor shall be enforced, restrained, molested, or burthened in his body or goods, or shall otherwise suffer, on account of his religious opinions or belief; but that all men shall be free to profess, and by argument to maintain, their opinions in matters of religion, and that the same shall in no wise diminish, enlarge, or affect their civil capacities.

Section III. And though we well know that this Assembly, elected by the people for their ordinary purposes of legislation only, have no power to restrain the acts of succeeding Assemblies, constituted with powers equal to our own, and that therefore to declare this act to be irrevocable would be of no effect in law; yet we are free to declare, and do declare, that the rights hereby asserted are of the natural rights of mankind, and that if any act shall be hereafter passed to repeal the present or to narrow its operations, such act will be an infringement of natural right.

Religion in Virginia

Notes on the State of Virginia, Query 17*

1781

THE first settlers in this country were emigrants from England, of the English Church, just at a point of time when it was flushed with complete victory over the religious of all other persuasions. Possessed, as they became, of the powers of making, administering, and executing the laws, they showed equal intolerance in this country with their Presbyterian brethren, who had emigrated to the northern government. The poor Quakers were flying from persecution in England. They cast their eyes on these new countries as asylums of civil and religious freedom; but they found them free only for the reigning sect. Several acts of the Virginia assembly of 1659, 1662, and 1693, had made it penal in parents to refuse to have their children baptized; had prohibited the unlawful assembling of Quakers; had made it penal for any master of a vessel to bring a Quaker into the State; had ordered those already here, and such as should come thereafter, to be imprisoned till they should abjure the country; provided a milder punishment for their first and second return, but death for their third; had inhibited all persons from suffering their meetings in or near their houses, entertaining them individually, or disposing of books which supported their tenets. If no execution took place here, as did in New England, it was not owing to the moderation of the church, or spirit of the legislature, as may be inferred from the law itself; but to historical circumstances which have not been handed down to us. The Anglicans retained full possession of the country about a century. Other opinions began then to creep in, and the great care of the government to support their own church, having

* See Preface to Part II, page 242, and *Autobiography*, Part I, page 58.

begotten an equal degree of indolence in its clergy, two-thirds of the people had become dissenters at the commencement of the present revolution. The laws, indeed, were still oppressive on them, but the spirit of the one party had subsided into moderation, and of the other had risen to a degree of determination which commanded respect.

The present state of our laws on the subject of religion is this. The convention of May 1776, in their declaration of rights, declared it to be a truth, and a natural right, that the exercise of religion should be free; but when they proceeded to form on that declaration the ordinance of government, instead of taking up every principle declared in the bill of rights, and guarding it by legislative sanction, they passed over that which asserted our religious rights, leaving them as they found them. The same convention, however, when they met as a member of the general assembly in October, 1776, repealed all *acts of Parliament* which had rendered criminal the maintaining any opinions in matters of religion, the forbearing to repair to church, and the exercising any mode of worship; and suspended the laws giving salaries to the clergy, which suspension was made perpetual in October, 1779. Statutory oppressions in religion being thus wiped away, we remain at present under those only imposed by the common law, or by our own acts of assembly. At the common law, *heresy* was a capital offence, punishable by burning. Its definition was left to the ecclesiastical judges, before whom the conviction was, till the statute of the 1 El. c. 1 circumscribed it, by declaring, that nothing should be deemed heresy, but what had been so determined by authority of the canonical scriptures, or by one of the four first general councils, or by other council, having for the grounds of their declaration the express and plain words of the scriptures. Heresy, thus circumscribed, being an offence against the common law, our act of assembly of October 1777, c. 17, gives cognizance of it to the general court, by declaring that the jurisdiction of that court shall be general in all matters at the common law. The execution is by the writ *De haeretico comburendo.* By our own act of assembly of 1705, c. 30, if a person brought up in the Christian religion denies the being of a God, or the Trinity, or asserts there are more gods than one, or denies the Christian religion to be true, or the scriptures to be of divine authority, he is punishable on the first offence by incapacity to hold any office or employment ecclesiastical, civil, or military; on the second by disability to sue, to take any gift or legacy, to be guardian, executor, or administrator, and by three years' imprisonment without bail. A father's right to the custody of his own children being founded in law on his right of guardianship, this being taken away, they may of course be severed from him, and put by the authority of a court into more orthodox hands. This is a summary view of that religious slavery under which a people have been willing to remain, who have lavished their lives and fortunes for the establishment of their civil freedom.* The error seems not sufficiently eradicated, that the operations of the mind, as well as the acts of the body, are subject to the coercion of the laws. But our rulers can have no authority over such natural rights, only as we have submitted to them. The rights of conscience we never submitted, we could not submit. We are answerable for them to our God. The legitimate powers of government extend to such acts only as are injurious to others. But it does me no injury for my neighbor to say there are twenty gods, or no God. It neither picks my pocket nor breaks my leg. If it be said, his testimony in a court of justice cannot be relied on, reject it then, and be the stigma on him. Constraint may make him worse by making him a hypocrite, but it will never make him a truer man. It may fix him obstinately in his errors, but will not cure them. Reason and free inquiry are the only effectual agents against error. Give a loose to them, they will support the true religion by bringing every false one to their tribunal, to the test of their investigation. They are the natural enemies of error, and of error only. Had not the Roman government permitted free inquiry, Christianity could never have been introduced. Had not free inquiry been indulged at the era of the reformation, the corruptions of Christianity could not have been purged away. If it be restrained now, the present corruptions will be protected, and new ones encouraged. Was the government to prescribe to us our medicine and diet, our bodies would be in such keeping as our souls are now. Thus in France the emetic was once forbidden as a medicine, and the potato as an article of food. Government is just as infal-

* *Furneaux passim.*—T.J.

lible, too, when it fixes systems in physics. Galileo was sent to the Inquisition for affirming that the earth was a sphere; the government had declared it to be as flat as a trencher, and Galileo was obliged to abjure his error. This error, however, at length prevailed, the earth became a globe, and Descartes declared it was whirled round its axis by a vortex. The government in which he lived was wise enough to see that this was no question of civil jurisdiction, or we should all have been involved by authority in vortices. In fact, the vortices have been exploded, and the Newtonian principle of gravitation is now more firmly established, on the basis of reason, than it would be were the government to step in, and to make it an article of necessary faith. Reason and experiment have been indulged, and error has fled before them. It is error alone which needs the support of government. Truth can stand by itself. Subject opinion to coercion: whom will you make your inquisitors? Fallible men; men governed by bad passions, by private as well as public reasons. And why subject it to coercion? To produce uniformity. But is uniformity of opinion desirable? No more than of face and stature. Introduce the bed of Procrustes then, and as there is danger that the large men may beat the small, make us all of a size, by lopping the former and stretching the latter. Difference of opinion is advantageous in religion. The several sects perform the office of a *censor morum* over each other. Is uniformity attainable? Millions of innocent men, women, and children, since the introduction of Christianity, have been burnt, tortured, fined, imprisoned; yet we have not advanced one inch towards uniformity. What has been the effect of coercion? To make one half the world fools, and the other half hypocrites. To support roguery and error all over the earth. Let us reflect that it is inhabited by a thousand millions of people. That these profess probably a thousand different systems of religion. That ours is but one of that thousand. That if there be but one right, and ours that one, we should wish to see the nine hundred and ninety-nine wandering sects gathered into the fold of truth. But against such a majority we cannot effect this by force. Reason and persuasion are the only practicable instruments. To make way for these, free inquiry must be indulged; and how can we wish others to indulge it while we refuse it ourselves. But every State, says an inquisitor, has established some religion. No two, say I, have established the same. Is this a proof of the infallibility of establishments? Our sister States of Pennsylvania and New York, however, have long subsisted without any establishment at all. The experiment was new and doubtful when they made it. It has answered beyond conception. They flourish infinitely. Religion is well supported; of various kinds, indeed, but all good enough; all sufficient to preserve peace and order; or if a sect arises, whose tenets would subvert morals, good sense has fair play, and reasons and laughs it out of doors, without suffering the State to be troubled with it. They do not hang more malefactors than we do. They are not more disturbed with religious dissensions. On the contrary, their harmony is unparalleled, and can be ascribed to nothing but their unbounded tolerance, because there is no other circumstance in which they differ from every nation on earth. They have made the happy discovery, that the way to silence religious disputes, is to take no notice of them. Let us too give this experiment fair play, and get rid, while we may, of those tyrannical laws. It is true, we are as yet secured against them by the spirit of the times. I doubt whether the people of this country would suffer an execution for heresy, or a three years' imprisonment for not comprehending the mysteries of the Trinity. But is the spirit of the people an infallible, a permanent reliance? Is it government? Is this the kind of protection we receive in return for the rights we give up? Besides, the spirit of the times may alter, will alter. Our rulers will become corrupt, our people careless. A single zealot may commence persecutor, and better men be his victims. It can never be too often repeated, that the time for fixing every essential right on a legal basis is while our rulers are honest, and ourselves united. From the conclusion of this war we shall be going down hill. It will not then be necessary to resort every moment to the people for support. They will be forgotten, therefore, and their rights disregarded. They will forget themselves, but in the sole faculty of making money, and will never think of uniting to effect a due respect for their rights. The shackles, therefore, which shall not be knocked off at the conclusion of this war, will remain on us long, will be made heavier and heavier, till our rights shall revive or expire in a convulsion.

Slavery

Notes on the State of Virginia, Query 18*

1781

THERE must doubtless be an unhappy influence on the manners of our people produced by the existence of slavery among us. The whole commerce between master and slave is a perpetual exercise of the most boisterous passions, the most unremitting despotism on the one part, and degrading submissions on the other. Our children see this, and learn to imitate it; for man is an imitative animal. This quality is the germ of all education in him. From his cradle to his grave he is learning to do what he sees others do. If a parent could find no motive either in his philanthropy or his self-love, for restraining the intemperance of passion towards his slave, it should always be a sufficient one that his child is present. But generally it is not sufficient. The parent storms, the child looks on, catches the lineaments of wrath, puts on the same airs in the circle of smaller slaves, gives a loose to the worst of passions, and thus nursed, educated, and daily exercised in tyranny, cannot but be stamped by it with odious peculiarities. The man must be a prodigy who can retain his manners and morals undepraved by such circumstances. And with what execration should the statesman be loaded, who, permitting one half the citizens thus to trample on the rights of the other, transforms those into despots, and these into enemies, destroys the morals of the one part, and the *amor patriae* of the other. For if a slave can have a country in this world, it must be any other in preference to that in which he is born to live and labor for another; in which he must lock up the faculties of his nature, contribute as far as depends on

* See Preface to Part II, page 242, and *Autobiography*, Part I, page 58.

his individual endeavors to the evanishment of the human race, or entail his own miserable condition on the endless generations proceeding from him. With the morals of the people, their industry also is destroyed. For in a warm climate, no man will labor for himself who can make another labor for him. This is so true, that of the proprietors of slaves a very small proportion indeed are ever seen to labor. And can the liberties of a nation be thought secure when we have removed their only firm basis, a conviction in the minds of the people that these liberties are of the gift of God? That they are not to be violated but with his wrath? Indeed I tremble for my country when I reflect that God is just; that his justice cannot sleep forever; that considering numbers, nature and natural means only, a revolution of the wheel of fortune, an exchange of situation is among possible events; that it may become probable by supernatural interference! The Almighty has no attribute which can take side with us in such a contest. But·it is impossible to be temperate and to pursue this subject through the various considerations of policy, of morals, of history natural and civil. We must be contented to hope they will force their way into everyone's mind. I think a change already perceptible, since the origin of the present revolution. The spirit of the master is abating, that of the slave rising from the dust, his condition mollifying, the way I hope preparing, under the auspices of heaven, for a total emancipation, and that this is disposed, in the order of events, to be with the consent of the masters, rather than by their extirpation.

PART THREE

Letters

PREFACE

LETTER-WRITING was a literary art in eighteenth-century Europe, and Jefferson was one of its fine practitioners in America. His letters show a versatility that still astonishes. They range over the whole spectrum of then-existing knowledge—from architecture and astronomy to yellow fever and zoology. Nothing seemed to be alien to Jefferson's unquenchable curiosity, as his magnificent book collection at Monticello showed. What Jefferson learned either through reading or conversation or direct observation, he was likely to put down on paper, often in a letter. The recipients of his letters were friends, collaborators, scholars, scientists, or quite simply general inquirers.

The number of Jefferson's letters, at least those that have been preserved, runs into the amazing number of eighteen thousand. He received no fewer than twenty-five thousand letters, from both Americans and Europeans. All this correspondence, together with Jefferson's other writings, is now in the process of publication by the Princeton University Press under the editorship of Julian P. Boyd. The first volume of *The Papers of Thomas Jefferson* appeared in 1950; others have been coming out at the rate of two or three a year. The whole collection, estimated at about sixty volumes, will constitute an invaluable treasury of Jeffersoniana as well as of American (and, for that matter, European) civilization.

Many Jefferson letters, as this necessarily short selection indicates, are a delight to read. They are illuminated by the play of ideas and, in addition, they are so sprightly as to whet the intellectual appetite. Jefferson was obviously a gifted literary man, even though his lifelong business was politics and public affairs.

Among other things, he was a keen judge of character. Note, in par-

·[309]·

ticular, his letter to Dr. Walter Jones with its memorable portrait of George Washington. The letters show Jefferson to be a master of the flashing phrase. Thus he writes of the "foggy" Plato as a sophist who "escaped the oblivion of his brethren . . . by the elegance of his diction." He referred to John Calvin as "an atheist . . . , his religion . . . daemonism." Patrick Henry he described as an empty orator who "said the strongest things in the finest language, without arrangement, desultorily." He characterized Aaron Burr as "a crooked gun . . . whose aim or shot you could never be sure of." Lafayette, whom Jefferson liked, he considered a man whose "foible is a canine appetite for popularity and fame." Of his friend Thomas Paine he wrote that he was a person who "thought more than he read."

Jefferson worked at his letters with thought and care, and loved writing them enough not to curb his spontaneity. His frankness got him into occasional trouble, especially when some letter was made public without authorization. Despite the pain such incidents caused him, he could not control them. "I sometimes expressly desire," he told a friend in 1821, "that my letter not be published; but this is so like requesting a man not to steal or cheat, that I am ashamed of it after I have done it."

As he grew older, Jefferson's voluminous correspondence became an almost intolerable burden. Letters kept pouring into Monticello unceasingly. In one year, Jefferson received 1,267 of them—many, as he complained to John Adams, "requiring answers of elaborate research, and all to be answered with due attention and consideration." He could not curtail the epistolary flood, which robbed him of his leisure. Answering the letters, he said, "keeps me at the drudgery of the writing-table all the prime hours of the day, leaving for the gratifications of my appetite for reading, only what I can steal from the hours of sleep."

The loss of leisure for Jefferson was a gain for posterity, as the letters in the following pages show.

S. K. P.

The Federal Constitution

Paris, December 20, 1787

≫ TO JAMES MADISON ≪   I like much the general idea of framing a government, which should go on of itself, peaceably, without needing continual recurrence to the State legislatures. I like the organization of the government into legislative, judiciary and executive. I like the power given the legislature to levy taxes, and for that reason solely, I approve of the greater House being chosen by the people directly. For though I think a House so chosen, will be very far inferior to the present Congress, will be very illy qualified to legislate for the Union, for foreign nations, and so forth, yet this evil does not weigh against the good, of preserving inviolate the fundamental principle, that the people are not to be taxed but by representatives chosen immediately by themselves. I am captivated by the compromise of the opposite claims of the great and little States, of the latter to equal, and the former to proportional influence. I am much pleased too, with the substitution of the method of voting by person, instead of that of voting by States; and I like the negative given to the Executive, conjointly with a third of either House; though I should have liked it better, had the judiciary been associated for that purpose, or invested separately with a similar power. There are other good things of less moment. I will now tell you

---

Madison (1751–1836), Jefferson's lifelong friend, succeeded him as President in 1809.

what I do not like. First, the omission of a bill of rights, providing clearly, and without the aid of sophism, for freedom of religion, freedom of the press, protection against standing armies, restriction of monopolies, the eternal and unremitting force of the habeas corpus laws, and trials by jury in all matters of fact triable by the laws of the land, and not by the laws of nations. To say, as Mr. Wilson does, that a bill of rights was not necessary, because all is reserved in the case of the general government which is not given, while in the particular ones, all is given which is not reserved, might do for the audience to which it was addressed; but it is surely a *gratis dictum*, the reverse of which might just as well be said; and it is opposed by strong inferences from the body of the instrument, as well as from the omission of the cause of our present Confederation, which had made the reservation in express terms. It was hard to conclude, because there has been a want of uniformity among the States as to the cases triable by jury, because some have been so incautious as to dispense with this mode of trial in certain cases, therefore, the more prudent States shall be reduced to the same level of calamity. It would have been much more just and wise to have concluded the other way, that as most of the States had preserved with jealousy this sacred palladium of liberty, those who had wandered, should be brought back to it; and to have established general right rather than general wrong. For I consider all the ill as established, which may be established. I have a right to nothing, which another has a right to take away; and Congress will have a right to take away trials by jury in all civil cases. Let me add, that a bill of rights is what the people are entitled to against every government on earth, general or particular; and what no just government should refuse, or rest on inference.

The second feature I dislike, and strongly dislike, is the abandonment, in every instance, of the principle of rotation in office, and most particularly in the case of the President. Reason and experience tell us, that the first magistrate will always be re-elected if he may be re-elected. He is then an officer for life. This once observed, it becomes of so much consequence to certain nations, to have a friend or a foe at the head of our affairs, that they will interfere with money and with arms.

A Galloman, or an Angloman, will be supported by the nation he be-
friends. If once elected, and at a second or third election outvoted by
one or two votes, he will pretend false votes, foul play, hold possession
of the reins of government, be supported by the States voting for him,
especially if they be the central ones, lying in a compact body themselves, and separating their opponents; and they will be aided by one
nation in Europe, while the majority are aided by another. The election
of a President of America, some years hence, will be much more interesting to certain nations of Europe, than ever the election of a King of
Poland was. Reflect on all the instances in history, ancient and modern,
of elective monarchies, and say if they do not give foundation for my
fears; the Roman Emperors, the Popes while they were of any importance, the German Emperors till they became hereditary in practice,
the Kings of Poland, the Deys of the Ottoman dependencies. It may be
said, that if elections are to be attended with these disorders, the less
frequently they are repeated the better. But experience says, that to
free them from disorder, they must be rendered less interesting by the
necessity of change. No foreign power, nor domestic party, will waste
their blood and money to elect a person who must go out at the end of a
short period. The power of removing every fourth year by the vote of
the people, is a power which they will not exercise, and if they were
disposed to exercise it, they would not be permitted. The King of Poland is removable every day by the diet. But they never remove him.
Nor would Russia, the Emperor, . . . permit them to do it. Smaller objections are, the appeals on matters of fact as well as laws; and the binding all persons, legislative, executive and judiciary by oath, to maintain
that constitution. I do not pretend to decide, what would be the best
method of procuring the establishment of the manifold good things in
this constitution, and of getting rid of the bad. Whether by adopting it,
in hopes of future amendment; or after it shall have been duly weighed
and canvassed by the people, after seeing the parts they generally dislike, and those they generally approve, to say to them, "We see now
what you wish. You are willing to give to your federal government
such and such powers; but you wish, at the same time, to have such and
such fundamental rights secured to you, and certain sources of convul-

sion taken away. Be it so. Send together deputies again. Let them establish your fundamental rights by a sacrosanct declaration, and let them pass the parts of the constitution you have approved. These will give powers to your federal government sufficient for your happiness."

This is what might be said, and would probably produce a speedy, more perfect and more permanent form of government. At all events, I hope you will not be discouraged from making other trials, if the present one should fail. We are never permitted to despair of the commonwealth. I have thus told you freely what I like, and what I dislike, merely as a matter of curiosity; for I know it is not in my power to offer matter of information to your judgment, which has been formed after hearing and weighing everything which the wisdom of man could offer on these subjects. I own, I am not a friend to a very energetic government. It is always oppressive. It places the governors indeed more at their ease, at the expense of the people. The late rebellion in Massachusetts has given more alarm, than I think it should have done. Calculate that one rebellion in thirteen States in the course of eleven years, is but one for each State in a century and a half. No country should be so long without one. Nor will any degree of power in the hands of government, prevent insurrections. In England, where the hand of power is heavier than with us, there are seldom half a dozen years without an insurrection. In France, where it is still heavier, but less despotic, as Montesquieu supposes, than in some other countries, and where there are always two or three hundred thousand men ready to crush insurrections, there have been three in the course of the three years I have been here, in every one of which greater numbers were engaged than in Massachusetts, and a great deal more blood was spilt. In Turkey, where the sole nod of the despot is death, insurrections are the events of every day. Compare again the ferocious depredations of their insurgents, with the order, the moderation and the almost self-extinguishment of ours. And say, finally, whether peace is best preserved by giving energy to the government, or information to the people. This last is the most certain, and the most legitimate engine of government. Educate and inform the whole mass of the people. Enable them to see that it is their interest to preserve peace and order, and they will preserve them. And it requires no very high degree of education to convince them of this. They are the only sure reliance for the preservation of our liberty. After all, it is my principle that the will of the majority should prevail. If they approve the proposed constitution in all its parts, I shall concur in it cheerfully, in hopes they will amend it, whenever they shall find it works wrong. This reliance cannot deceive us, as long as we remain virtuous; and I think we shall be so, as long as agriculture is our principal object, which will be the case, while there remains vacant lands in any part of America. When we get piled upon one another in large cities, as in Europe, we shall become corrupt as in Europe, and go to eating one another as they do there. I have tired you by this time with disquisitions which you have already heard repeated by others, a thousand and a thousand times; and, therefore, shall only add assurances of the esteem and attachment with which I have the honor to be, dear sir, your affectionate friend and servant.

The French Revolution

Philadelphia, January 3, 1793

≫ TO WILLIAM SHORT ≪ My last private letter to you was of October 16, since which I have received your Nos. 103, 107, 108, 109, 110, 112, 113 and 114 and yesterday your private one of September 15, came to hand. The tone of your letters had for some time given me pain, on account of the extreme warmth with which they censured the proceedings of the Jacobins of France. I considered that sect as the same with the republican patriots, and the Feuillants as the monarchical patriots, well known in the early part of the Revolution, and but little distant in their views, both having in object the establishment of a free constitution, differing only on the question whether their chief executive should be hereditary or not. The Jacobins (as since called) yielded to the Feuillants, and tried the experiment of retaining their hereditary executive. The experiment failed completely, and would have brought on the re-establishment of despotism had it been pursued. The Jacobins knew this, and that the expunging that office was of absolute necessity. And the nation was with them in opinion, for however they might have been formerly for the constitution framed by the first assembly, they were come over from their hope in it, and were now generally Jacobins.

Short (1759–1849) was Jefferson's secretary in Paris and occupied diplomatic posts in Holland and Spain.

In the struggle which was necessary, many guilty persons fell without the forms of trial, and with them some innocent. These I deplore as much as anybody, and shall deplore some of them to the day of my death. But I deplore them as I should have done had they fallen in battle. It was necessary to use the arm of the people, a machine not quite so blind as balls and bombs, but blind to a certain degree. A few of their cordial friends met at their hands the fate of enemies. But time and truth will rescue and embalm their memories, while their posterity will be enjoying that very liberty for which they would never have hesitated to offer up their lives. The liberty of the whole earth was depending on the issue of the contest, and was ever such a prize won with so little innocent blood? My own affections have been deeply wounded by some of the martyrs to this cause, but rather than it should have failed I would have seen half the earth desolated; were there but an Adam and an Eve left in every country, and left free, it would be better than as it now is. I have expressed to you my sentiments, because they are really those of ninety-nine in a hundred of our citizens. The universal feasts, and rejoicings which have lately been had on account of the successes of the French, showed the genuine effusions of their hearts. You have been wounded by the sufferings of your friends, and have by this circumstance been hurried into a temper of mind which would be extremely disrelished if known to your countrymen.

On Personal Relations

⋙ TO MARIA JEFFERSON EPPES ⋘ I acknowledged, my dear Maria, the receipt of yours in a letter I wrote to Mr. Eppes. It gave me the welcome news that your sprain was well. But you are not to suppose it entirely so. The joint will remain weak for a considerable time, and give you occasional pains much longer. The state of things at ——— is truly distressing. Mr. ———'s habitual intoxication will destroy himself, his fortune, and family. Of all calamities, this is the greatest. I wish my sister could bear his misconduct with more patience. It would lessen his attachment to the bottle, and at any rate would make her own time more tolerable. When we see ourselves in a situation which must be endured and gone through, it is best to make up our minds to it, meet it with firmness, and accommodate everything to it in the best way practicable. This lessens the evil, while fretting and fuming only serves to increase our own torments. The errors and misfortunes of others should be a school for our own instruction. Harmony in the married state is the very first object to be aimed at. Nothing can preserve affections uninterrupted but a firm resolution never to differ in will, and a determination in each to consider the love of

Jefferson's youngest daughter Maria married John Wayles Eppes on October 13, 1797.

the other as of more value than any object whatever on which a wish had been fixed. How light, in fact, is the sacrifice of any other wish, when weighed against the affections of one with whom we are to pass our whole life. And though opposition, in a single instance, will hardly of itself produce alienation, yet every one has their pouch into which all these little oppositions are put: while that is filling, the alienation is insensibly going on, and when filled it is complete. It would puzzle either to say why; because no one difference of opinion has been marked enough to produce a serious effect by itself. But he finds his affections wearied out by a constant stream of little checks and obstacles. Other sources of discontent, very common indeed, are the little cross purposes of husband and wife, in common conversation, a disposition in either to criticize and question whatever the other says, a desire always to demonstrate and make him feel himself in the wrong, and especially in company. Nothing is so goading. Much better, therefore, if our companion views a thing in a light different from what we do, to leave him in quiet possession of his view. What is the use of rectifying him, if the thing be unimportant; and if important, let it pass for the present, and wait a softer moment and more conciliatory occasion of revising the subject together. It is wonderful how many persons are rendered unhappy by inattention to these little rules of prudence. I have been insensibly led, by the particular case you mention, to sermonize you on the subject generally; however, if it be the means of saving you from a single heartache, it will have contributed a great deal to my happiness—but before I finish the sermon, I must add a word on economy. The unprofitable condition of Virginia estates in general, leaves it now next to impossible for the holder of one to avoid ruin. And this condition will continue until some change takes place in the mode of working them. In the meantime, nothing can save us and our children from beggary, but a determination to get a year beforehand, and restrain ourselves vigorously this year to the clear profits of the last. If a debt is once contracted by a farmer, it is never paid but by a sale. The article of dress is perhaps that in which economy is the least to be recommended. It is so important to each to continue to please the other, that the happiness of both requires the most pointed attention to whatever may contribute to it—and the more as time makes greater inroads on our person. Yet, generally, we become slovenly in proportion as personal decay requires the contrary. I have great comfort in believing that your understanding and dispositions will engage your attention to these considerations; and that you are connected with a person and family who, of all within the circle of my acquaintance, are most in the dispositions which will make you happy. Cultivate their affections, my dear, with assiduity. Think every sacrifice a gain, which shall tend to attach them to you. My only object in life is to see yourself and your sister, and those deservedly dear to you, not only happy, but in no danger of becoming unhappy.

Socrates and Jesus

Washington, April 9, 1803

≫ TO JOSEPH PRIESTLEY ≪ While on a short visit lately to Monticello, I received from you a copy of your comparative view of Socrates and Jesus, and I avail myself of the first moment of leisure after my return to acknowledge the pleasure I had in the perusal of it, and the desire it excited to see you take up the subject on a more extended scale. In consequence of some conversation with Dr. Rush, in the year 1798–99, I had promised some day to write him a letter giving him my view of the Christian system. I have reflected often on it since, and even sketched the outlines in my own mind. I should first take a general view of the moral doctrines of the most remarkable of the ancient philosophers, of whose ethics we have sufficient information to make an estimate, say Pythagoras, Epicurus, Epictetus, Socrates, Cicero, Seneca, Antoninus. I should do justice to the branches of morality they have treated well; but point out the importance of those in which they are deficient. I should then take a view of the deism and ethics of the Jews, and show in what a degraded state they were, and the necessity they presented of a reformation. I should proceed to a view of the life, character, and doctrines of Jesus, who sensible of incorrectness of

---

Priestley (1733–1804), the famous English scientist who discovered oxygen, was also a Unitarian minister whose ideas on religion influenced those of Jefferson.

their ideas of the Deity, and of morality, endeavored to bring them to the principles of a pure deism, and juster notions of the attributes of God, to reform their moral doctrines to the standard of reason, justice and philanthropy, and to inculcate the belief of a future state. This view would purposely omit the question of his divinity, and even his inspiration. To do him justice, it would be necessary to remark the disadvantages his doctrines had to encounter, not having been committed to writing by himself, but by the most unlettered of men, by memory, long after they had heard them from him; when much was forgotten, much misunderstood, and presented in every paradoxical shape. Yet such are the fragments remaining as to show a master workman, and that his system of morality was the most benevolent and sublime probably that has been ever taught, and consequently more perfect than those of any of the ancient philosophers. His character and doctrines have received still greater injury from those who pretend to be his special disciples, and who have disfigured and sophisticated his actions and precepts, from views of personal interest, so as to induce the unthinking part of mankind to throw off the whole system in disgust, and to pass sentence as an impostor on the most innocent, the most benevolent, the most eloquent and sublime character that ever has been exhibited to man. This is the outline; but I have not the time, and still less the information which the subject needs. It will therefore rest with me in contemplation only. You are the person of all others would do it best, and most promptly. You have all the materials at hand, and you put together with ease. I wish you could be induced to extend your late work to the whole subject. I have not heard particularly what is the state of your health; but as it has been equal to the journey to Philadelphia, perhaps it might encourage the curiosity you must feel to see for once this place, which nature has formed on a beautiful scale, and circumstances destine for a great one. As yet we are but a cluster of villages; we cannot offer you the learned society of Philadelphia; but you will have that of a few characters whom you esteem, and a bed and hearty welcome with one who will rejoice in every opportunity of testifying to you his high veneration and affectionate attachment.

The Separation of Church and State

Washington, January 23, 1808

≫ TO SAMUEL MILLER ≪ I consider the government of the United States as interdicted by the Constitution from intermeddling with religious institutions, their doctrines, discipline, or exercises. This results not only from the provision that no law shall be made respecting the establishment or free exercise of religion, but from that also which reserves to the States the powers not delegated to the United States. Certainly, no power to prescribe any religious exercise, or to assume authority in religious discipline, has been delegated to the general government. It must then rest with the States, as far as it can be in any human authority. But it is only proposed that I should *recommend*, not prescribe a day of fasting and prayer. That is, that I should *indirectly* assume to the United States an authority over religious exercises, which the Constitution has directly precluded them from. It must be meant, too, that this recommendation is to carry some authority, and to be sanctioned by some penalty on those who disregard it; not indeed of fine and imprisonment, but of some degree of proscription, perhaps in public opinion. And does the change in the nature of the penalty make the

Samuel Miller (1769–1850), Presbyterian clergyman and moderator, was a minister in New York City until 1813 and later became professor of church history at the Princeton Theological Seminary.

·[323]·

recommendation less a *law* of conduct for those to whom it is directed? I do not believe it is for the interest of religion to invite the civil magistrate to direct its exercises, its discipline, or its doctrines; nor of the religious societies, that the general government should be invested with the power of effecting any uniformity of time or matter among them. Fasting and prayer are religious exercises; the enjoining them an act of discipline. Every religious society has the right to determine for itself the times for these exercises, and the objects proper for them, according to their own particular tenets; and this right can never be safer than in their own hands, where the Constitution has deposited it.

I am aware that the practice of my predecessors may be quoted. But I have ever believed, that the example of State executives led to the assumption of that authority by the general government, without due examination, which would have discovered that what might be a right in a State government, was a violation of that right when assumed by another. Be this as it may, every one must act according to the dictates of his own reason, and mine tells me that civil powers alone have been given to the President of the United States, and no authority to direct the religious exercises of his constituents.

I again express my satisfaction that you have been so good as to give me an opportunity of explaining myself in a private letter, in which I could give my reasons more in detail than might have been done in a public answer; and I pray you to accept the assurances of my high esteem and respect.

On Behavior

Washington, November 24, 1808

❧ TO THOMAS JEFFERSON RANDOLPH ❧ My dear Jefferson, Your situation, thrown at such a distance from us, and alone, cannot but give us all great anxieties for you. As much has been secured for you, by your particular position and the acquaintance to which you have been recommended, as could be done towards shielding you from the dangers which surround you. But thrown on a wide world, among entire strangers, without a friend or guardian to advise, so young too, and with so little experience of mankind, your dangers are great, and still your safety must rest on yourself. A determination never to do what is wrong, prudence and good humor, will go far towards securing to you the estimation of the world. When I recollect that at fourteen years of age, the whole care and direction of myself was thrown on myself entirely, without a relation or friend qualified to advise or guide me, and recollect the various sorts of bad company with which I associated from time to time, I am astonished I did not turn off with some of them, and become as worthless to society as they were. I had the good fortune to become acquainted very early with some characters of very high standing, and to feel the incessant wish that I could ever become what

---

Jefferson's grandson, who was sent to school in Philadelphia at the age of 15. He was born in 1792 and died in 1875.

they were. Under temptations and difficulties, I would ask myself what would Dr. Small, Mr. Wythe, Peyton Randolph do in this situation? What course in it will insure me their approbation? I am certain that this mode of deciding on my conduct, tended more to correctness than any reasoning powers I possessed. Knowing the even and dignified line they pursued, I could never doubt for a moment which of two courses would be in character for them. Whereas, seeking the same object through a process of moral reasoning, and with the jaundiced eye of youth, I should often have erred. From the circumstances of my position, I was often thrown into the society of horse racers, card players, fox hunters, scientific and professional men, and of dignified men; and many a time I have asked myself, in the enthusiastic moment of the death of a fox, the victory of a favorite horse, the issue of a question eloquently argued at the bar, or in the great council of the nation, well, which of these kinds of reputation should I prefer? That of a horse jockey, a fox hunter, an orator, or the honest advocate of my country's rights? Be assured, my dear Jefferson, that these little returns into ourselves, this self-catechising habit, is not trifling nor useless, but leads to the prudent selection and steady pursuit of what is right.

I have mentioned good humor as one of the preservatives of our peace and tranquillity. It is among the most effectual, and its effect is so well imitated and aided, artificially, by politeness, that this also becomes an acquisition of first rate value. In truth, politeness is artificial good humor, it covers the natural want of it, and ends by rendering habitual a substitute nearly equivalent to the real virtue. It is the practice of sacrificing to those whom we meet in society, all the little conveniences and preferences which will gratify them, and deprive us of nothing worth a moment's consideration; it is the giving a pleasing and flattering turn to our expressions, which will conciliate others, and make them pleased with us as well as themselves. How cheap a price for the good will of another! When this is in return for a rude thing said by another, it brings him to his senses, it mortifies and corrects him in the most salutary way, and places him at the feet of your good nature, in the eyes of the company. But in stating prudential rules for our government in society, I must not omit the important one of never entering into dispute or argument with another. I never saw an instance of one of two disputants convincing the other by argument. I have seen many, on their getting warm, becoming rude, and shooting one another. Conviction is the effect of our own dispassionate reasoning, either in solitude, or weighing within ourselves, dispassionately, what we hear from others, standing uncommitted in argument ourselves. It was one of the rules which, above all others, made Doctor Franklin the most amiable of men in society, "never to contradict anybody." If he was urged to announce an opinion, he did it rather by asking questions, as if for information, or by suggesting doubts. When I hear another express an opinion which is not mine, I say to myself, he has a right to his opinion, as I to mine; why should I question it? His error does me no injury, and shall I become a Don Quixote, to bring all men by force of argument to one opinion? If a fact be misstated, it is probable he is gratified by a belief of it, and I have no right to deprive him of the gratification. If he wants information, he will ask it, and then I will give it in measured terms; but if he still believes his own story, and shows a desire to dispute the fact with me, I hear him and say nothing. It is his affair, not mine, if he prefers error. There are two classes of disputants most frequently to be met with among us. The first is of young students, just entered the threshold of science, with a first view of its outlines, not yet filled up with the details and modifications which a further progress would bring to their knowledge. The other consists of the ill-tempered and rude men in society, who have taken up a passion for politics. (Good humor and politeness never introduce into mixed society a question on which they foresee there will be a difference of opinion.) From both of those classes of disputants, my dear Jefferson, keep aloof, as you would from the infected subjects of yellow fever or pestilence. Consider yourself, when with them, as among the patients of Bedlam, needing medical more than moral counsel. Be a listener only, keep within yourself, and endeavor to establish with yourself the habit of silence, especially on politics. In the fevered state of our country, no good can ever result from any attempt to set one of these fiery zealots to rights, either in fact or principle. They are determined as to the facts they will believe, and the opinions on which they will act. Get by them, therefore, as you would by an angry bull; it is not for a man of sense to dispute the road with such an animal. You will be more exposed than others to have these animals shaking their horns at you, because of the relation in which you stand with me. Full of political venom, and willing to see me and to hate me as a chief in the antagonist party, your presence will be to them what the vomit grass is to the sick dog, a nostrum for producing ejaculation. Look upon them exactly with that eye, and pity them as objects to whom you can administer only occasional ease. My character is not within their power. It is in the hands of my fellow citizens at large, and will be consigned to honor or infamy by the verdict of the republican mass of our country, according to what themselves will have seen, not what their enemies and mine shall have said. Never, therefore, consider these puppies in politics as requiring any notice from you, and always show that you are not afraid to leave my character to the umpirage of public opinion. Look steadily to the pursuits which have carried you to Philadelphia, be very select in the society you attach yourself to, avoid taverns, drinkers, smokers, idlers, and dissipated persons generally; for it is with such that broils and contentions arise; and you will find your path more easy and tranquil. The limits of my paper warn me that it is time for me to close with my affectionate adieu.

P.S. Present me affectionately to Mr. Ogilvie, and, in doing the same to Mr. Peale, tell him I am writing with his polygraph, and shall send him mine the first moment I have leisure enough to pack it.

The Invention of Elevators

Monticello, August 13, 1813

⫸ TO ISAAC McPHERSON ⫷ Your letter of August 3d asking information on the subject of Mr. Oliver Evans' exclusive right to the use of what he calls his Elevators, Conveyers, and Hopper-boys, has been duly received. My wish to see new inventions encouraged, and old ones brought again into useful notice, has made me regret the circumstances which have followed the expiration of his first patent. I did not expect the retrospection which has been given to the reviving law. For although the second proviso seemed not so clear as it ought to have been, yet it appeared susceptible of a just construction; and the retrospective one being contrary to natural right, it was understood to be a rule of law that where the words of a statute admit of two constructions, the one just and the other unjust, the former is to be given them. The first proviso takes care of those who had lawfully used Evans' improvements under the first patent; the second was meant for those who had lawfully erected and used them after that patent expired, declaring they "should not be liable to damages therefor." These words may indeed be restrained to uses already past, but as there is parity of reason for those to come, there should be parity of law. Every

McPherson was a Baltimore inventor who had written Jefferson concerning scientific matters.

man should be protected in his lawful acts, and be certain that no *ex post facto* law shall punish or endamage him for them. But he is endamaged, if forbidden to use a machine lawfully erected, at considerable expense, unless he will pay a new and unexpected price for it. The proviso says that he who erected and used lawfully should not be liable to pay damages. But if the proviso had been omitted, would not the law, construed by natural equity, have said the same thing? In truth both provisos are useless. And shall useless provisos, inserted *pro majori cautela* only, authorize inferences against justice? The sentiment that *ex post facto* laws are against natural right, is so strong in the United States, that few, if any, of the State constitutions have failed to proscribe them. The federal constitution indeed interdicts them in criminal cases only; but they are equally unjust in civil as in criminal cases, and the omission of a caution which would have been right, does not justify the doing what is wrong. Nor ought it to be presumed that the legislature meant to use a phrase in an unjustifiable sense, if by rules of construction it can be ever strained to what is just. The law books abound with similar instances of the care the judges take of the public integrity. Laws, moreover, abridging the natural right of the citizen, should be restrained by rigorous constructions within their narrowest limits.

Your letter, however, points to a much broader question, whether what have received from Mr. Evans the new and proper name of Elevators, are of his invention. Because, if they are not, his patent gives him no right to obstruct others in the use of what they possessed before. I assume it is a Lemma, that it is the invention of the machine itself, which is to give a patent right, and not the application of it to any particular purpose, of which it is susceptible. If one person invents a knife convenient for pointing our pens, another cannot have a patent right for the same knife to point our pencils. A compass was invented for navigating the sea; another could not have a patent right for using it to survey land. A machine for threshing *wheat* has been invented in Scotland; a second person cannot get a patent right for the same machine to thresh *oats*, a third *rye*, a fourth *peas*, a fifth *clover*, &c. A string of buckets is invented and used for raising water, ore, &c., can a second have a patent right to the same machine for raising wheat, a third oats, a fourth rye, a fifth peas, &c.? The question then whether such a string of buckets was invented first by Oliver Evans, is a mere question of fact in mathematical history. Now, turning to such books only as I happen to possess, I find abundant proof that this simple machinery has been in use from time immemorial. Doctor Shaw, who visited Egypt and the Barbary coast in the years 1727–8–9, in the margin of his map of Egypt, gives us the figure of what he calls a Persian wheel, which is a string of round cups or buckets hanging on a pulley, over which they revolved, bringing up water from a well and delivering it into a trough above. He found this used at Cairo, in a well 264 feet deep, which the inhabitants believe to have been the work of the patriarch Joseph. Shaw's travels, 341, Oxford edition of 1738 in folio, and the Universal History, I. 416, speaking of the manner of watering the higher lands in Egypt, says, "formerly they made use of Archimedes's screw, thence named the Egyptian pump, but they now generally use wheels (wallowers) which carry a rope or chain of earthen pots holding about seven or eight quarts apiece, and draw the water from the canals. There are besides a vast number of wells in Egypt, from which the water is drawn in the same manner to water the gardens and fruit trees; so that it is no exaggeration to say, that there are in Egypt above 200,000 oxen daily employed in this labor." Shaw's name of Persian wheel has been since given more particularly to a wheel with buckets, either fixed or suspended on pins, at its periphery. Mortimer's husbandry, I. 18, Duhamel III. II., Ferguson's Mechanic's plate, XIII; but his figure, and the verbal description of the Universal History, prove that the string of buckets is meant under that name. His figure differs from Evans' construction in the circumstances of the buckets being round, and strung through their bottom on a chain. But it is the principle, to wit, a string of buckets, which constitutes the invention, not the form of the buckets, round, square, or hexagon; nor the manner of attaching them, nor the material of the connecting band, whether chain, rope, or leather. Vitruvius, L. x. c. 9, describes this machinery as a windlass, on which is a chain descending to the water, with vessels of copper attached to it; the windlass being turned, the chain moving on it will raise the vessel, which in passing over the windlass will empty the water they have brought up into a reservoir. And Perrault, in his edition of Vitruvius, Paris, 1684, fol. plates 61, 62, gives us three forms of these water elevators, in one of which the buckets are square, as Mr. Evans' are. Bossut, Histoire des Mathématiques, i. 86, says, "the drum wheel, the wheel with buckets and the *Chapelets*, are hydraulic machines which come to us from the ancients. But we are ignorant of the time when they began to be put into use." The *Chapelets* are the revolving bands of the buckets which Shaw calls the Persian wheel, the moderns a chain-pump, and Mr. Evans elevators. The next of my books in which I find these elevators is Wolf's Cours de Mathématiques, i. 370, and plate I, Paris 1747, 8vo; here are two forms. In one of them the buckets are square, attached to two chains, passing over a cylinder or wallower at top, and under another at bottom, by which they are made to revolve. It is a nearly exact representation of Evans' Elevators. But a more exact one is to be seen in Desagulier's Experimental Philosophy, ii. plate 34; in the Encyclopédie de Diderot et D'Alembert, 8vo edition of Lausanne, 1st volume of plates in the four subscribed Hydraulique. Norie, is one where round eastern pots are tied by their collars between two endless ropes suspended on a revolving lantern or wallower. This is said to have been used for raising ore out of a mine. In a book which I do not possess, L'Architecture Hydraulique de Belidor, the 2d volume of which is said [De la Lande's continuation of Montuclas' Histoire de Mathématiques, iii. 711] to contain a detail of all the pumps, ancient and modern, hydraulic machines, fountains, wells, &c., I have no doubt this Persian wheel, chain-pump, chapelets, elevators, by whichever name you choose to call it, will be found in various forms. The last book I have to quote for it is Prony's Architecture Hydraulique i., Avertissement vii., and § 648, 649, 650. In the latter of which passages he observes that the first idea which occurs for raising water is to lift it in a bucket by hand. When the water lies too deep to be reached by hand, the bucket is suspended by a chain and let down over a pulley or windlass. If it be desired to raise a continued stream of water, the simplest means which offers itself to the mind is to attach to an endless chain or cord a number of pots or buckets, so disposed that, the chain being suspended on a lanthorn or wallower above, and plunged in water below, the buckets may descend and ascend alternately, filling themselves at bottom and emptying at a certain height above, so as to give a constant stream. Some years before the date of Mr. Evans' patent, a Mr. Martin of Caroline county in this State, constructed a drill-plough, in which he used the band of buckets for elevating the grain from the box into the funnel, which let them down into the furrow. He had bands with different sets of buckets adapted to the size of peas, of turnip seed, &c. I have used this machine for sowing Benni seed also, and propose to have a band of buckets for drilling Indian Corn, and another for wheat. Is it possible that in doing this I shall infringe Mr. Evans' patent? That I can be debarred of any use to which I might have applied my drill, when I bought it, by a patent issued after I bought it?

These verbal descriptions, applying so exactly to Mr. Evans' elevators, and the drawings exhibited to the eye, flash conviction both on reason and the senses that there is nothing new in these elevators but their being strung together on a strap of leather. If this strap of leather be an invention, entitling the inventor to a patent right, it can only extend to the strap, and the use of the string of buckets must remain free to be connected by chains, ropes, a strap of hempen girthing, or any other substance except leather. But, indeed, Mr. Martin had before used the strap of leather.

The screw of Archimedes is as ancient, at least, as the age of that mathematician, who died more than 2,000 years ago. Diodorus Siculus speaks of it, L. i., p. 21, and L. v., p. 217, of Stevens' edition of 1559, folio; and Vitruvius, xii. The cutting of its spiral worm into sections for conveying flour or grain, seems to have been an invention of Mr. Evans, and to be a fair subject of a patent right. But it cannot take away from others the use of Archimedes' screw with its perpetual spiral, for any purposes of which it is susceptible.

The hopper-boy is an useful machine, and so far as I know, original.

It has been pretended by some (and in England especially), that inventors have a natural and exclusive right to their inventions, and not merely for their own lives, but inheritable to their heirs. But while it is a moot question whether the origin of any kind of property is derived from nature at all, it would be singular to admit a natural and even an hereditary right to inventors. It is agreed by those who have seriously considered the subject, that no individual has, of natural right, a separate property in an acre of land, for instance. By an universal law, indeed, whatever, whether fixed or movable, belongs to all men equally and in common, is the property for the moment of him who occupies it; but when he relinquishes the occupation, the property goes with it. Stable ownership is the gift of social law, and is given late in the progress of society. It would be curious then, if an idea, the fugitive fermentation of an individual brain, could, of natural right, be claimed in exclusive and stable property. If nature has made any one thing less susceptible than all others of exclusive property, it is the action of the thinking power called an idea, which an individual may exclusively possess as long as he keeps it to himself; but the moment it is divulged, it forces itself into the possession of everyone, and the receiver cannot dispossess himself of it. Its peculiar character, too, is that no one possesses the less, because every other possesses the whole of it. He who receives an idea from me, receives instruction himself without lessening mine; as he who lights his taper at mine, receives light without darkening me. That ideas should freely spread from one to another over the globe, for the moral and mutual instruction of man, and improvement of his condition, seems to have been peculiarly and benevolently designed by nature, when she made them, like fire, expansible over all space, without lessening their density in any point, and like the air in which we breathe, move, and have our physical being, incapable of confinement or exclusive appropriation. Inventions then cannot, in nature, be a subject of property. Society may give an exclusive right to the profits arising from them, as an encouragement to men to pursue ideas which may produce utility, but this may or may not be done, according to the will and convenience of the society, without claim or complaint from anybody. Accordingly, it is a fact, as far as I am informed, that England was, until we copied her, the only country on earth which ever, by a general law, gave a legal right to the exclusive use of an idea. In some other countries it is sometimes done, in a great case, and by a special and personal act, but, generally speaking, other nations have thought that these monopolies produce more embarrassment than advantage to society; and it may be observed that the nations which refuse monopolies of invention, are as fruitful as England in new and useful devices.

Considering the exclusive right to invention as given not of natural right, but for the benefit of society, I know well the difficulty of drawing a line between the things which are worth to the public the embarrassment of an exclusive patent, and those which are not. As a member of the patent board for several years, while the law authorized a board to grant or refuse patents, I saw with what slow progress a system of general rules could be matured. Some, however, were established by that board. One of these was, that a machine of which we were possessed, might be applied by every man to any use of which it is susceptible, and that this right ought not to be taken from him and given to a monopolist, because the first perhaps had occasion so to apply it. Thus a screw for crushing plaster might be employed for crushing corn-cobs. And a chain-pump for raising water might be used for raising wheat: this being merely a change of application. Another rule was that a change of material should not give title to a patent. As the making a ploughshare of cast rather than of wrought iron; a comb of iron instead of horn or of ivory, or the connecting buckets by a band of leather rather than of hemp or iron. A third was that a mere change of form should give no right to a patent, as a high-quartered shoe instead of a low one; a round hat instead of a three-square; or a square bucket instead of a round one. But for this rule, all the changes of fashion in dress would have been under the tax of patentees. These were among the rules which the uniform decisions of the board had already established, and under each of them Mr. Evans' patent would have been refused. First, because it was a mere change of application of the chain-pump, from raising water to raise wheat. Secondly, because the using a leathern instead of a hempen band, was a mere change of material; and thirdly, square buckets instead of round, are only a change of form, and the ancient forms, too, appear to have been indifferently square or round. But there were still abundance of cases which could not be brought under rule, until they should have presented themselves under all their aspects; and these investigations occupying more time of the members of the board than they could spare from higher duties, the whole was turned over to the judiciary, to be matured into a system, under which everyone might know when his actions were safe and lawful. Instead of refusing a patent in the first instance, as the board was authorized to do, the patent now issues of course, subject to be declared void on such principles as should be established by the courts of law. This business, however, is but little analogous to their course of reading, since we might in vain turn over all the lubberly volumes of the law to find a single ray which would lighten the path of the mechanic or the mathematician. It is more within the information of a board of academical professors, and a previous refusal of patent would better guard our citizens against harassment by law-suits. But England had given it to her judges, and the usual predominancy of her examples carried it to ours.

It happened that I had myself a mill built in the interval between Mr. Evans' first and second patents. I was living in Washington, and left the construction to the mill-wright. I did not even know he had erected elevators, conveyers and hopper-boys, until I learnt it by an application from Mr. Evans' agent for the patent price. Although I had no idea he had a right to it by law (for no judicial decision had then been given), yet I did not hesitate to remit to Mr. Evans the old and moderate patent price, which was what he then asked, from a wish to encourage even the useful revival of ancient inventions. But I then expressed my opinion of the law in a letter, either to Mr. Evans or to his agent.

I have thus, Sir, at your request, given you the facts and ideas which occur to me on this subject. I have done it without reserve, although I have not the pleasure of knowing you personally. In thus frankly committing myself to you, I trust you will feel it as a point of honor and candor, to make no use of my letter which might bring disquietude on myself. And particularly, I should be unwilling to be brought into any difference with Mr. Evans, whom, however, I believe too reasonable to take offence at an honest difference of opinion. I esteem him much, and sincerely wish him wealth and honor. I deem him a valuable citizen, of uncommon ingenuity and usefulness. And had I not esteemed still more the establishment of sound principles, I should now have been silent. If any of the matter I have offered can promote that object, I have no objection to its being so used; if it offers nothing new, it will of course not be used at all. I have gone with some minuteness into the mathematical history of the elevator, because it belongs to a branch of science in which, as I have before observed, it is not incumbent on lawyers to be learned; and it is possible, therefore, that some of the proofs I have quoted may have escaped on their former arguments. On the law of the subject I should not have touched, because more familiar to those who have already discussed it; but I wished to state my own view of it merely in justification of myself, my name and approbation being subscribed to the act. With these explanations, accept the assurance of my respect.

Philosophy and Religion

⇒ TO JOHN ADAMS ⇐ Since mine of August the 22d, I have received your favors of August the 16th, September the 2d, 14th, 15th, and —, and Mrs. Adams' of September the 20th. I now send you, according to your request, a copy of the syllabus. To fill up this skeleton with arteries, with veins, with nerves, muscles and flesh, is really beyond my time and information. Whoever could undertake it would find great aid in Enfield's judicious abridgment of Brucker's History of Philosophy, in which he has reduced five or six quarto volumes, of one thousand pages each of Latin closely printed, to two moderate octavos of English open type.

To compare the morals of the Old, with those of the New Testament, would require an attentive study of the former, a search through all its books for its precepts, and through all its history for its practices, and the principles they prove. As commentaries, too, on these, the philosophy of the Hebrews must be inquired into, their Mishna, their Gemara, Cabbala, Jezirah, Sohar, Cosri, and their Talmud, must be examined and understood, in order to do them full justice. Brucker, it

---

John Adams (1735–1826), second President of the United States, resumed a delightful correspondence with Jefferson in 1812, after an estrangement of about a dozen years.

would seem, has gone deeply into these repositories of their ethics, and Enfield his epitomizer, concludes in these words: "Ethics were so little understood among the Jews, that in their whole compilation called the Talmud, there is only one treatise on moral subjects. Their books of morals chiefly consisted in a minute enumeration of duties. From the law of Moses were deduced six hundred and thirteen precepts, which were divided into two classes, affirmative and negative, two hundred and forty-eight in the former, and three hundred and sixty-five in the latter. It may serve to give the reader some idea of the low state of moral philosophy among the Jews in the middle age, to add that of the two hundred and forty-eight affirmative precepts, only three were considered as obligatory upon women, and that in order to obtain salvation, it was judged sufficient to fulfill any one single law in the hour of death; the observance of the rest being deemed necessary, only to increase the felicity of the future life. What a wretched depravity of sentiment and manners must have prevailed, before such corrupt maxims could have obtained credit! It is impossible to collect from these writings a consistent series of moral doctrine." . . . It was the reformation of this "wretched depravity" of morals which Jesus undertook. In extracting the pure principles which he taught, we should have to strip off the artificial vestments in which they have been muffled by priests, who have travestied them into various forms, as instruments of riches and power to themselves. We must dismiss the Platonists and Plotinists, the Stagyrites and Gamalielites, the Eclectics, the Gnostics and Scholastics, their essences and emanations, their logos and demiurgos, æons and dæmons, male and female, with a long train of . . . or, shall I say at once, of nonsense. We must reduce our volume to the simple evangelists, select, even from them, the very words only of Jesus, paring off the amphibologisms into which they have been led, by forgetting often, or not understanding, what had fallen from him, by giving their own misconceptions as his dicta, and expressing unintelligibly for others what they had not understood themselves. There will be found remaining the most sublime and benevolent code of morals which has ever been offered to man. I have performed this operation for my own use, by cutting verse by verse out of the printed book, and arranging the matter which is evidently his, and which is as easily distinguishable as diamonds in a dunghill. The result is an octavo of forty-six pages, of pure and unsophisticated doctrines, such as were professed and acted on by the *unlettered* Apostles, the Apostolic Fathers, and the Christians of the first century.* Their Platonizing successors, indeed, in after times, in order to legitimate the corruptions which they had incorporated into the doctrines of Jesus, found it necessary to disavow the primitive Christians, who had taken their principles from the mouth of Jesus himself, of his Apostles, and the Fathers contemporary with them. They excommunicated their followers as heretics, branding them with the opprobrious name of Ebionites or Beggars.

For a comparison of the Grecian philosophy with that of Jesus, materials might be largely drawn from the same source. Enfield gives a history and detailed account of the opinions and principles of the different sects. These relate to the Gods, their natures, grades, places and powers; the demi-Gods and dæmons, and their agency with man; the universe, its structure, extent and duration; the origin of things from the elements of fire, water, air and earth; the human soul, its essence and derivation; the *summum bonum* and *finis bonorum*; with a thousand idle dreams and fancies on these and other subjects, the knowledge of which is withheld from man; leaving but a short chapter for his moral duties, and the principal section of that given to what he owes himself, to precepts for rendering him impassible, and unassailable by the evils of life, and for preserving his mind in a state of constant serenity.

Such a canvas is too broad for the age of seventy, and especially of one whose chief occupations have been in the practical business of life. We must leave, therefore, to others, younger and more learned than we are, to prepare this euthanasia for Platonic Christianity, and its restoration to the primitive simplicity of its founder. I think you give a just outline of the theism of the three religions, when you say that the principle of the Hebrew was the fear, of the Gentile the honor, and of the Christian the love of God.

An expression in your letter of September the 14th, that "the human

* The selection of passages "extracted textually" from the Gospels has been published under such titles as *The Jefferson Bible* and *The Life and Morals of Jesus of Nazareth.*

understanding is a revelation from its maker," gives the best solution that I believe can be given of the question, "what did Socrates mean by his Dæmon?" He was too wise to believe, and too honest to pretend, that he had real and familiar converse with a superior and invisible being. He probably considered the suggestions of his conscience, or reason, as revelations or inspirations from the Supreme mind, bestowed, on important occasions, by a special superintending Providence.

I acknowledge all the merit of the hymn of Cleanthes to Jupiter, which you ascribe to it. It is as highly sublime as a chaste and correct imagination can permit itself to go. Yet in the contemplation of a being so superlative, the hyperbolic flights of the Psalmist may often be followed with approbation, even with rapture; and I have no hesitation in giving him the palm over all the hymnists of every language and of every time. Turn to the 148th Psalm, in Brady and Tate's version. Have such conceptions been ever before expressed? Their version of the 15th Psalm is more to be esteemed for its pithiness than its poetry. Even Sternhold, the leaden Sternhold, kindles, in a single instance, with the sublimity of his original, and expresses the majesty of God descending on the earth, in terms not unworthy of the subject:

> The Lord descended from above,
> And bowed the heav'ns most high;
> And underneath his feet he cast
> The darkness of the sky.
> On Cherubim and Seraphim
> Full royally he rode;
> And on the wings of mighty winds
> Came flying all abroad.
> —*Psalm xviii, 9, 10.*

The best collection of these psalms is that of the Octagonian dissenters of Liverpool, in their printed form of prayer; but they are not always the best versions. Indeed, bad is the best of the English versions; not a ray of poetical genius having ever been employed on them. And how much depends on this may be seen by comparing Brady and Tate's 15th Psalm with Blacklock's *Justum et tenacem propositi virum* of Horace, quoted in Hume's history, Car. 2, ch. 65. A translation of David in this style, or in that of Pompei's Cleanthes, might give us some idea of the merit of the original. The character, too, of the poetry of these hymns is singular to us; written in monostichs, each divided into strophe and anti-strophe, the sentiment of the first member responded with amplification or antithesis in the second.

On the subject of the postscript of yours of August the 16th and of Mrs. Adams' letter, I am silent. I know the depth of the affliction it has caused, and can sympathize with it the more sensibly, inasmuch as there is no degree of affliction, produced by the loss of those dear to us, which experience has not taught me to estimate. I have ever found time and silence the only medicine, and these but assuage, they never can suppress, the deep drawn sigh which recollection forever brings up, until recollection and life are extinguished together. Ever affectionately yours.

A Portrait of George Washington

Monticello, January 2, 1814

✸ TO WALTER JONES ✸   You say that in taking General Washington on your shoulders, to bear him harmless through the federal coalition, you encounter a perilous topic. I do not think so. You have given the genuine history of the course of his mind through the trying scenes in which it was engaged, and of the seductions by which it was deceived, but not depraved. I think I knew General Washington intimately and thoroughly; and were I called on to delineate his character, it should be in terms like these.

His mind was great and powerful, without being of the very first order; his penetration strong, though not so acute as that of a Newton, Bacon, or Locke; and as far as he saw, no judgment was ever sounder. It was slow in operation, being little aided by invention or imagination, but sure in conclusion. Hence the common remark of his officers, of the advantage he derived from councils of war, where, hearing all suggestions, he selected whatever was best; and certainly no general ever planned his battles more judiciously. But if deranged during the course of the action, if any member of his plan was dislocated by sudden circumstances, he was slow in a readjustment. The consequence was that

---

Jones (1745–1815) was a Virginia physician and member of Congress from 1797 to 1799 and from 1803 to 1811.

he often failed in the field, and rarely against an enemy in station, as at Boston and York. He was incapable of fear, meeting personal dangers with the calmest unconcern. Perhaps the strongest feature in his character was prudence, never acting until every circumstance, every consideration, was maturely weighed; refraining if he saw a doubt, but, when once decided, going through with his purpose, whatever obstacles opposed. His integrity was most pure, his justice the most inflexible I have ever known, no motives of interest or consanguinity, of friendship or hatred, being able to bias his decision. He was, indeed, in every sense of the words, a wise, a good, and a great man. His temper was naturally irritable and high-toned; but reflection and resolution had obtained a firm and habitual ascendency over it. If ever, however, it broke its bonds, he was most tremendous in his wrath. In his expenses he was honorable, but exact; liberal in contributions to whatever promised utility; but frowning and unyielding on all visionary projects, and all unworthy calls on his charity. His heart was not warm in its affections; but he exactly calculated every man's value, and gave him a solid esteem proportioned to it. His person, you know, was fine, his stature exactly what one would wish, his deportment easy, erect and noble; the best horseman of his age, and the most graceful figure that could be seen on horseback. Although, in the circle of his friends, where he might be unreserved with safety, he took a free share in conversation, his colloquial talents were not above mediocrity, possessing neither copiousness of ideas, nor fluency of words. In public, when called on for a sudden opinion, he was unready, short, and embarrassed. Yet he wrote readily, rather diffusely, in an easy and correct style. This he had acquired by conversation with the world, for his education was merely reading, writing, and common arithmetic, to which he added surveying at a later day. His time was employed in action chiefly, reading little, and that only in agriculture and English history. His correspondence became necessarily extensive, and, with journalizing his agricultural proceedings, occupied most of his leisure hours within doors. On the whole, his character was, in its mass, perfect, in nothing bad, in few points indifferent; and it may truly be said, that never did nature and fortune combine more perfectly to make a man great, and to place him in the same constellation with whatever worthies have merited from man an everlasting remembrance. For his was the singular destiny and merit, of leading the armies of his country successfully through an arduous war, for the establishment of its independence; of conducting its councils through the birth of a government, new in its forms and principles, until it had settled down into a quiet and orderly train; and of scrupulously obeying the laws through the whole of his career, civil and military, of which the history of the world furnishes no other example.

How, then, can it be perilous for you to take such a man on your shoulders? I am satisfied the great body of republicans think of him as I do. We were, indeed, dissatisfied with him on his ratification of the British treaty. But this was short lived. We knew his honesty, the wiles with which he was encompassed, and that age had already begun to relax the firmness of his purposes; and I am convinced he is more deeply seated in the love and gratitude of the republicans, than in the Pharisaical homage of the federal monarchists. For he was no monarchist from preference of his judgment. The soundness of that gave him correct views of the rights of man, and his severe justice devoted him to them. He has often declared to me that he considered our new Constitution as an experiment on the practicability of republican government, and with what dose of liberty man could be trusted for his own good; that he was determined the experiment should have a fair trial, and would lose the last drop of his blood in support of it. And these declarations he repeated to me the oftener and more pointedly, because he knew my suspicions of Colonel Hamilton's views, and probably had heard from him the same declarations which I had, to wit, "that the British constitution, with its unequal representation, corruption, and other existing abuses, was the most perfect government which had ever been established on earth, and that a reformation of those abuses would make it an impracticable government." I do believe that General Washington had not a firm confidence in the durability of our government. He was naturally distrustful of men, and inclined to gloomy apprehensions; and I was ever persuaded that a belief that we must at length end in something like a British constitution, had some weight in his adoption of the ceremonies of levees, birthdays, pompous meetings with

Congress, and other forms of the same character, calculated to prepare us gradually for a change which he believed possible, and to let it come on with as little shock as might be to the public mind.

These are my opinions of General Washington, which I would vouch at the judgment-seat of God, having been formed on an acquaintance of thirty years. I served with him in the Virginia Legislature from 1769 to the Revolutionary war, and again, a short time in Congress, until he left us to take command of the army. During the war and after it we corresponded occasionally, and in the four years of my continuance in the office of Secretary of State, our intercourse was daily, confidential, and cordial. After I retired from that office, great and malignant pains were taken by our federal monarchists, and not entirely without effect, to make him view me as a theorist, holding French principles of government, which would lead infallibly to licentiousness and anarchy. And to this he listened the more easily, from my known disapprobation of the British treaty. I never saw him afterwards, or these malignant insinuations should have been dissipated before his just judgment, as mists before the sun. I felt on his death, with my countrymen, that "verily a great man hath fallen this day in Israel."

More time and recollection would enable me to add many other traits of his character; but why add them to you, who knew him well? And I cannot justify to myself a longer detention of your paper.

Vale, proprieque tuum, me esse tibi persuadeas.

Psychology and Ethics

Monticello, June 13, 1814

⫸ TO THOMAS LAW ⫷ Of all the theories on this question, the most whimsical seems to have been that of Wollaston, who considers *truth* as the foundation of morality. The thief who steals your guinea does wrong inasmuch as he acts a lie in using your guinea as if it were his own. Truth is certainly a branch of morality, and a very important one to society. But presented as its foundation, it is as if a tree taken up by the roots had its stem reversed in the air, and one of its branches planted in the ground. Some have made the *love of God* the foundation of morality. This, too, is but a branch of our moral duties, which are generally divided into duties to God and duties to man. If we did a good act merely from the love of God and a belief that it is pleasing to Him, whence arises the morality of the atheist? It is idle to say, as some do, that no such being exists. We have the same evidence of the fact as of most of those we act on, to wit: their own affirmations, and their reasonings in support of them. I have observed, indeed, gen-

---

Law (1759–1834), a writer on economic subjects, was born in England and in 1793 settled in the U. S., where he married Eliza Parke Custis, Martha Washington's granddaughter. William Wollaston (1650–1724), an English philosophical writer, was the author of books on religion, including *The Religion of Nature Delineated* (1722).

erally, that while in Protestant countries the defections from the Platonic Christianity of the priests is to Deism, in Catholic countries they are to Atheism. Diderot, D'Alembert, D'Holbach, Condorcet, are known to have been among the most virtuous of men. Their virtue, then, must have had some other foundation than the love of God.

The Το καλόν of others is founded in a different faculty, that of taste, which is not even a branch of morality. We have indeed an innate sense of what we call beautiful, but that is exercised chiefly on subjects addressed to the fancy, whether through the eye in visible forms, as landscape, animal figure, dress, drapery, architecture, the composition of colors . . . or to the imagination directly, as imagery, style, or measure in prose or poetry, or whatever else constitutes the domain of criticism or taste, a faculty entirely distinct from the moral one. Self-interest, or rather self-love, or *egoism*, has been more plausibly substituted as the basis of morality. But I consider our relations with others as constituting the boundaries of morality. With ourselves we stand on the ground of identity, not of relation, which last, requiring two subjects, excludes self-love confined to a single one. To ourselves, in strict language, we can owe no duties, obligation requiring also two parties. Self-love, therefore, is no part of morality. Indeed it is exactly its counterpart. It is the sole antagonist of virtue, leading us constantly by our propensities to self-gratification in violation of our moral duties to others. Accordingly, it is against this enemy that are erected the batteries of moralists and religionists, as the only obstacle to the practice of morality. Take from man his selfish propensities, and he can have nothing to seduce him from the practice of virtue. Or subdue those propensities by education, instruction or restraint, and virtue remains without a competitor. Egoism, in a broader sense, has been thus presented as the source of moral action. It has been said that we feed the hungry, clothe the naked, bind up the wounds of the man beaten by thieves, pour oil and wine into them, set him on our own beast and bring him to the inn, because we receive ourselves pleasure from these acts. So Helvetius, one of the best men on earth, and the most ingenious advocate of this principle, after defining "interest" to mean not merely that which is pecuniary, but whatever may procure us pleasure or withdraw us from pain, [*De l'esprit* 2, 1,] says, [*ib.* 2, 2,] "the humane man is he to whom the sight of misfortune is insupportable, and who to rescue himself from this spectacle, is forced to succor the unfortunate object." This indeed is true. But it is one step short of the ultimate question. These good acts give us pleasure, but how happens it that they give us pleasure? Because nature hath implanted in our breasts a love of others, a sense of duty to them, a moral instinct, in short, which prompts us irresistibly to feel and to succor their distresses, and protests against the language of Helvetius, [*ib.* 2, 5,] "what other motive than self-interest could determine a man to generous actions? It is as impossible for him to love what is good for the sake of good, as to love evil for the sake of evil." The Creator would indeed have been a bungling artist, had he intended man for a social animal, without planting in him social dispositions. It is true they are not planted in every man, because there is no rule without exceptions; but it is false reasoning which converts exceptions into the general rule. Some men are born without the organs of sight, or of hearing, or without hands. Yet it would be wrong to say that man is born without these faculties, and sight, hearing, and hands may with truth enter into the general definition of man. The want or imperfection of the moral sense in some men, like the want or imperfection of the senses of sight and hearing in others, is no proof that it is a general characteristic of the species. When it is wanting, we endeavor to supply the defect by education, by appeals to reason and calculation, by presenting to the being so unhappily conformed, other motives to do good and to eschew evil, such as the love, or the hatred, or rejection of those among whom he lives, and whose society is necessary to his happiness and even existence; demonstrations by sound calculation that honesty promotes interest in the long run; the rewards and penalties established by the laws; and ultimately the prospects of a future state of retribution for the evil as well as the good done while here. These are the correctives which are supplied by education, and which exercise the functions of the moralist, the preacher, and legislator; and they lead into a course of correct action all those whose disparity is not too profound to be eradicated. Some have argued against the existence of a moral sense, by saying that if nature had given us such a sense, impelling us to vir-

tuous actions, and warning us against those which are vicious, then nature would also have designated, by some particular ear-marks, the two
sets of actions which are, in themselves, the one virtuous and the other
vicious. Whereas, we find, in fact, that the same actions are deemed
virtuous in one country and vicious in another. The answer is that nature has constituted *utility* to man the standard and best of virtue. Men
living in different countries, under different circumstances, different
habits and regimens, may have different utilities; the same act, therefore, may be useful, and consequently virtuous in one country which is
injurious and vicious in another differently circumstanced. I sincerely,
then, believe with you in the general existence of a moral instinct. I
think it the brightest gem with which the human character is studded,
and the want of it as more degrading than the most hideous of the
bodily deformities. I am happy in reviewing the roll of associates in
this principle which you present in your second letter, some of which
I had not before met with. To these might be added Lord Kames,* one
of the ablest of our advocates, who goes so far as to say, in his Principles
of Natural Religion,† that a man owes no duty to which he is not
urged by some impulsive feeling. This is correct, if referred to the
standard of general feeling in the given case, and not to the feeling of a
single individual. Perhaps I may misquote him, it being fifty years
since I read his book.

---

* Henry Home, Lord Kames (1696–1782), was a Scottish jurist and philosopher.
† *Essays on the Principles of Morality and Natural Religion*, published in 1751.

On the Constitution

Monticello, July 12, 1816

❧ TO SAMUEL KERCHEVAL ❦ Some men look at constitutions with sanctimonious reverence, and deem them like the ark of the covenant, too sacred to be touched. They ascribe to the men of the preceding age a wisdom more than human, and suppose what they did to be beyond amendment. I knew that age well; I belonged to it, and labored with it. It deserved well of its country. It was very like the present, but without the experience of the present; and forty years of experience in government is worth a century of book-reading; and this they would say themselves, were they to rise from the dead. I am certainly not an advocate for frequent and untried changes in laws and constitutions. I think moderate imperfections had better be borne with; because, when once known, we accommodate ourselves to them, and find practical means of correcting their ill effects. But I know also, that laws and institutions must go hand in hand with the progress of the human mind. As that becomes more developed, more enlightened, as new discoveries are made, new truths disclosed, and manners and opinions change with the change of circumstances, institutions must advance also, and keep pace with the times. We might as well require

---

Kercheval (1786–1845?), a writer from the western part of Virginia, published *A History of the Valley of Virginia in 1833.*

a man to wear still the coat which fitted him when a boy, as civilized society to remain ever under the regimen of their barbarous ancestors. It is this preposterous idea which has lately deluged Europe in blood. Their monarchs, instead of wisely yielding to the gradual change of circumstances, of favoring progressive accommodation to progressive improvement, have clung to old abuses, entrenched themselves behind steady habits, and obliged their subjects to seek through blood and violence rash and ruinous innovations, which, had they been referred to the peaceful deliberations and collected wisdom of the nation, would have been put into acceptable and salutary forms. Let us follow no such examples, nor weakly believe that one generation is not as capable as another of taking care of itself, and of ordering its own affairs. Let us, as our sister States have done, avail ourselves of our reason and experience, to correct the crude essays of our first and unexperienced, although wise, virtuous, and well-meaning councils. And lastly, let us provide in our constitution for its revision at stated periods. What these periods should be, nature herself indicates. By the European tables of mortality, of the adults living at any one moment of time, a majority will be dead in about nineteen years. At the end of that period then, a new majority is come into place; or, in other words, a new generation. Each generation is as independent of the one preceding, as that was of all which had gone before. It has then, like them, a right to choose for itself the form of government it believes most promotive of its own happiness; consequently, to accommodate to the circumstances in which it finds itself, that received from its predecessors; and it is for the peace and good of mankind, that a solemn opportunity of doing this every nineteen or twenty years, should be provided by the constitution; so that it may be handed on, with periodical repairs, from generation to generation, to the end of time, if anything human can so long endure. It is now forty years since the constitution of Virginia was formed. The same tables inform us, that, within that period, two-thirds of the adults then living are now dead. Have then the remaining third, even if they had the wish, the right to hold in obedience to their will, and to laws heretofore made by them, the other two-thirds, who, with themselves, compose the present mass of adults? If they have not, who has? The dead? But the dead have no rights. They are nothing; and nothing cannot own something. Where there is no substance, there can be no accident. This corporeal globe, and everything upon it, belong to its present corporeal inhabitants, during their generation. They alone have a right to direct what is the concern of themselves alone, and to declare the law of that direction; and this declaration can only be made by their majority. That majority, then, has a right to depute representatives to a convention, and to make the constitution what they think will be the best for themselves. But how collect their voice? This is the real difficulty. If invited by private authority, or county or district meetings, these divisions are so large that few will attend; and their voice will be imperfectly, or falsely pronounced. Here, then, would be one of the advantages of the ward divisions I have proposed. The mayor of every ward, on a question like the present, would call his ward together, take the simple yea or nay of its members, convey these to the county court, who would hand on those of all its wards to the proper general authority; and the voice of the whole people would be thus fairly, full, and peaceably expressed, discussed, and decided by the common reason of the society. If this avenue be shut to the call of sufferance, it will make itself heard through that of force, and we shall go on, as other nations are doing, in the endless circle of oppression, rebellion, reformation; and oppression, rebellion, reformation, again; and so on forever.

These, sir, are my opinions of the governments we see among men, and of the principles by which alone we may prevent our own from falling into the same dreadful track. I have given them at greater length than your letter called for. But I cannot say things by halves; and I confide them to your honor, so to use them as to preserve me from the gridiron of the public papers. If you shall approve and enforce them, as you have done that of equal representation, they may do some good. If not, keep them to yourself as the effusions of withered age and useless time. I shall, with not the less truth, assure you of my great respect and consideration.

On His Personal Life

≫ TO VINE UTLEY ≪ Sir, Your letter of February the 18th came to hand on the 1st and the request of the history of my physical habits would have puzzled me not a little, had it not been for the model with which you accompanied it, of Doctor Rush's answer to a similar inquiry. I live so much like other people, that I might refer to ordinary life as the history of my own. Like my friend the Doctor, I have lived temperately, eating little animal food, and that not as an aliment so much as a condiment for the vegetables, which constitute my principal diet. I double, however, the Doctor's glass and a half of wine, and even treble it with a friend; but halve its effects by drinking the weak wines only. The ardent wines I cannot drink, nor do I use ardent spirits in any form. Malt liquors and cider are my table drinks, and my breakfast, like that also of my friend, is of tea and coffee. I have been blest with organs of digestion which accept and concoct, without ever murmuring, whatever the palate chooses to consign to them, and I have not yet lost a tooth by age. I was a hard student until I entered on the business of life, the duties of which leave no idle time to those disposed to fulfill them; and now, retired, and at the age of seventy-six, I am again a hard

---

Little is known about Vine Utley, except that he was a Connecticut doctor, living around Lyme, and an ardent Jeffersonian.

—often ahead of American troops—to obtain information for the later use of our occupation forces.

Saul K. Padover's travels, lectures, fellowships, and honors have been many since then. His numerous works on Jefferson have sold about a million copies; and a biography, *Thomas Jefferson*, and *Thomas Jefferson on Democracy* have been translated into forty languages. Evidently Jefferson's ideas have the powerful appeal to the rest of the world that they had to our young nation. Not only have the Padover books gone to the four corners of the globe, but so has the author. He has lectured on Jefferson from Rangoon to Mandalay and from Salzburg to Sendai. Professor Padover lives in Brooklyn, New York, with his wife, Margaret, whom he married in 1957 on April 13. (Does that date ring a bell?)

III

ILLUSTRATING *The Writings of Thomas Jefferson* certainly called for a special combination of technical skill and imagination, which is why we feel lucky to have gotten Lynd Ward to do it. He is no newcomer to you or us, having begun his Club career in 1940 with *Beowulf*, and the most recent of his many commissions was for *The Master of Ballantrae*, which we published last summer.

Lynd Ward was born in Chicago in 1905. He attended schools there, in Massachusetts, and in New Jersey, eventually landing at Teachers College, Columbia, as a fine-arts major. While there he edited the famous *Columbia Jester* (a job which had been held a few years earlier by George Macy, who was the founder of The Heritage Club). He was graduated in 1926, whereupon he spent a year in Europe studying graphic arts, etching, lithography, and woodcuts under such masters as Alois Kolb, Georg Mathey, and Hans Alexander Mueller. Since then Lynd Ward, one of the premier artists of our time, has illustrated more than one hundred books of all varieties and shapes, from paperbacks to the most sumptuous limited editions. Two of his famous wordless novels-in-wood-cuts, *God's Man* and *Wild Pilgrimage*, published respectively in 1929 and 1932, are still in print. Lynd Ward's media include pen-and-ink, wash, and water color.

For *The Writings of Thomas Jefferson* our man Lynd Ward created sixteen fine lithographs, each in blue and black and each filling a full page in the book. In addition to that, he made thirty-six part-page monochrome drawings. Why are the lithographs in *blue* and black? you might ask.

"When you go into the front door at Monticello," Lynd Ward told us, "you encounter a gray-blue on the walls—considerably lighter than the blue used in this volume but enough of a blue to establish a strong feeling of blue for the whole experience. And blue somehow is associated in my mind with the Federal government." So blue it is.

Those drawings, and the text, were printed on a specially made paper that came from the Cohoes, N.Y., mill of the Mohawk Paper Company. It is a gray-toned laid sheet, and it was fabricated according to the specifications agreed upon by Lynd Ward and Roderick Stinehour, the designer of our volume, and was printed under the watchful eyes and skilled hand of Ed Wilson's New York Lithographing Company.

The appropriate grandeur of Rocky Stinehour's excellent design stems in part from his choice of Monotype Bell for the typeface, the text being set in twelve-point with three points of leading. (It's not the same bell we have been ringing on April 13.) John Austin cut this type back in 1788 for John Bell. It is often referred to as the first English modern face, and its sharply cut serifs help it give a pleasing sparkle on the printed page.

There's another touch of grandeur, we think, in the cover design, in both the vellum cloth of the shelfback and the harmonizing marbled paper on the sides.

IN A LETTER he wrote to Benjamin Rush in 1800, Jefferson said at one point, "I have sworn upon the altar of God eternal hostility against every form of tyranny over the mind of man." As you stand in the Jefferson Memorial in Washington, you look up and see these words in the frieze of the main entablature, far overhead. The man who found the phrase, and suggested that it be inscribed in the Memorial, was Saul K. Padover, who, we think we can safely say, is the leading authority on Jefferson. That was in 1940, when the Memorial was being constructed. Padover was then assistant to Secretary of the Interior Ickes who had asked him to do some digging on the subject. The significance for those fortunate people who possess The Heritage Club edition of *The Writings of Thomas Jefferson* is that Professor Padover has edited and made the selections and presented with them a trenchant, appreciative Introduction, and with sectional Prefaces that enhance immeasurably one's understanding of the man and his works.

Chairman of the Department of Political Science of the prestigious New School for Social Research in New York, Saul K. Padover was born in Austria in 1905 on April 13. (Does that date ring a bell?) His father, an American citizen, brought him to this country in 1920. He was graduated from Wayne University *cum laude*, attended graduate classes at Yale, 1928–29, took his M.A. at the University of Chicago the next year, and his Ph.D. there in 1932. Professor Padover taught, researched, and lectured on history at various universities, and studied under a Guggenheim Fellowship in 1936–37 in Paris, Vienna, and London. It was in 1938 that he joined the staff of Secretary Ickes, an appointment that led Dr. Padover into many facets of government work, culminating in intelligence assignments for O.S.S. which called upon him to move into Germany in 1944–45

your copy of *The Writings of Thomas Jefferson.* His greatest personal tragedy struck in September, 1782: the death of his wife, who had been ill since the birth of their last daughter in May. After a period of deep mourning, Jefferson was finally in a mood to enter public life again. In 1783 he was back in Philadelphia as a member of the Congress, and a year later was appointed Minister Plenipotentiary to assist Franklin and Adams in their commercial negotiations with European countries.

When he returned to the United States in 1789, Washington appointed him Secretary of State in the first Cabinet.

Jefferson was elected Vice-President under John Adams in 1796, and four years later became our third President, serving two terms. Probably the most notable achievement of his two terms was the Louisiana Purchase, by which he took the responsibility of acquiring from France the land between the Mississippi and the Rockies for $15,000,000.

Jefferson's Presidential term expired on March 3, 1809; after forty years of public service, he was at last permitted to retire to Monticello.

Jefferson's last years were devoted to the establishment of the University of Virginia. He anticipated most of the now accepted ideas about the aim, administration, and curriculum of American universities. By his own estimation, this was one of his greatest achievements, for he chose for his tomb the epitaph:

Here was buried

THOMAS JEFFERSON

Author of the Declaration of American Independence, of the Statute of Virginia for religious freedom, & Father of the University of Virginia.

The great man even breathed his last at a moment of great significance: on July 4, 1826, the fiftieth anniversary of the day that revolutionized a world.

Summary View of the Rights of British America, and in other public documents. As for his personal story, he wrote an Autobiography which covered the first half of his life, and then a sort of diary of his years as Secretary of State which he called the "Anas," or "loose scraps." The most consequential and interesting of all these works have been brought together in the volume you now have before you.

I

THE MAN WHO MADE UP those famous words—"all men are created equal"—was born with a silver spoon in his mouth on April 13, 1743, at Shadwell, the biggest of his father's tobacco plantations in Virginia. Young Tom enjoyed books, horses, and all the fine things that went with aristocracy; Peter Jefferson died when his son was four-teen and left it all to him. The boy's classical education started early, first at Mr. Maury's school near Shadwell, and it continued when, at the age of seventeen, he entered William and Mary College.

Among the intellectuals whom he im-pressed was George Wythe, the brilliant legal eagle, and after graduation from Wil-liam and Mary in 1762, Jefferson studied law under him for five years. But a political career offered more challenge to his far-ranging mind and interests. He heard Patrick Henry orate in the House of Burgesses debates in 1765; he became a member of that body in 1769, where the first thing he did was to in-troduce a bill allowing owners to free their slaves. (It failed to pass.)

Relations with Britain worsened, and among the most active Virginia patriots was Jefferson. He began producing reso-lutions and tracts on natural rights and law that attracted much attention. In 1774 came *A Summary View of the Rights of British Amer-ica,* in which he offered such arguments as "our emigration to this country gave England no more rights over us than the emigration of the Danes and Saxons gave to the present authorities of their mother country over England." Though considered a bit extreme, it was widely read, impressing many not only with its viewpoint but with its author's skill as a stylist.

In 1775 Jefferson arrived in Philadelphia as a Virginia delegate to the Second Continental Congress, where he exhibited what John Adams called "a reputation for literature, science, and a happy talent for composition." His pen was enlisted in the cause of inde-pendence; the following year he was given an assignment which made history: the drafting of a formal declaration of inde-pendence from Great Britain. The Declara-tion that was finally approved by the Con-gress July 4, 1776, was cut and changed here and there by others, but essentially it was Jefferson's.

The Declaration of Independence was a high point in the life of this young man, but he was just getting going. He drafted a constitution for Virginia; as a member of its House of Delegates he set about reforming the laws of the new state, reorganizing the courts, abolishing primogeniture, battling for separation of Church and State, and proposing a state-supported system of edu-cation including elementary, grammar, and classical schools, a library, and a college or university. Jefferson was a central figure in the plans to revise the penal code; eventually capital punishment was abolished for all crimes but murder and treason, and other humanitarian changes were effected. His at-tempts to have slavery abolished failed, but he did have a law passed barring the impor-tation of slaves.

Jefferson served two terms as Governor of Virginia and then in June of 1781 retired to Monticello, which had been built after Shadwell was destroyed by fire in 1770. At this time he wrote his only published work, a remarkable book called *Notes on Virginia,* two excerpts from which you will find in

THE HERITAGE CLUB

Sandglass

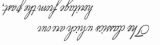

The classics which are our heritage from the past, in Editions which will be the heritage of the future

NUMBER II:33

ISSUED MONTHLY TO THE MEMBERS OF
THE HERITAGE CLUB
207 WEST 25TH STREET, NEW YORK 10001

How Thomas Jefferson Got Plastered

IN THE SUMMER of 1825, James Madison wrote to Thomas Jefferson, praising a New York sculptor named John Browere, who had recently made busts of Madison himself, his wife Dolly, Lafayette, and De Witt Clinton. So it was with interest that Jefferson made an appointment for twenty minutes with Browere in the east wing sun-room at Monticello.

Browere had the old man remove his coat and shirt and lie down on a couch. Then he stuck breathing straws in his nostrils, oiled his face, and began brushing on layers of thin, warm plaster. Thrice twenty minutes went by while the ex-President struggled for breath through the straws and the plaster hardened.

George Randolph, his seventeen-year-old grandson, looking through the window and seeing his grandfather partially encased in plaster, wheezing through straws, and a stranger hammering away at him with mallet and chisel, was alarmed enough to call his mother. With several servants they burst into the sun-room just as Browere had removed the main parts of the mold. Plaster still stuck to Jefferson's ears and a few other places, and the crowd commented disapprovingly, har-rying the sculptor to pick at it until it was gone. Exhausted, the ex-President lay down for a half-hour to recover.

Always the gentleman and the gracious host, he did not complain to Browere about the discomfort of the experience, but rather invited him to stay for dinner and spend the night at Monticello. When he returned to New York the artist used the mold to cast a remarkable head of Jefferson which is now preserved at Fenimore House in Cooperstown, New York.

Jefferson sent a letter to Madison telling him all about it. Describing the final stages of the operation, he said that "there became real danger that the ears would separate from the head sooner than from the plaister." The letter was one of thousands that Jefferson penned, in a day when a person usually sat down and laboriously wrote them out.

Jefferson's thoughts and ideas on politics and government, freedom, education, toler-ance, and the many other matters which deeply concerned the nation then as now were expressed in many of these letters. In addition, his philosophy still lives in his eloquent Declaration of Independence, in his reasoned Inaugural Addresses, in his radical

[1]

student. Indeed, my fondness for reading and study revolts me from the drudgery of letter writing. And a stiff wrist, the consequence of an early dislocation, makes writing both slow and painful. I am not so regular in my sleep as the Doctor says he was, devoting to it from five to eight hours, according as my company or the book I am reading interests me; *and I never go to bed without an hour, or half an hour's previous reading of something moral, whereon to ruminate in the intervals of sleep.* But whether I retire to bed early or late, I rise with the sun. I use spectacles at night, but not necessarily in the day, unless in reading small print. My hearing is distinct in particular conversation, but confused when several voices cross each other, which unfits me for the society of the table. I have been more fortunate than my friend in the article of health. So free from catarrhs that I have not had one (in the breast, I mean) on an average of eight or ten years through life. I ascribe this exemption partly to the habit of bathing my feet in cold water every morning, for sixty years past. A fever of more than twenty-four hours I have not had above two or three times in my life. A periodical headache has afflicted me occasionally, once, perhaps, in six or eight years, for two or three weeks at a time, which seems now to have left me; and, except on a late occasion of indisposition, I enjoy good health; too feeble, indeed, to walk much, but riding without fatigue six or eight miles a day, and sometimes thirty or forty. I may end these egotisms, therefore, as I began, by saying that my life has been so much like that of other people, that I might say with Horace, to every one, *"nomine mutato, narratur fabula de te."** I must not end, however, without due thanks for the kind sentiments of regard you are so good as to express towards myself; and with my acknowledgments for these, be pleased to accept the assurances of my respect and esteem.

* "With the name changed, the story can be told of you."

On His Personal Philosophy

Monticello, October 31, 1819

➤➤ TO WILLIAM SHORT ❧ As you say of yourself, I too am an Epicurean. I consider the genuine (not the imputed) doctrines of Epicurus as containing everything rational in moral philosophy which Greece and Rome have left us. Epictetus, indeed, has given us what was good of the Stoics; all beyond, of their dogmas, being hypocrisy and grimace. Their great crime was in their calumnies of Epicurus and misrepresentations of his doctrines; in which we lament to see the candid character of Cicero engaging as an accomplice. Diffuse, vapid, rhetorical, but enchanting. His prototype Plato, eloquent as himself, dealing out mysticisms incomprehensible to the human mind, has been deified by certain sects usurping the name of Christians; because, in his foggy conceptions, they found a basis of impenetrable darkness whereon to rear fabrications as delirious, of their own invention. These they fathered blasphemously on him whom they claimed as their founder, but who would disclaim them with the indignation which their caricatures of his religion so justly excite. Of Socrates we have nothing genuine but in the Memorabilia of Xenophon; for Plato makes him one of his collocutors merely to cover his own whimsies under the mantle of

Short (1759–1849), Jefferson's friend and one-time secretary, was an American diplomat.

his name; a liberty of which we are told Socrates himself complained. Seneca is indeed a fine moralist, disfiguring his work at times with some stoicisms, and affecting too much of antithesis and point, yet giving us on the whole a great deal of sound and practical morality. But the greatest of all the reformers of the depraved religion of his own country, was Jesus of Nazareth. Abstracting what is really his from the rubbish in which it is buried, easily distinguished by its luster from the dross of his biographers, and as separable from that as the diamond from the dunghill, we have the outlines of a system of the most sublime morality which has ever fallen from the lips of man; outlines which it is lamentable he did not live to fill up.* Epictetus and Epicurus give laws for governing ourselves, Jesus a supplement of the duties and charities we owe to others. The establishment of the innocent and genuine character of this benevolent moralist, and the rescuing it from the imputation of imposture, which has resulted from artificial systems,† invented by ultra-Christian sects, unauthorized by a single word ever uttered by him, is a most desirable object, and one to which Priestley‡ has successfully devoted his labors and learning. It would in time, it is to be hoped, effect a quiet euthanasia of the heresies of bigotry and fanaticism which have so long triumphed over human reason, and so generally and deeply afflicted mankind; but this work is to be begun by winnowing the grain from the chaff of the historians of his life. I have sometimes thought of translating Epictetus (for he has never been tolerably translated into English) by adding the genuine doctrines of Epicurus from the Syntagma of Gassendi, and an abstract from the Evangelists of whatever has the stamp of the eloquence and fine imagination of Jesus. The last I attempted too hastily some twelve or fifteen years ago. It was the work of two or three nights only, at Washington, after getting through the evening task of reading the letters and papers of the day. But with one foot in the grave, these are now idle projects for me. My

---

* See also Jefferson's letter to John Adams, October 13, 1813, and the footnote on page 332.
† E.g. The immaculate conception of Jesus, his deification, the creation of the world by him, his miraculous powers, his resurrection and visible ascension, his corporeal presence in the Eucharist, the Trinity; original sin, atonement, regeneration, election, orders of Hierarchy. . . .—T.J.
‡ Jefferson's friend, the scientist Joseph Priestley, organized the first Unitarian Church in the United States and wrote many philosophical works on religion.

business is to beguile the wearisomeness of declining life, as I endeavor to do, by the delights of classical reading and of mathematical truths, and by the consolations of a sound philosophy, equally indifferent to hope and fear.

I take the liberty of observing that you are not a true disciple of our master Epicurus, in indulging the indolence to which you say you are yielding. One of his canons, you know, was that "the indulgence which prevents a greater pleasure, or produces a greater pain, is to be avoided." Your love of repose will lead, in its progress, to a suspension of healthy exercise, a relaxation of mind, an indifference to everything around you, and finally to a debility of body, and hebetude of mind, the farthest of all things from the happiness which the well-regulated indulgences of Epicurus ensure; fortitude, you know, is one of his four cardinal virtues. That teaches us to meet and surmount difficulties; not to fly from them, like cowards; and to fly, too, in vain, for they will meet and arrest us at every turn of our road. Weigh this matter well; brace yourself up.

The Doctrines of Jesus

Monticello, June 26, 1822

⇒ TO BENJAMIN WATERHOUSE ⇐ The doctrines of Jesus are simple, and tend all to the happiness of man.

1. That there is only one God, and he all perfect.

2. That there is a future state of rewards and punishments.

3. That to love God with all thy heart and thy neighbor as thyself, is the sum of religion. These are the great points on which he endeavored to reform the religion of the Jews. But compare with these the demoralizing dogmas of Calvin.

1. That there are three Gods.

2. That good works, or the love of our neighbor, are nothing.

3. That faith is everything, and the more incomprehensible the proposition, the more merit in its faith.

4. That reason in religion is of unlawful use.

5. That God, from the beginning, elected certain individuals to be saved, and certain others to be damned; and that no crimes of the former can damn them; no virtues of the latter save.

Now, which of these is the true and charitable Christian? He who believes and acts on the simple doctrines of Jesus? Or the impious dog-

---

Waterhouse (1754–1846) was a physician, professor of medicine at Harvard, author, pioneer in vaccination, and a follower of Jefferson in politics.

matists, as Athanasius and Calvin? Verily I say these are the false shepherds foretold as to enter not by the door into the sheepfold, but to climb up some other way. They are mere usurpers of the Christian name, teaching a counter-religion made up of the *deliria* of crazy imaginations, as foreign from Christianity as is that of Mahomet. Their blasphemies have driven thinking men into infidelity, who have too hastily rejected the supposed author himself, with the horrors so falsely imputed to him. Had the doctrines of Jesus been preached always as pure as they came from his lips, the whole civilized world would now have been Christian. I rejoice that in this blessed country of free inquiry and belief, which has surrendered its creed and conscience to neither kings nor priests, the genuine doctrine of one only God is reviving, and I trust that there is not a young man now living in the United States who will not die a Unitarian.

But much I fear, that when this great truth shall be re-established, its votaries will fall into the fatal error of fabricating formulas of creed and confessions of faith, the engines which so soon destroyed the religion of Jesus, and made of Christendom a mere Aceldama; that they will give up morals for mysteries, and Jesus for Plato. How much wiser are the Quakers, who, agreeing in the fundamental doctrines of the gospel, schismatize about no mysteries, and, keeping within the pale of common sense, suffer no speculative differences of opinion, any more than of feature, to impair the love of their brethren. Be this the wisdom of Unitarians, this the holy mantle which shall cover within its charitable circumference all who believe in one God, and who love their neighbor!

A Decalogue on Conduct

Monticello, February 21, 1825

❧ TO THOMAS JEFFERSON SMITH ❦ This letter will, to you, be as one from the dead. The writer will be in the grave before you can weigh its counsels. Your affectionate and excellent father has requested that I would address to you something which might possibly have a favorable influence on the course of life you have to run, and I too, as a namesake, feel an interest in that course. Few words will be necessary, with good dispositions on your part. Adore God. Reverence and cherish your parents. Love your neighbor as yourself, and your country more than yourself. Be just. Be true. Murmur not at the ways of·Providence. So shall the life into which you have entered, be the portal to one of eternal and ineffable bliss. And if to the dead it is permitted to care for the things of this world, every action of your life will be under my regard. Farewell.

[Accompanying the letter:]

A Decalogue of Canons for Observation in Practical Life
1. Never put off till tomorrow what you can do today.
2. Never trouble another for what you can do yourself.

Thomas Jefferson Smith was the son of Jefferson's old friend Samuel Harrison Smith, one-time editor of the *National Intelligencer*.

3. Never spend your money before you have it.
4. Never buy what you do not want because it is cheap; it will be dear to you.
5. Pride costs us more than hunger, thirst, and cold.
6. We never repent of having eaten too little.
7. Nothing is troublesome that we do willingly.
8. How much pain have cost us the evils which have never happened.
9. Take things always by their smooth handle.
10. When angry, count ten before you speak; if very angry, a hundred.